THE RYUKYUS

A HISTORY OF THE ISLAND KINGDOM AND THE BIRTH OF OKINAWA

Ibrahim Jalal

The Ryukyus
By Ibrahim Jalal

ISBN-13: 978-988-8843-21-3

© 2023 Ibrahim Jalal

HISTORY / Asia

EB193

All rights reserved. No part of this book may be reproduced in material form, by any means, whether graphic, electronic, mechanical or other, including photocopying or information storage, in whole or in part. May not be used to prepare other publications without written permission from the publisher except in the case of brief quotations embodied in critical articles or reviews. For information contact info@earnshawbooks.com

Published in Hong Kong by Earnshaw Books Ltd.

Prologue

In the Forbidden City, the vast imperial palace in Beijing, news has reached the Emperor that the king of one of his many tributary states has passed away. With the former king's heir apparent set to ascend the throne, the Emperor orders the formation of an over five-hundred-man delegation of diplomats, scholars, musicians and cooks, who are to make immediate preparations and sail east. Rare goods from both within the Middle Kingdom and the empire's tributary states scattered throughout Asia are carefully loaded onto huge junks, themselves a reminder of the Emperor's vast power.

The upper section of each junk is coated in heavy black paint with red accents around the edges, and on the each side of the bow two wide eyes have been painted. In contrast to the somber tone of the ships upper section, the hull is a fluorescent white. The junks are all equipped with three tear-shaped sails, each fixed to three separate battens. The smallest of these sails is at the ship's stern, with a marginally larger sale sitting at the bow. The largest of the sails, more than double the size of the smaller counterparts is unfurled from the mainmast at the ship's center. Amongst the rare goods that loaded onto the junks is royal clothing fit for the new king and a black crown studded with assorted jewels.

The junks set sail from the port of Fuzhou, tracing the flow of the Min River as it pours out into the Pacific. The junks cross the great ocean, pulling away from the shallow waters surrounding the mainland and heading into the deep blue waters of the Pacific. Having completed their journey, the ships anchor in the port of Naha, where the delegation will spend the next half year. This tributary state has been expecting them, and the delegation is promptly guided to a special building constructed for their very purpose, designed to meet their every need during their stay here.

Before attending the enthronement ceremony, some of the Chinese delegation pay homage to the kings of yore at a Buddhist temple not far from ocean. When the day of the enthronement ceremony begins, the delegation marches ceremonially with pomp towards the castle that sits at the heart of the kingdom. As the procession proceeds to the royal capital of Shuri, curious locals look on in awe. The procession moves along roads paved with coral limestone tiles, passing ancient Banyan trees with their long roots stretching down from the canopies to the ground, blood red Hibiscus flowers from which long stamen protrude and fruit trees of citruses.

The heir apparent meets the delegation at one of the castle's gates, Shureimon. A towering structure of red lacquered wood, a roof of red and white tiles, and a central plaque on which 'Land of Propriety' engraved in golden Chinese characters. The heir apparent and the delegation together make their way to the castle, situated on a hill overlooking the city below, complete with zig-zagging walls that cut across the landscape. Like Shureimon, At the center of the castle complex sits a building of red lacquered wood and red and white tiles. In the castle's courtyard precious objects from the Emperor are presented in a building constructed for this very occasion. A declaration is read in classical Chinese and Chinese instruments play during the enthronement ceremony. At last, the heir apparent is presented with the royal clothes and crown that had so carefully been transported across the ocean. He is now recognized by the Emperor of China as the King of Ryukyu, and like his predecessors is granted access to

PROLOGUE

the Middle Kingdom's tributary states, opening up a world of international trade for his small island nation.

This small kingdom to which the Emperors of China would dispatch delegations from time and time across the centuries, is the Ryukyu Kingdom, the historic predecessor of today's Okinawa.

Okinawa first came to the wider world's attention in the dying days of World War II. The Japanese military chose to make a stand there and the Battle of Okinawa from April 1 to June 22, 1945, was one of the most ferocious engagements of the entire war, one that appeared to foreshadow an even more gruesome and bloody invasion of the Japanese home islands. It saw Kamikaze aircraft attacks, suicide charges and a gruelling slog though mud and mortar fire as the Allies slowly prized control of the island away from the Japanese. The Imperial Japanese army fought with such reckless abandon because for the first time they were fighting to protect what they saw as their home soil. One quarter of the entire population were killed in the fighting, many of them compelled by Japanese troops to commit suicide rather than surrender to the Allied forces.

The former mayor of Koza, Ōyama Chōjō (1901–1999) described the suffering succinctly:

"In March of 1945, the American army landed and the Battle of Okinawa began...from children to the elderly...it was awful and ghastly. The battle continued for three months during which I lost my young brother and sister, who had such bright futures ahead of them, and also my mother and older brother. Such a deeply sad experience is not unique to me. There is not a single household who did not lose a member of their family or relative in the Battle of Okinawa.[1]"

---

1 Ōta Masahide. Okinawa No Jiritsu to Nihon: Fukki Yonjūnen No Toikake. Iwanamishoten, 2003, 7.

THE RYUKYUS

After the war was brought to a shuddering halt, not by a mass invasion but by the ignition of two atomic bombs in August, less than two months after Okinawa succumbed, Okinawa and its many associated islands became part of America's 'Keystone of the Pacific' a floating military base that provided superior access to East and Southeast Asia. The Americans made efforts not only to revive Okinawa socially and economically, but also to revive the identity of the people as independent from Japan and harking back to the days of the Ryukyu Kingdom, an independent mercantile nation that was for long periods a tributary state to China, trading with Japan, Korea and Southeast Asia.

The Americans, during the administration after 1945, made increasing references to 'Ryukyu' such as in the naming of the United States Civil Administration of the Ryukyu Islands (the civil administration government), the holding of a Commodore Perry centennial event in 1953 to mark the relationship between the peoples of the former Ryukyu Kingdom and America, and even the establishment of Ryukyu University — pointedly not called Okinawa University — the first university to ever be established in the Ryukyu Islands. The site was purposefully chosen on the bombed-out remains of Shuri Castle, the royal capital of the Ryukyu kings, to stress the American commitment to respecting the long history and culture of the Ryukyu people.

Regardless of all this, in time the majority of Okinawans eventually settled for a return to Japan, although the Americans continue to operate a number of large military bases there. Okinawa was frequently referred to by the US as the 'Keystone of the Pacific', strategically located perfectly in between Japan, the Korean Peninsula, China and close to Southeast Asia, a crucial location for maintaining stability in Cold War Asia. During the Vietnam war, for example, Okinawa was vital in dispatching troops to Southeast Asia. Some would argue the military

PROLOGUE

presence on the islands continues to ensure peace in the region today, while others protest that the bases are no longer needed. The issue is a contentious one in Okinawa and Japan.

This book takes you on the journey of how this tiny island state played a pivotal role in the history of East and Southeast Asia, its rise, its decline and ultimate transformation into Japan's most southern prefecture, Okinawa and its role today as a strategic location for the US military.

Let us first set the scene. The Ryukyu Archipelago is a collection of over 150 islands. Some of these are large enough that it would take days to cross on foot, others are so small the ocean can always be seen and the waves always heard. Some of these islands have been inhabited by humans since prehistoric times, others have been largely left to nature and remain uninhabited.[i] Those who call the islands home number some 1.5 million people, residing at what could be considered a crossroads of East Asia, almost directly between Japan, Korea and China. It is precisely because of this special location that these islands have played such a significant role in the history, society and culture of the region.

The Ryukyu Archipelago today is Okinawa and is Japan's most southern prefecture, the only one to be composed solely of islands. The territory of the former Ryukyu Kingdom, which lasted from 1429 to 1879, also included the southern islands of Kagoshima Prefecture which extend southwards from mainland Japan.

This book will take the reader on a journey from the time of the first people to enter these islands, to the rise and fall of the Ryukyu Kingdom in a narrative history that whenever possible will present the life, thoughts and motivations of those who lived here in their own words.

THE RYUKYUS

Since history as a discipline began in Ancient Greece and Ancient China, there have been many different styles of writing. Herodotus (BCE 484—425) 'the Father of History' took a more narrative approach compared to Thucydides (BCE 460—400) who shunned 'storytelling' for a more a more matter-of-fact approach. History today has changed and developed and is now generally divided into two styles of writing: academic works and works for the general public.

This book has not been written with an academic audience in mind, instead I hope to attract readers who may have little familiarity with the region but who may already have an interest in Japanese, Southeast Asian, or Chinese history. This book aims to introduce much of the knowledge that is currently locked away in the Japanese language to a wider audience in English.

I have provided sources for the reader for orientation in the text in the case of quotations from historical figures, scholar's interpretations and statistical information. This has been provided as footnotes with standard numerals, while a full list of texts used in this work can be found in the bibliography. Endnotes are in Roman numerals and have been used to provide extra information that would distract from the flow of the text, or Japanese language words that would be difficult to find if searched for with the Roman alphabet for those who do have an understanding of Chinese or Japanese but who would like to investigate further.

In places, I have created other narrative-like sections derived from history to give the reader a sense of place. These sections are based on historic sources and local legends, while at other times I have taken to quoting contemporaries directly where the opportunity arises.

Ryukyu prospered during its time as a Chinese tributary state; trading of goods developed between Korea, Japan and

PROLOGUE

China in the East, and distant Malaya and the islands now part of Indonesia to the south-west. During this golden age, the Ryukyu Kingdom developed a high culture, established diplomatic links throughout Asia and successfully brought the entirety of the Ryukyu Archipelago under the domain of one central authority for the first time in history. This international mercantilism was such a point of pride for the kings of Ryukyu that a 721 kilogram bronze bell was cast declaring the small maritime kingdom 'The Bridge of Nations', and Ryukyu's prosperity, culture and history entirely depended on this internationalism.

Yet this era of prosperity was not to last. By the early 17th century the first Europeans, the Portuguese and Spanish, had begun to enter Asia and other European nations soon followed. These very same Europeans began to topple Ryukyu's trading partners, the Sultanate of Malacca, the Kingdom of Ayutthaya and eventually threatened the heart of the East Asian tributary system itself, China.

But it was not the Europeans who bought an end to the Ryukyu kingdom's independence. Closer to home, the Satsuma samurai of Japan launched an invasion of Ryukyu in 1609, annexing the northern island of Amami and bringing it under their direct control. South of Amami, the Ryukyu Kingdom was reborn as a puppet state that was now partially integrated into the Shogunate system, the samurai government of Japan. Over this period, trade declined and agriculture became the main staple of the Ryukyu economy, leading to a booming population, albeit one that was constantly in flux due to natural disasters and famine. North of the kingdom, in what had become Satsuma-controlled Amami, sugarcane developed into a cash crop enriching the southern samurai in the process and creating a class of indentured servants amongst many of the common people of Amami. Under *de facto* Japanese rule, a ban on Christianity was enforced throughout the archipelago, with stone beacons erected in the most southern islands so that the sight of any foreign ships could be rapidly relayed to Shuri, then to the Satsuma and ultimately to the Shogun. Despite being under the control of the Satsuma, the Ryukyu Kingdom still governed the majority of the archipelago and while the Satsuma samurai were pulling the strings, this would have been hardly noticed by the majority of the kingdom's peasants whose daily struggles continued as before.

As much as possible, the Satsuma attempted to keep their dominance of the Ryukyu Kingdom a secret, allowing a degree of Ryukyu tribute to China from which they could profit. At the same time, the archipelago came under the *Sakoku* policy of Japan in which the Shogun in *de jure* terms at least, forbade any foreigners from making landfall in Japan, while also preventing any Japanese leaving.

In an increasingly imperialistic 19th century, such isolationist polices were impossible to maintain, and beginning in the 1850s the Shogunate was forced to concede access to numerous ports, following America's use of 'gunboat diplomacy' to force the country open.

During this tumultuous period, debate erupted in Japan about where the country was heading. Some scorned the Shogunate, with many samurai rallying under the phrase 'revere the emperor and expel the barbarians'. While the emperor had 'ruled' Japan since ancient times, the real power was in the hands of military generals, the successive dynasties of shoguns who had ruled since the early 14th Century. Those who rallied around this phrase believed that restoring the emperor to his rightful place would prevent the decline of the nation.

This tension culminated in the Meiji Restoration of 1868 in which power was forcibly taken from the Shogunate and the

PROLOGUE

emperor was restored to power as a figurehead. But the Ryukyu Kingdom did not fit neatly into the fledgling nation state, and questions arose about what to do with the islands and its people. Both the Qing dynasty (1636-1912) of China and the Meiji government of Japan asserted claims to the Ryukyu Archipelago. Questions about who rightfully controlled the Ryukyus were put to rest in 1895 when Japan defeated the Qing in the first Sino-Japanese War (1894—1895). Following this, the Ryukyu Kingdom was abolished and succeeded by Okinawa Prefecture. The last king of Ryukyu was exiled to Tokyo in 1879.

Now formally part of Japan, Okinawa was caught up in a wave of reforms taking place across the nation that sought to establish a national conscious, the quashing of regionalism and the creation of a pan-Japanese identity. These reforms were particularly keenly felt in Okinawa as it had a larger cultural and linguistic gap to bridge than the mainland prefectures.

The assimilation of Okinawa was also crucial to the Meiji Oligarchs, the politicians overseeing this new order, as they saw the Ryukyu Archipelago as the southern entry point into Japan. It was from here they were vulnerable should the country be attacked in war. It was therefore important that those on Japan's southern doorstep think of themselves as citizens of Japan, and preferably lose any identity related to the former kingdom's history and indigenous customs.

While the official policy sought to assimilate Ryukuans, in their daily interactions with mainlanders they often became targets of discrimination whether at home in the islands, in mainland Japan and even within Japanese communities abroad. Okinawan attempts to become more like their mainlander counterparts were imposed top-down by the government, but these ideas were also proactively taken up by many Okinawans, with references to how they should even 'sneeze like mainlanders.'

THE RYUKYUS

There is also a parallel Okinawan history during this era that takes us away from the islands themselves — that of the Okinawans who migrated abroad in the 19th Century. These migrants travelled as far away as Brazil, North America and even to islands in the south-west Pacific including New Caledonia.

The Three Divisions of the Ryukyu Archipelago

The Ryukyu Archipelago is a vast island chain that stretches over a thousand kilometers across the Pacific Ocean. The islands arch from just off the coast of Japan's Kyushu in the north to just over one hundred kilometers from Taiwan in the south. In these subtropical islands, the temperature rarely diverges by more than 11 or 12 degrees centigrade throughout the year. Even in winter, temperatures below ten degrees are rare, with the average temperature between 15 and 18 degrees, while in midsummer the average is between 27 and 29.

Throughout the year, more than 2,000mm of rain fall and humidity is at a consistently high level. Much of the rain comes from the monsoon and typhoon seasons. These islands are warmed by the Kuroshiro Current, an ocean stream that brings warmer water from the Philippines north through the Ryukyu Archipelago and past Japan, allowing for the world's northernmost coral reefs to flourish. In summer, these islands are visited by the Pacific High, a subtropical anticyclone, which ensures hot summer days and clear blue skies. The winter brings its counterpart, the Siberian High, a cold dry air bringing strong winds, clouds and rain.

A wide range of ecological, historical and cultural differences is to be found throughout this chain of islands. The Ryukyu Archipelago can be broken up into three distinct divisions: Northern Ryukyu, Central Ryukyu and Southern Ryukyu. Northern Ryukyu begins with the Tokara Islands, a 150-kilometer

PROLOGUE

chain of twelve small islands that stretch from the Japanese home island of Kyushu down to the second section of the Archipelago, the Amami Islands. Unlike the Tokara Islands, Amami has numerous small islands with the larger Amami Ōshima, of over seven-hundred square kilometers, at its center. Tokara and Amami, are categorized as Northern Ryukyu and today they are part of Japan's Kagoshima Prefecture.

South from Amami, we move into Okinawa Prefecture. Here are the Okinawa Islands including the main island of Okinawa, it is the fifth largest island in Japan and the largest of the archipelago. it is home to hundreds of thousands of people, the most populous island of the Ryukyu Archipelago. Okinawa is also the historic home of the Ryukyu Kingdom, and as a result it is Okinawa which has come to have the greatest cultural and historical influence on the islands north and south of the archipelago. This core section is referred to as Central Ryukyu.

While Okinawa, Amami and Tokara are relatively close together, there is a gulf of two-hundred kilometers of open ocean separating them from Southern Ryukyu, which is made up of the Sakishima Islands. The Sakishima Islands themselves are generally broken up into two clusters: the Miyako Islands, a group with the main island of Miyako surrounded by smaller outlying islands and further west, the Yaeyama Islands, the most southern collection of islands throughout the archipelago.

The island with the biggest population in Yaeyama is Ishigaki Island, on which over forty thousand people live. Traditionally they have been confined to the coastal areas away from the jungles and mountains of the interior. To the west of Ishigaki is Iriomote Island, a heavily forested island which is the third largest within the Ryukyu Archipelago and the second largest in Okinawa Prefecture. Further west still is the more isolated Yonaguni Island. A relatively small island of only twenty-seven square kilometers, but notable due to its proximity to Taiwan, making Yonaguni the most western point of all Japan. As with Amami, Okinawa and Miyako there are also many smaller outlying islands to be found throughout Yaeyama.

The largest islands in the Ryukyu Archipelago

Rank	Island	Approx. Surface Area	Location
1	Okinawa Island	1,207 square kilometers (S)	Central Ryukyu
2	Amami Ōshima	712 square kilometers	Northern Ryukyu
3	Iriomote	290 square kilometers	Southern Ryukyu (Sakishima)
4	Ishigaki	222 square kilometers	Southern Ryukyu (Sakishima)
5	Miyako Island	159 square kilometers	Southern Ryukyu (Sakishima)

Geology and Wildlife

In the Ryukyu Archipelago the larger islands are generally formed of the same rock as the mainland Japanese islands, while the smaller islands tend to be formed from Ryukyu limestone born from the movement of the earth's crust compacting coral reefs.

The makeup of the islands has had an enduring legacy on the architecture with buildings made of Ryukyu limestone throughout Okinawa. This limestone is used in both traditional and modern architecture in stone walls and pieces are also sold as souvenirs, often engraved with a phrase in the Okinawan language. Often present within the stone are shells and creatures that have been preserved as fossils from tens of thousands of years ago.

PROLOGUE

Numerous caves known as *Gama* in Okinawan, are a unique feature of the landscape. There are about two-thousand limestone caves throughout Okinawa Prefecture formed from coral. Take for example the cave of Gyokusendo in Okinawa, where stalactites grow at a pace of one millimeter every three years. This relatively rapid rate of growth is due to the sub-tropical climate bringing large quantities of rainwater into the cave, this coupled with high levels of carbon dioxide allows microbes to thrive in this warm environment, speeding up the erosion of the limestone.

Generally large islands such as Iriomote and Amami Ōshima broke away from continental Asia millions of years ago, while smaller island such as Taketomi, Kohama and Kuroshima were formed from this limestone. Other islands are a combination, such as Okinawa Island, the south of which is composed of the latter and the north the former, as is the case with Ishigaki. Yonaguni is a smaller island that is not formed of Ryukyu limestone, and like Ishigaki and Iriomote has a more intense topography compared to that of limestone islands such as Taketomi or Miyako.

The formation of the Ryukyu Archipelago is tied to that of the wider Japanese Archipelago. During the last ice age, what would become the Ryukyu Archipelago was a land bridge between what is now Taiwan and Kyushu. About 1.5 million years ago, the northern part of Ryukyu began to pull away from this land bridge. This movement, followed by rising water levels, led to the creation of part of the Ryukyu Archipelago. About 500,000 years ago an upheaval of coral caused by movement of the Philippine Plate created the archipelago's coral islands.

The geological formation of each of the Ryukyu Archipelago's islands has in turn shaped life and geography on each island. On Iriomote and Ishigaki, there are *Itaji* trees (*castanoposis sieboldii*) and oak trees (*quercus salicina*) which came from the ancient days when these islands were still part of the Eurasian continent. Wildlife also varies depending on the island, such as with unique species including the Iriomote Mountain Cat, a tiny relative of the leopard, which was in the jungles of Iriomote when the island was still part of the continent.

The isolation of these islands has also led to the development of a unique range of wildlife. Rare animals that can be found in Ryukyu include the coconut crab, which can weigh as much as four kilograms, the Ryukyu flying fox, a giant bat with a wingspan of over one meter and the Okinawan rail, a small flightless bird found in the Yanbaru rainforest.

The islands are akin to the Galapagos, with diversity a central feature of the islands; the number of species of bird throughout Okinawa contributes to 73% of the total bird species in Japan and the same is true for 75% of Japan's reptiles. Mammals throughout the Ryukyu Archipelago are relatively small, of these, fourteen species are unique to the Ryukyu archipelago, including the Amami Black Rabbit.

Language at the Crossroads of East Asia
Amid this unique geography and wildlife there is an equally unique culture, and just like the flora and fauna, this differs from island to island all the way from Amami in the north to Yaeyamain the south.

Those who visit Okinawa Prefecture will likely notice a distinct difference to mainland Japan. One example are the characteristic Shisa guardian lions displayed on the roofs, walls or in the grounds of homes, restaurants, hotels, or indeed almost any building. The Shisa come in many forms, some are fierce creatures with ragged manes like a bellowing fire, sharp claws and piercing eyes. Others are more friendly, including brightly colored lions with round faces and big eyes and gaping smiles.

PROLOGUE

There are so many variations of Shisa throughout these islands that you can spot hundreds of pairs just walking through the streets of Naha, the capital of Okinawa prefecture.

Then there are the bright traditional orange tiled roofs of Ryukyu which make a vibrant contrast to the turquoise blue of the surrounding ocean. These tiles are often decorated with a flower design on the eves and sometimes are covered with white accents; very different to the somber ashen tiles that often make up the roofs of castles and temples in mainland Japan.

Then there is the regional language where even a tourist who is not familiar with the Japanese language will likely pick up on the greeting '*Haisai*' in place of the Japanese '*Konichiwa*'.

Okinawa is often contrasted with Japan but there is also a strong regional identity present at the level of the individual islands. This identity is reflected in the languages of the archipelago which, while closely related to Japanese, are mutually unintelligible. In standard Japanese, the word for welcome is '*Yōkoso*' or '*Irashiamase*', in the language of Okinawa (called *Uchināguchi* and not to be confused with Okinawan Japanese), this phrase is '*Mensōrē*'.

Differences do not end here, the same phrase in the Miyako language (*Myākufutsu*) is '*Nmyāchi*', in the language of Yaeyama (*Yaimamuni*) it is '*Ōritōri*' and further away in the Yonaguni language (*Dunanmunui*) this same phrase is '*Wāri*'.

If you visit Okinawa prefecture and travel throughout the Ryukyu Archipelago, you may notice signs with each of these phrases in common use at ports, markets and airports.

While Okinawans now speak standard Japanese as their first language, native words from each region continue to be used alongside in everyday speech and traditional and contemporary songs.

Much of the culture within the Ryukyu Archipelago stems

THE RYUKYUS

from centuries of interactions with people in China, Japan and throughout Southeast Asia whether this be dances, alcohol, music or religion introduced from elsewhere. Such things were blended and adapted into something new within the Ryukyu Kingdom and continue to live on in Okinawa. The Ryukyu archipelago then was a literal 'bridge of nations' and a crossroads in East Asia whose historical and cultural legacy continue to be felt in these islands.

1

Prehistoric Ryukyu to the Gusuku Period

Paleolithic Era

Much of how the first people entered the Ryukyu Archipelago remains shrouded in mystery. In the archaeological record, there is evidence of people arriving from the south, and at other times from the north, bringing with them different material cultures. At times some of these people would have struggled to survive, and the bones and artifacts they left behind may have little relation to the people who inhabit these islands today.

The first people to enter the archipelago arrived during the Paleolithic era, about 20,000 to 30,000 years ago, when a land bridge connected it to mainland Japan. Bones from this era have been discovered in Okinawa and Miyako, with the oldest remains found in Yamashita Cave in Naha. These remains appear to be of an eight-year-old girl; radiocarbon dating suggests these bones are approximately 32,000 years old. The most famous remains were found in southern Okinawa, those of the 18,000-year-old Minatogawa Man. It has been proposed that the Minatogawa Man is related to Wadjak Man from Java, and Liujiang Man from southern China, suggesting that the Minatogawa Man entered the Ryukyu Archipelago from Southeast Asia.

However, it may have been difficult for the Minatogawa Man to have survived in the Ryukyu Archipelago. The Anthropologist, Takamiya Hiroto has argued that hunter-gatherers, seeking new sources of food may have entered the Ryukyu Archipelago only to go extinct there. At present, it is difficult to establish the genetic connection between Minatogawa Man and contemporary Okinawans as DNA is not well preserved in remains due to Ryukyu's humid climate.[2]

The key to cracking part of the mystery can be found through DNA analysis of contemporaneous Okinawans and Japanese. The biggest genetic difference between Okinawans and mainland Japanese is the high presence of the haplogroup M7a, which seems to have entered Japan from the south. M7a, which is thought to relate to the Jōmon people, can be found in about 7% of the population throughout mainland Japan, in Okinawa this is as high as 25%.[3] It is possible that the origins of Minatogawa Man will become more apparent with more advanced DNA analysis in the future, but for now it remains difficult to say whether or not he is the direct ancestor of the Okinawan people.[ii]

Southern and Northern Cultures in the Archaeological Record

In the archaeological record there are also signs that people entered these islands from Southeast Asia and southern China. The archaeologist, Katō Shinpei points to how stone tools found in Amami resemble those found in the aforementioned regions.[4] The picture is more complicated than just one group entering the archipelago from the south, as there appears to be two spheres of paleolithic culture in the archipelago, one in the south and another in the north.

In comparison to Amami, where artifacts are classified as deriving from the southern paleolithic cultural sphere, further

---

2   Kenichi Shinoda, *Nihonjin Ni Natta Sosen Tachi: DNA Kara Kaimei Suru Sono Tagenteki Kōzō* (NHK Books, 2007), 137.
3   *DNA Kara Kaimei Suru Sono Tagenteki Kōzō*, 140.
4   Kazuyuki Tomiyama, *Ryūkyū, Okinawa Shi No Sekai* (Yoshikawa Kōbunkan, 2003), 89.

north in Tanegashima and Kyushu, stone blades and microliths appear to come from a northern paleolithic cultural sphere. This northern paleolithic sphere which covered most of Japan seems to have had its borders around southern Kyushu and the most northern islands of the Ryukyu Archipelago.

Yet southern paleolithic culture also appears to have existed as far north as southern Kyushu. An archaeological excavation at Minami-Satsuma City in Kagoshima Prefecture in the early 1990s discovered Jōmon culture remains dating from about 12,000 years ago. At the site, scrapers used to make canoes, like those throughout Southeast Asia have been discovered alongside stone axes.

The southern Paleolithic culture may have come to an end following the massive Akahoya eruption from the Kikai Caldera, around 4350 BCE. The Kikai Caldera is a mostly submerged volcano and holds the record for the largest recorded eruption on the planet in the past 10,000 years. This eruption led to vast pyroclastic flows across southern Kyushu, with parts of the island and further up the Japanese archipelago to the home island of Shikoku being transformed into deserts; the area becoming uninhabitable for centuries. The Akahoya eruption ejected 150 cubic kilometers of magma, more than three times the 1815 Tambora eruption in Indonesia and would have been devastating to nearby life. The scale of the eruption was so large that ash layers from the eruption can be found as far away as Japan's northern home island of Hokkaido, around 1,000 miles away.

After the eruption, about 6,000 years ago, pottery with characteristic patterns formed by pressing fingers into the clay creating grooves began to appear in Kyushu alongside other plain pottery, although the lineage of these pottery styles remains unclear.[iii] About 1,000 years after the appearance of this pottery, Todoroki Pottery and Sobata Pottery, characteristic of the northern culture were found in Kyushu and as far south as Okinawa.[iv] Alongside this, obsidian tools made from rock in Kyushu and Ichiki pottery, also characteristic of the northern culture, became widespread, showing the influence of the northern culture extending south as far as Okinawa.[v]

While there was a direct connection between what would become Japan and Ryukyu, rising sea levels cut off the Ryukyu Archipelago from Kyushu and culture in the two regions would dramatically diverge over the following centuries.

The Shell Mound Period

During the period from 5000 BCE to the 12th century, Okinawa and Amami entered the Shell Mound Period, in which life developed along the island's coral reefs. During the early half of the Shell Mound Period, the Jōmon Period in Japan would shift to the Yayoi Period (300BCE-300CE), as mainland immigrants from China and the Korean Peninsula brought rice farming, ending the predominantly hunter-gatherer lifestyle of the Jōmon people in parts of southern and central Japan. Some have classified Okinawa's Shell Mound Period as an extension of Japan's Jōmon period, although there are significant cultural differences.

As far north as Hokkaido and as far south as Kyushu, the Jōmon people in Japan created ceramic figures known as Dogū. Although the purpose of these figures remains unknown, it is possible they were used in rituals. The appearance of Dogū can vary; some having bulbous eyes, such as the 'goggle-eyed' Dogū.[vi] Others resemble different humanoid creatures entirely such as the 'Hollow Dogū' and the 'Jōmon Venus'.[vii] These Dogū however, have not been found in Okinawa. Likewise, there are cultural elements that can be found in Okinawa that are not present on the mainland, such as geometrical carvings on

PREHISTORIC RYUKYU TO THE GUSUKU PERIOD

Dugong bone.[viii]

The people in both Okinawa and mainland Japan, while closely related genetically, were experiencing a cultural divergence. Perhaps the biggest factor for this was the advent of coral reefs. During the Shell Mound Period, people throughout the archipelago made their living closer to the ocean, the reefs providing a vital and stable source of food. The coral reefs of the Ryukyu Archipelago are the only coral reefs in all of East Asia, and are the most northern in the world. It is therefore not difficult to imagine the profound effect this could have on the lifestyle and culture of the people of Ryukyu.

With parts of mainland Japan shifting into the Yayoi period the culture of these new people would begin to extend into Northern and Central Ryukyu, however any cultural exchange that did take part in this period did not extend to the practice of mainland agriculture, the Ryukyu Archipelago would continue to develop without rice cultivation. There also appears to be a greater genetic divergence that took place in this period, with the people of Ryukyu, northern Japan and Hokkaido maintaining higher levels of DNA associated with the Jōmon than the mainland Japanese who were increasingly composed of Yayoi migrants from continental Asia. This genetic difference remains in the people of Okinawa and the Ainu of Hokkaido in the present day. Genetic differences can even be seen in dogs and other animals. Ryukyu and Ainu dog breeds share genetic connections which are far less present in Shiba-Inu dogs typical of mainland Japan. As with the mainland Japanese, the Shiba dogs have DNA more closely tied to breeds common in the Korean peninsula, which is not as present in Ryukyu and Ainu dog breeds.

Cultural connections between Northern and Central Ryukyu and mainland Japan came about through trade. Amongst the coral reefs there was an abundance of conch and green turban shells — a highly coveted treasure throughout the ancient world. Green turban shells have a thick layer of mother-of-pearl inside them, spiralled in shape, they are colored a speckled green and brown, while the conchs can be a florescent pink, pale white or motley brown and are characterized by a distinct siphonal canal. These shells were akin to precious gemstones and many cultures throughout the world used such shells not only as jewellery but also as a form of currency. In Kyushu these shells were used by chieftains and religious leaders to show their power or spiritual authority. One such example can be found almost five hundred miles north of Okinawa in the Japanese home island of Kyushu where the grave of an individual from the Yayoi period (1000 BCE – 300 CE) was unearthed with a bracelet of conch shells from far away Okinawa as a grave item.

In return for these shells, those in Northern and Central Okinawa received pottery. With demand for these shells growing, people throughout the Ryukyu Archipelago began collecting them in shell mounds in anticipation of trade, and these shells were carried as far away as Hokkaido and the Korean Peninsula. The creation of shell mounds led to an increasingly stratified society with local leaders overseeing trade, laying the foundations for territorial disputes throughout Okinawa from the 12th Century. In the island of Kumejima, off the east coast of Okinawa, coins from China's Warring States Period and Tang Period (618-907 CE) have been discovered suggesting the trade in Kyushu's shells went as far as China, well beyond the Japanese mainland.

Stratification between Ryukyu and Japan
Throughout the first centuries of the Common Era cultural and economic developments in Japan would greatly outpace those of the Ryukyu Archipelago. Ryukyu largely remained unchanged throughout the Shell Mound Period. Beginning in 538CE, Japan

PREHISTORIC RYUKYU TO THE GUSUKU PERIOD

entered the Asuka Period, lasting until 645, where it would see the introduction of Buddhism and subsequent construction of vast temples and pagodas to celebrate the new religion. Following this was the Nara period (710-794) and the creation of a capital city in present day Nara, attracting merchants from Korea, China and as far away as India. The Heian period followed from 794-1185, in which court culture reached a golden age in the new capital inspiring Japanese classics such as the *Tales of Genji*, one of the world's first novels which was in circulation from 1008 onwards. During this period agriculture transitioned to rice farming, administrative and criminal codes (*Ritsuryō* codes) were established, and further temples were constructed.

While all this change was happening in the north, the lives for the people of the Ryukyu Archipelago remained relatively unchanged, continuing their hunter-gatherer lifestyle while collecting and trading shells from the shallow lagoons surrounding the coral reefs.

The continuation of hunter-gatherer societies in this period occurred at both extremities of what is now the nation of Japan, the Ryukyu Archipelago in the south and the indigenous Ainu in northern Honshu and Hokkaido beyond. The continuation of the hunter-gatherer lifestyle does not necessarily mean that these societies were inferior to their rice-cultivating neighbors. Both societies had bountiful supplies to sustain their populations and hunters benefited from working fewer hours than their more labor-intensive farming counterparts. Jared Diamond has also pointed out that many societies made the shift to farming only when hunting became difficult, and often people in farming societies were more malnourished than their hunting counterparts.[5]

---

[5] Jared Diamond, *The Worst Mistake in the History of the Human Race*, Discovery Magazine, UCLA School of Medicine, 1987, 64-66.

THE RYUKYUS

Differences in Southern Ryukyu

The islands of Northern Ryukyu and Central Ryukyu are close together. They begin in the north with Tanegashima off the cost of Kyushu arching south towards the island of Okinawa. Today, Amami in Northern Ryukyu and Okinawa in Central Ryukyu are largely thought of as separate entities, the former belonging to Kagoshima prefecture and the latter Okinawa prefecture, but these islands for the most part had a shared history up until the early 17th century. The same cannot be said for Southern Ryukyu which is separated from Okinawa by 270-kilometers of open ocean called the Miyako Strait.

At times, this gulf of ocean would act as a barrier between the societies living on the Sakishima islands in the south and the rest of the archipelago. As such, divergent cultures can be found in the archaeological record between Miyako and Yaeyama in the Sakishima islands and the islands in northern and central Ryukyu.

Around 4,300 to 3,300 years ago, Yaeyama and Miyako were in the 'Red Pottery Period'. While this pottery has not been found in China, Taiwan, or Okinawa, it is still a possibility that this culture was adopted from southern China or Southeast Asia, making its way from the west into Yaeyama via Taiwan.

These people possibly crossed into Yaeyama in search of new grounds to hunt and fish. Pottery of this era is referred to as *Shimotabaru*, its name derives from the shell mound on the island of Hateruma with the same name in which it was first discovered.[ix] A characteristic of the *Shimotabaru* pottery is the particular thickness of its walls which are 1.5 to 2cm thick compared to the 8mm to 1cm thickness of the pottery found in Okinawa.

The Red Pottery Period disappeared from Yaeyama and Miyako followed by an eight-hundred-year blank period in the

PREHISTORIC RYUKYU TO THE GUSUKU PERIOD

archaeological record. It is not clear what happened to the people who made *Shimotabaru* pottery, but it is possible that they met a natural disaster; famine was always a risk and faults in the Ryukyu oceanic trench can unleash devastating earthquakes. It is also possible, although perhaps less likely, that they moved on from Miyako and Yaeyama to elsewhere. Other theories suggest pottery fell out of use in favor of wooden containers that are absent from the archeological record. If this were the case, the methods for making pottery could have disappeared from the peoples of Yaeyama and Miyako over generations without any intervening external event.

About seven hundred years after this, 1,500 years ago, the Sakishima Islands entered a period classified as the No Pottery Period, in which shell axes emerge in the archaeological record for the first time. These axes were likely used in the construction of canoes. However, as with the Red Pottery Period many unanswered questions remain. Heated stones used for cooking, which also appear during this period, can be seen in other Pacific island cultures, and while the custom could have developed independently, there is the possibility of an as yet unknown connection. Shell axes have also been discovered in the Philippines but known examples are at least 2,000 years older than those found in Yaeyama and Miyako. More puzzling is that similar axes cannot be found in Taiwan, which would have been a likely source had people entered the Sakishima Islands from the Philippines.

Because of the differences between Southern Ryukyu and the rest of the archipelago, one might expect the peoples of Sakishima to be genetically different from their northern cousins, but this is not the case. It seems that if the people of Sakishima were genetically different once, the people throughout the archipelago became more homogeneous over time. The same is true for the languages of Miyako and Yaeyama, which are part of the Ryukyu language family sharing many similarities to Okinawan.

The Gusuku Period

A degree of homogeneity came about during the archipelago's next epoch which saw increasing connections throughout the islands. During the Gusuku Period (12th Century – 15th Century) the same ocean that had once been a barrier, became a bridge through superior vessels facilitating a crossing between the islands once more.

With plentiful resources, the societies of the Ryukyu Archipelago inevitably saw a growth in their populations which in turn led to fiercer competition for these resources. It is from the Gusuku Period that archaeologists have discovered carbonated rice and wheat, as well as knives made of iron together with the beginning of agricultural settlements throughout the islands. People also began living on plateaus and hills, making use of spring water for farming with some focus shifting away from a dependence on the coral reefs. Although production of iron had started during the late Shell Mound Period, production greatly accelerated in the Gusuku period with iron production in Southern Okinawa rising tenfold.[x]

The name of the period, 'Gusuku' is the Okinawan word for castle, and can be traced to the remains of stone buildings built from the 13th Century. These castles with their towering stone walls continue to be a feature of the landscape today and you will encounter them across Okinawa.

The men who controlled these castles were known as *Aji* or *Anji*, and as with the feudal lords in mainland Japan, there were power struggles among themselves to increase their hegemony throughout the island.

The historian Tomiyama Kazuyuki has divided the Gusuku

PREHISTORIC RYUKYU TO THE GUSUKU PERIOD

Period into two uneven parts, the early part of the Gusuku Period becoming the 'Proto-Gusuku' period. During the Proto-Gusuku Period in the 12th Century, the foundations for the building of Gusuku were laid, although it would not be until the 13th Century that they began to appear across the landscape of Okinawa in their full castle form.[6] It is not clear exactly when castle walls were erected on these sites, it could have been as early as between the 13th and 14th Centuries as it is known the *Aji* were fighting for control of land, although more archaeological evidence still needs to be found.

By the 15th Century it is known that Zakimi castle had walls constructed from blocks of cut stone, complete with masonry and arched entrances. While these Gusuku were often built on hills suggesting functionality as castles, they may have initially been religious sites, store houses, or a mixture of all three.

Most Gusuku throughout Okinawa have several characteristic features: a main hall located within a series of walls, an inner garden called an *Unā*, stores houses and holy sites. These features can be seen throughout Katsuren, Nakijin and Zakimi Gusuku, all of which were built between the 14th and 16th Centuries.[xi]

As the *Aji* of these Gusuku vied with each other for power, the number of abandoned Gusuku increased as territory became consolidated into fewer and fewer hands of increasingly powerful *Aji*. The ruins of many of these Gusuku remain scattered throughout the Okinawan landscape.

Increasing Trade in the Gusuku period

It was during the Gusuku Period that there was an increase in international trade. From around the 11th Century, stone pots from Nagasaki, beneficial for being able to maintain high degrees

---

6   *Ryūkyū, Okinawa Shi No Sekai*, 103.

of heat, began to appear throughout the entirety of the Ryukyu Archipelago. It is likely that these pots were traded for shells, and it is important to note how unlike they are to pottery in the Shell Mound Period as these goods managed to cross the gulf between Okinawa and Miyako. While pottery could be found before the Gusuku Period, these pots are far more widely distributed and in greater numbers.

Porcelain from China was obtained in unprecedented levels beginning in the 13th Century, and by the following century porcelain from Southeast Asia begins to appear in increasing volume also. The island of Tokunoshima in Northern Ryukyu, became a center of pottery production, and this 'Sue Pottery' was circulated throughout the Archipelago.[xii] Another pottery that appears in Tokunoshima is 'Kamui Pottery', from the 11th to 14th Centuries; more than one hundred kilns can be found on this relatively small island.[xiii] Kamui Pottery is present at the sites of numerous Gusuku, and possibly originated in Korea as tiles found at Urasoe Gusuku are in the style of Korea's Goryeo Kingdom (918-1392). Similar tiles can be found throughout Katsuren Gusuku and Shuri Castle. At Urasoe, it is not clear whether these tiles were bought directly from Korea, or were made by a similar technique somewhere in Ryukyu, such as Tokunoshima. There are numerous theories of how the production *Kamui* Pottery began in Northern Ryukyu; the practice could have been from Koreans who moved to Tokunoshima, or it could have been bought to the island via Kyushu merchants.

The presence of both *Sue* and *Kamui* Pottery throughout the archipelago demonstrates that from the 12th Century the culture of the Sakishima Islands in Southern Ryukyu was becoming more similar to that of Okinawa and Amami in the north.

It was not only pottery from further north that entered the Sakishima Islands. When Yaeyama entered a period equivalent

PREHISTORIC RYUKYU TO THE GUSUKU PERIOD

to the Gusuku Period in Okinawa, porcelain from China began to appear on much greater level here also with the Sakishima Islands conducting their own independent trade with China.[xiv]

Yaeyama's equivalent to the Gusuku castles were 'Suku' which also served a similar purpose. The most famous archaeological site is the Furusutobaru Castle site where mounds of earth overlooking the sea at Ōhama on Ishikgaki have been found. The former walls of the site have been reconstructed and pieces of pottery and metal unearthed on the site indicate the people of Yaeyama were trading beyond their shores.[xv]

Some archaeologists have posited the theory that the Ryukyu languages were formed throughout the Gusuku Period, with Japanese merchants, blacksmiths and potters settling on Ryukyu and raising families with the local population, establishing similarities to Japanese. This theory also offers possible answers to why the languages of Yaeyama and Miyako resemble the other Ryukyuan languages despite a different archaeological record. On the other hand, the linguist Uemura Yukio has proposed much earlier dates for the formation of the Ryukyu languages, somewhere between the Yayoi or Nara Periods, although Uemura does recognize that the languages of Sakishima were likely later developments of the Ryukyu Language family.[7]

The early half of the Gusuku Period in the Ryukyu Archipelago corresponds with the Heian Period (794-1192) and Kamakura Period (1185-1333) in mainland Japan, in which a new class of samurai began to shift power away from the imperial court and into their own hands, establishing the country's first shogunate. The latter half of the Gusuku Period corresponds with the Muromachi Period (1338-1573) in which the Ashikaga Shogunate disposed of the *de facto* imperial government. However, as local

---

7   *Ryūkyū, Okinawa Shi No Sekai*, 104-105.

THE RYUKYUS

samurai leaders (Daimyō) began to increase in power Japan fell into the Sengoku or the warring states period in the 15th Century and the martial prowess these samurai built up fighting each other would have dire consequences for the Ryukyu archipelago centuries down the line.

2

THE THREE KINGDOMS

Three Kingdoms

In Ryukyu, by the early 14th Century, the vying *Aji* had consolidated power into three domains, and this period is known as the "Three Kingdoms Period" (1322-1429). The Three Kingdoms constituted the island of Okinawa, with Hokuzan in the north, Chūzan in the center, and Nanzan in the south.[xvi]

In each of these kingdoms, the center of power was a particular Gusuku. In Hokuzan this was Nakijin Gusuku, which lies on a peninsula jutting out from Okinawa's north-west side. The high stone walls of Nakijin remain standing today. At 1.5 kilometers in length and 8 meters tall, at their highest points, from a distance it appears as if a miniature Great Wall of China is cutting across the landscape. From within the castle walls one can look down from the high ground onto the forest which gives way to the shallows and ocean further beyond. The *Aji* of Nakijin extended their rule across northern Okinawa and Amami.[xvii]

In terms of space, Hokuzan rule extended across more than half of the landmass of Okinawa, however much of this was rural and sparse populations were surrounded by vast swathes of the Yanbaru rainforest. Perhaps because of this, there is less information remaining about the kings of Hokuzan, although Nakijin itself is extolled in the *Omorosaushi*, a volume of songs composed between the 12th and 17th Centuries that capture much of the history of the Ryukyu Kingdom, calling Nakijin 'renowned' and how it 'conquered many *Aji*'.[xviii]

South of Hokuzan is the kingdom of Chūzan with Urasoe Gusuku at its center. Its layered walls are reminiscent of a wedding cake as they climb up the plateau. The central Gusuku of each kingdom was not necessarily fixed, and the center of Chūzan would later be moved to Shuri Castle.[xix]

The center of Nanzan, the most southern kingdom, appears to have been even more fluid than that of Chūzan, with theories that both Shimashii-Ōsato Gusuku and Shimashiri-Ōsato (also known as Nanzan Gusuku) were the center of hegemony in the south. Compared to the castles of the two kingdoms in the north, both are currently in a state of disrepair. Shimashii-Ōsato Gusuku can be found in Nanjō City and only a few walls remain, most of which have crumbled to large stones; the same is true of Shimashiri-Ōsato Gusuku in present-day Itoman, the most southern city on the island of Okinawa.

The Official History
Much of what we know about the Three Kingdoms Period comes from official histories of the Ryukyu Kingdom. The Ryukyu Kingdom had its origins in Chūzan which came to absorb both its northern and southern neighbors. Much of this history therefore shows Chūzan as a benevolent state in contrast to the corruption of the kings of Hokuzan and Nanzan.

Numerous scholars have also proposed that there never were three 'kingdoms' on the island of Okinawa — it is far more likely that there were collections of *Aji* who shared a similar culture forming the primary three domains of control. Within these regions, unity was not absolute and *Aji* could be disposed of which may also explain why there are two castles at Nanzan. If this theory is correct, each region only became a 'kingdom' with

THE THREE KINGDOMS

the hindsight of the Ryukyu Kingdom centuries later, spinning a grand narrative about how the kingdom came into being many centuries after these events took place.

Therefore, while these official histories likely have an undercurrent of truth, they are amalgamated with exaggerations and self-justifications: these histories were written with the aim to justify legitimacy of the regime and their record cannot be taken completely at face value.

Sources from the Ryukyu Kingdom are not the only historical records we have from this period. The first descriptions of the Ryukyu Archipelago come from Chinese sources, and it is from these continental neighbors that the term 'Ryukyu' was first used.

In the *Book of Sui* (completed in the mid-7th Century) a naval report refers to an island that can be seen to the east on a clear Spring or Autumn day.[xx] The report is by a naval officer dispatched by Emperor Yang of Sui (569-618); China's first recorded discovery of a 'Ryukyu'. This 'Ryukyu' could be referring to Taiwan or possibly Yonaguni, the most western of Yaeyama's islands which can be seen with the naked eye from Taiwan under a clear sky.

As the islands of Okinawa cannot be seen from mainland China or Taiwan, it is highly unlikely that 'Ryukyu' originally referred to Okinawa. The first time 'Ryukyu' is used explicitly in reference to Okinawa, is in the *Ming Shilu* (compiled between 1368 and 1644), by this time the term 'Ryukyu' had been applied specifically to Okinawa, and would eventually become a term referring to the entirety of the archipelago.[xxi] Chinese works would use a range of different characters to emulate the sound of the word 'Ryukyu' eventually settling on 琉球 which would also be taken up by the later Ryukyu Kingdom.[xxii]

The naming of these islands, in a map from the Ming dynasty

era, also demonstrates their importance, classifying Okinawa as 'Greater Ryukyu', and Taiwan as 'Minor Ryukyu'. Such monikers signal that it was Okinawa that the Ming primarily sought for diplomatic and commercial links rather than Taiwan.[xxiii] This naming convention would eventually make its way into European languages, first in Portuguese as *'Lequio Loochoo'* during the Age of Exploration (15th to 17th Century) and then as *'Great Loochoo'* in English. Why did China's Ming Dynasty (1368-1644) place such high value on the islands of 'Great Ryukyu'? To understand this, it is necessary to look at the environment in which China's Ming Dynasty came to be.

The Birth of China's Ming Dynasty

Before the Ming Dynasty, there was the Yuan dynasty (1279-1368) which was formed by the Mongols following the conquering of the Han Chinese Song Dynasty (920-1279). The emergence of a Mongol Empire can be traced back to 1206, when Genghis Khan succeeded in unifying the people of the Mongolian steppes. The Mongols first became a direct threat when they began encroaching on China's northern frontier in 1215, with the capture of present day Beijing (formerly the capital of the Jin Dynasty (266-420), and the establishment of the new capital of Khanbaliq. The Mongols finally subjugated southern China by overthrowing the ethnically Chinese Song Dynasty in 1279.

This consolidation of power in China came under Genghis Khan's grandson, Kublai Khan (1215-1294). But the Mongol dynasty was not destined to last: only eighty years later China's new imperial power was facing increasing resistance and revolts against the Mongols sprang up throughout China.

It was against this backdrop that Zhu Yuanzhang (1328-1398) emerged as one of the opposing leaders. By 1364, it appeared that Zhu had the Mandate of Heaven and had conquered almost all of China, declaring Nanjing his new capital. In 1368, Zhu and his army occupied Khanbaliq, driving the Mongols to the Eurasian Steps. Initiating his reign as the Hongwu Emperor, Zhu began carrying out reforms to centralize the new regime.

While the Yuan dynasty had been toppled, fighting with the Mongols continued north of the Great Wall. To stabilize the country, the Ming began to send delegates throughout Asia, in the process establishing a diplomatic network that would affirm the Ming's place as the new authority in China.

One of the main threats the Ming faced were the Wakō pirates who were prevalent in the western Pacific. These pirates primarily raided the coastlines of China and Korea but were also operating along the coast of Japan, in fact the term Wakō has often been translated as 'Japanese pirates', and many in China viewed the pirates as a problem stemming from Japan. Yet there are accounts of Wakō originating from China and Korea and it would be a mistake to assume that all Wakō were Japanese, this evidence can even be found in Chinese and Korean texts. *The History of Ming* suggests that by the 16th Century more than half the Wakō were Chinese.[xxiv] While on the Korean Peninsula an official history of the Kingdom of Goryeo records that the Wakō were bandits from Korea.[xxv] *The Annals of the Joseon Dynasty*, written under the regime which succeeded Goryeo—records that Koreans wearing similar clothes to Japanese were often pirates.[xxvi] The Historian Murai Shōsuke has proposed that the Wakō pirates were dropouts from mainstream society throughout East Asia, away from the constraints of emperors and kings, they lived free as 'marginal men'.[8]

The Wakō also likely participated in trade as well as pillaging, and the historian Takara Kurayoshi has suggested that the god

---

8   Naoki Yoshinari and Hiromi Fuku, *Ryūkyū Ōkoku to Wakō Omoro No Kataru Rekishi* (Shinwasha, 2008), 23.

of warriors, agriculture and fishing, *Hachiman* may have been bought to Ryukyu by Wakō from Japan who came to trade in Naha.[9]

To the Ming, the Wakō were a constant annoyance and in 1371 a maritime ban was introduced to counteract their activities. The consequences of the ban meant that any Chinese wishing to trade privately had no choice aside from smuggling, furthermore the Chinese people already scattered throughout Asia were no longer allowed to return home. This is in part the reason for Chinese communities remaining widespread throughout Southeast Asia.

The tributary system was not a historical inevitability, China had the power to extend trade networks and even establish colonies overseas. The most striking example of this potential is under the third Ming Emperor Zhu Di (1402–1424), the Yongle Emperor, who sent Admiral Zheng He (1371–1433/35) to report on the world beyond China's borders. Across seven voyages between 1405 and 1433 Zheng's fleet visited Southeast Asia, South Africa, and western and eastern Africa. Yet instead of pursuing this path of international trade, one that would have led to a very different world history, China decided to close its borders and trade via a tributary system, this provided a special opportunity for not only Ryukyu but individuals throughout East and Southeast Asia.

The Ming's Tributary Network

Under the tributary system, a state that paid tribute to the imperial throne recognized the ultimate authority of the Emperor. They would pay homage to the Emperor at a fixed time of so many years, arriving in Chinese ports designated for them by the Ming government. They would bring offerings from their

---

9   Kurayoshi Takara, Kenichi Tanigawa, and Ringorō Ōyama, *Okinawa Amami to Yamato* (Doseisha, 1986), 11.

THE THREE KINGDOMS

dominion and in turn be rewarded with Chinese goods that were more than compensatory for the journey and far exceeding the value of the goods given by them as tribute. Under the tributary system, this was the only legal way for foreign states to obtain Chinese goods.

Over the reigns of the first three Ming Emperors, a vassalage network was built up to include Goryeo (Korea), Japan, Annam and Champa (Vietnam), Siam (Thailand), Malacca, Sumatra, the Mongolian Plains and India. Due to Ryukyu and Japan's proximity to China, they were some of the first states to enter this tributary network under the reign of the first Ming Emperor.[xxvii]

The first Chinese envoy to Japan was sent early in 1369, only one year after the foundation of the Ming empire. The Hongwu Emperor dispatched a delegation led by Yang Zai (Yosai in Japanese) with a sovereign letter that announced the foundations of the new regime in the neighboring continent and a request that Japan suppress the Wakō pirates active in its waters.

By bringing Japan into the tributary system, Ming China hoped that it could also bring an end to piracy, although this was not to be the case. In 1401, the Muromachi Shogun Ashikaga Yoshimitsu (1358-1408) sent an envoy to China along with tribute. The following year, the Jianwen Emperor (1377-1402) sent an envoy in turn, recognizing Yoshimitsu as the 'King of Japan.'

Ryukyu's beginnings as a vassal state

A few years after sending the first envoy to Japan, Yang Zai was once again sent in 1372 on a diplomatic mission, this time to King Satto (1321-1395) of Chūzan in Ryukyu. As with many of the early kings of the three kingdoms not much is known about Satto, although one legend in the official history shows off his mystical powers.

Building a tower one night, a *Habu* (yellow spotted pit viper) bit into the king's left hand, before the poison could spread through his veins, he cut off his hand. Shocked by his king's sacrifice, a loyal retainer cut off his own hand and donated it to Satto. Ever since this, the king's left hand was said to be darker and hairier than his right. The purpose of such a legend is likely to show the benevolence of Satto, a king so just that his loyal retainers were even willing to make such sacrifices for their lord.[xxviii]

Why did the Chinese envoy first arrive in the Kingdom of Chūzan instead of Hokuzan or Nanzan? Chūzan had some of the finest ports in Okinawa, such as Naha, Tomari and Maki and this would have made the middle Okinawan kingdom the most accessible place for a Chinese envoy.

In the *Ming Shilu* it is recorded that Yang Zai was dispatched to Chūzan by the Hongwu Emperor where he told King Satto of China's long rule by the Mongols and of how the Mandate of Heaven had been rightfully restored to the Han Chinese. Under the benevolence of the Hongwu Emperor this new empire had been christened the 'Great Ming'. Now the Emperor was sending delegations across the world to tell them of the new world order in China.

Bringing Ryukyu into China's tributary network of course served to bolster the system, yet as with Japan there were other ulterior motives for sending the delegation to Ryukyu.

Despite the overthrow of the Yuan Dynasty, the Ming still faced the threat of the Mongols beyond the Great Wall of China. In Ryukyu, there were precious commodities required to hold off the Mongol hordes: sulfur, a prerequisite for gunpowder, and horses, a means to carry supplies to the front lines respectively.

Yang Zai was not the first Chinese to visit Ryukyu, the historian Harada Nobuo has pointed out that there was already a network of Chinese in Ryukyu who shared a common language with their homeland, which can be seen in the archaeological record with Chinese pottery found throughout the Ryukyu Archipelago from a much earlier date than the foundation of the Ming Dynasty.[10]

These connections to China were not focused in just Central and Northern Ryukyu, Chinese pottery unearthed from the 14th and 15th Centuries at Miyako also suggests that Miyako and Yaeyama had their own links with China since at least the 14th Century. This network of Chinese was a factor that enabled the Ming to make inroads throughout East and Southeast Asia with relative ease.

Responding to the Ming's call, in December of the same year, King Satto arranged for his brother Taiki to lead a tributary mission to the Ming. It is not known when Taiki arrived, or in which port the delegation anchored, but it is recorded that the Emperor was given a letter from the King of Chūzan alongside other tributary items and that in turn the delegation was given items including the finest silks and other provisions.

Taiki then crossed the East China Sea and made it back safely to Ryukyu, which is confirmed in the *Ming Shilu* as Taiki made numerous further expeditions to China.

Under King Satto and his successor Bunei (1356-1406), Chūzan would send over thirty delegations to the Ming between 1372 and 1403. The items Chūzan sent to China included horses and sulfur from Ryukyu and palm trees and pepper from Southeast Asia. This record of pepper and palms being given by Chūzan shows that even in this early stage, some form of trade between the Ryukyu Archipelago and Southeast Asia was already underway.

The *Ming Shilu* also mentions the kings of Hokuzan and Nanzan. It is recorded that the king of Nanzan, Shō-Satto (or

---

10 Nobuo Harada, *Ryūkyū To chūgoku: Wasurerareta Sakuhōshi* (Yoshikawakōbunkan, 2003), 13.

alternatively Ufusato) paid tribute to the Ming in 1380 and continued paying tribute from then on, in total seven times until 1398.[xxix]

Shō-Satto's first delegation was sent seven years after Taiki first ventured to China. Later in the *Ming Shilu*, there is also mention of the king of Hokuzan, Haniji who first sent a tributary delegation in 1383, three years after the king of Nanzan sent his mission. Rather than being under direct rule by China, the three kingdoms shared cultural and economic ties. Each kingdom would bring goods to the Ming court and be rewarded with Chinese goods many times more valuable than their initial tribute. The kingdoms could then keep these goods or sell them throughout Asia.

Tribute was rewarding for the kingdoms as they could send delegations to China on multiple occasions. The *Ming Shilu* records that Nanzan alone sent 35 tributary missions to China between 1380 and 1429. By recognizing the emperor, each king was bestowed clothing suitable to their rank and a crown called the *Hibenkan*.[xxx] The *Hibenkan* were tall round hats studded with gold, silver and jewels. An 18th Century example of a *Hibenkan* has twelve gold stripes, and over seven types of jewels, with twenty-four covering the hat in total. An ornate hairpin goes through the crowns, and on this example the heads of dragons were finely carved into them.[xxxi]

Benefits to the three kingdoms extended beyond economic support. In 1392, both Chūzan and Nanzan sent students to the Guozijian (國子監), effectively China's Imperial college.[xxxii] At this establishment, students from Ryukyu would learn to read and write Chinese at the highest levels, something which would continue into the following era of the Ryukyu Kingdom and throughout China's Ming and Qing dynasties. This made Ryukyu the state that continued to send students to the college

THE THREE KINGDOMS

for the longest period.

But the foreign relations of the three kingdoms were not only tied to China. In 1398, Chūzan sent Utsuchi on an expedition to Goryeo (Korea) to return Koreans who had been the victims of Wakō pirates.[xxxiii] Along with returning the Koreans, Utsuchi's delegation also bought with them sulfur, palms, pepper and turtle shells. Later that year, Goryeo sent a delegation to Ryukyu to give thanks.

Chūzan also received tribute from Miyako and Yaeyama. One of the most notable cases was in 1390 when the hegemon of Miyako, Yonahasedo Tuyumya stayed at the port of Tomari in Chūzan for three years, learning the Okinawan language. During this period both Miyako and Yaeyama were outside of the control of any of the three kingdoms on Okinawa and would not be brought under the control of Okinawa until the birth of the Ryukyu Kingdom.

3

WAR AND REGICIDE

The Throne of Chūzan

Despite having the power to send out tributary missions to China, the three kingdoms themselves were considerably unstable. In the *Annals of the Joseon Dynasty*, it is recorded that in the Kingdom of Nanzan, when the uncle of Shō-Satto usurped the throne, the former king fled to the Korean peninsula. Then in September of 1394, a delegation from Chūzan requested Shō Satto's return.

The changes between the central Gusuku at Nanzan also suggest internal fighting amongst the *Aji* of the same 'kingdom'. It is also recorded that when, in the New Year of 1383, the emissaries of Satto and Shō-Satto met with the Hongwu Emperor in Nanjing, he urged them to stop feuding and end their disputes so that the people of Ryukyu could live in peace.

Just as the archaeological record has shown links between the Ryukyu Archipelago and a wider East Asia, it is in the late 14th and early 15th centuries that pottery begins to become more unanimous signifying a single kingdom that came to rule these islands.

According to the official histories of Chūzan, the figure who would go on to found the kingdom was only 150 centimeters (4 feet 11 inches) in height, born in 1372 and inherited his father's rank as the Sashiki *Aji* in the Kingdom of Nanzan in 1402. Due to his small size, he has been called 'the little *Aji* of Sashiki'. This figure would later go on to take the name Shō Hashi, as the founder of the Ryukyu Kingdom.

Shō Hashi's father was a local chief with a Gusuku at Sashiki. While he held some regional power, he was not a particularly influential figure in Nanzan, let alone Okinawa.

But a change of fortune came for Shō Hashi when King Satto of Chūzan passed away on October 5, 1396 at the age of 75 and his son Bunei ascended the throne. In the official histories of the Ryukyu Kingdom, Bunei is described as an impudent ruler, enjoying the benefits of the people of Chūzan's labors and offering no respect in return. In 1406 Shō Hashi led an attack on the center of Chūzan, Urasoe Gusuku, toppling Bunei from the throne. It is not clear whether Shō Hashi led a preemptive strike against Bunei from his base in Sashiki, or if the *Aji* within Chūzan allied with him and assisted in the coup. Having conquered Chūzan Shō Hashi installed his father, Shō Shishō (1354-1421) on the throne.[xxxiv]

In the *Omorosaushi*, a collection of Ryukyu epics, Shō Shishō is described as an eagle, a symbol of quick wittedness and of the king's right to rule. Such a king was destined to bring prosperity to his people. Yoshinari Naoki believes the description of Shō Shishō as an eagle is an influence derived from Okinawa's interactions with the Korean Peninsula. In Korean texts, such as the *Samguk Yusa*, the eagle is a symbol of absolute rule.[11]

The Subjugation of the Kingdom of Hokuzan

The following year, in 1407 Shō Shishō sent a delegation to the Ming court informing them that he was Bunei's chosen successor. While the father and son had overthrown Bunei, it seems they

---

11   *Ryūkyū Ōkoku to Wakō Omoro No Kataru*, 205-215.

thought there would be a question their legitimacy, a theme that can be seen throughout the official histories of the kingdoms of Ryukyu.

In 1416, news reached Chūzan that the king of Hokuzan, Hananchi (reign 1401-1416) was planning to launch an offensive on Chūzan. In response, Shō Hashi led an army of three-thousand men to attack Nakijin Gusuku. Hananchi was defeated and the kingdom of Hokuzan disappeared from the *Ming Shilu*. The north and center of Okinawa now became one kingdom, with Chūzan extending to the Yanbaru rainforest in the north.

In 1421 Shō Shishō passed away, with Shō Hashi finally ascending the throne at the age of 49. The next year, in 1422, Shō Hashi appointed his son Shō Chū (1391-1444) as the custodian of Hokuzan at Nakijin, and Shō Chū would become the third king of Ryukyu in 1440. It is around this time that Shō Hashi moved the capital of Chūzan from Urasoe to Shuri, possibly after the Ming recognized him as the heir to the throne, or it could have been the base he had used to attack Hokuzan. When exactly this move happened is unclear but by at least 1427 Shuri had become the seat of royal power. Shuri castle would go on to become a symbol of not just the Ryukyu Kingdom but Okinawa itself.[xxxv]

There is an epitaph that is now in the Okinawa Prefectural Museum that commemorates how Huái Jī (Kaiki in Japanese) came to Chūzan as a representative of the Ming under the reign of Shō Hashi.[xxxvi] Under Huái Jī, Shuri was developed in accordance with the principles of Feng Shui—this saw the construction of gardens, the digging of a pond called *Ryūtan* and the planting of trees and flowers. Takara Kurayoshi has noted the year these projects at Shuri began was the year after Shō Hashi's conquest of Hokuzan, and the project probably commemorated a celebration of the kingdom's new domain.[xxxvii]

WAR AND REGICIDE

The fall of Nanzan and the Birth of a Unified Island of Okinawa
Over a decade after conquering Hokuzan, in 1429 Shō Hashi led an army against the king of Nanzan, Taromai (or Tarumii, reign 1415-1429).[xxxviii] Taromai is recorded in the official histories as a covetous king, his greed and indifference to his subjects were such that he traded a spring from which his people could obtain fresh water for a frivolous golden folding screen.

As with the stories surrounding Hokuzan, it was likely internal disputes within Nanzan that gave Chūzan the opportunity to launch an offensive, but the concept of a just ruler taking over from the corrupt is a recurring theme that continues until the stability of the second Ryukyu dynasty was established in 1469. Having conquered Nanzan, the island of Okinawa was at last unified under one political entity. As the founder of what had become the Ryukyu Kingdom, in 1430 Shō Hashi sent a delegation to meet with the Chinese Xuande Emperor (1399-1435), and according to *Chūzan Seifu* the following message was delivered:

> "I report to your Majesty that in our country of Ryukyu, three kings have been fighting ceaselessly for more than one-hundred years, with the people struggling under this distress. Being unable to bare this state of affairs, I [Shō Hashi] raised an army to chastise Hananchi in the north and subjugate Taromai in the south. Now society is at peace and the people's lifestyle has become settled."[12]

Thus, Shō Hashi had finally fulfilled the request of the Hongwu Emperor: the creation of a stable Okinawa. With the Kingdom of

---

12 Kurayoshi Takara, *Ryūkyū Ōkoku* (Iwanami Shoten, 2005), 51.

Chūzan at the center of the unification of Okinawa, the title 'King of Chūzan' would continue to be used within Ryukyu, although it would come to mean the entirety of Ryukyu, and the characters of Chūzan (中山) can be seen throughout Shuri Castle.

The unification of the Ryukyu Kingdom came centuries later than the formation of states in China, Korea and Japan. Around this same time the dome of the Florence cathedral was being constructed and Portuguese traders were delivering their first cargo of slaves to Lisbon in Europe. Closer to home, Beijing had become the largest city in the world and this would bring more prosperity to this nascent island kingdom.

This was also a time of turbulence to the north. While Ryukyu and China were in periods of relative stability, not long after the Ryukyu Kingdom's formation Japan descended into a period of warring states as Daimyō (feudal lords) fought each other for hegemony. The growing power of Europe and the militarization of Japan would have stark consequences, eventually bringing an end to the Ryukyu Kingdom — although this would not be for another four hundred years in 1879.

Ryukyu's conquest of Amami

Having conquered Okinawa, the first Shō dynasty began to expand its power to the outlying islands of Okinawa and eventually north towards the islands of Amami. While the Japanese records *Nihon-Shoki* and *Zoku-Nihonki* recorded that islands in the south (Amami) were part of Japan's *Ritsuryō* system, this likely meant that they only paid tribute to the Yamato court, rather than under direct rule by Japan.[xxxix]

For the Ryukyu Kingdom, Amami being just north of Okinawa was ripe for the picking and these islands likely became part of the Ryukyu Kingdom between the late 14th and early 15th Century.

The connection between Amami and Okinawa was close even before their formal integration under the Ryukyu Kingdom. The southern Amami islands of Yoronto and Okinoerabu are less than 100 kilometers off the coast of Okinawa. As these islands had no trees for firewood, their denizens made numerous trips back and forth to the kingdom of Hokuzan during the days of the Three Kingdoms and were probably some of the earliest islands in Amami to become absorbed by the Ryukyu Kingdom.

Amami Ōshima, the second largest island in the archipelago, became part of the Ryukyu Kingdom in 1441, although there would be a twenty-four-year gap before the neighboring island Kikaijima was integrated into the kingdom. This expansion north was evidently a gradual process.

The legacy of this integration of Amami from the south continues to be seen today. Traditional Ryukyu ballads known as *Ryūka* continue to be created on Okinoerabu but not on Amami Ōshima. While Amami is today part of Kagoshima Prefecture, many of Amami's traditions resemble those in Okinawa, and the Amami dialect is closer to Okinawan than that of Kagoshima.[xl]

An Unstable Dynasty

While Shō Hashi had succeeded in founding the first united Okinawa, the instability of the Three Kingdoms Period continued into the first dynasty of the Ryukyu Kingdom. The kings of the first dynasty tended to have their lives cut short due to internal fighting and disputes over succession.

The average reign of a king during the first Shō dynasty was just six years, and even the longest reigning, Shō Toku (1441-1469), who was the grandson of Shō Hashi and the last king of the first dynasty, was only on the throne for nine years. The king with the shortest reign during the first Shō dynasty was Shō Kinpuku (1398-1453) who ruled for just five years.

This instability came to the fore during succession crises, such as on the death of Shō Kinpuku between the heir to the throne, Shiro and the king's brother, Furi. This tension broke out into the Shiro-Furi revolt in which both parties would lose their lives, destroying much of the royal capital by fire in the process.[xli] With both heirs dead, it was the king's younger brother who would ascend the throne as Shō Taikyu (1415-1460) in 1454.

Trouble would also come from eager contenders outside of the royal household. Five years later in August 1458 the Gosamaru-Amawari revolt broke out under Shō Taikyu's reign.[xlii] The instigator of the revolt was either Gosamaru or Amawari; in most versions of the story Gosamaru is the hero and Amawari the villain.

Gosamaru of Nakijin had assisted the dynasty's founder, Shō Hashi during his 1416 offensive on the Kingdom of Hokuzan when he was in his twenties. For his loyalty Gosamaru was entrusted to guard the north, and then ordered to construct Zakimi Gusuku as a defensive outpost north of Shuri.

To the east of Shuri is the Katsuren Peninsula that juts out from Okinawa extending out into the Pacific. This was the domain of the *Aji* Amawari who had married Shō Tai's eldest daughter, and had grown rich through trade.[xliii] Under King Shō Chū, Gosamaru was ordered to restore Naka Gusuku and moved there in 1440 to watch over Amawari whose power was growing and there were suspicions that he had his eye on the throne of Ryukyu.

Events did not play out in the loyal Gosamaru's favor, and in 1458 Amawari reported that it was Gosamaru who was planning a revolt, not he. When the king's soldiers came to Naka Gusuku, rather than betray his king, Gosamaru chose to commit suicide. When Amawari's treachery was discovered he was next to be disposed of.[xliv] While there are numerous versions of this story and theories to accompany it, the Gosamaru-Amawari rebellion shows that even a few decades after the formation of the Ryukyu Kingdom there remained *Aji* who were willing to fight to establish their own regimes, and while the Shiro-Furi and Gosamaru-Amawari rebellions make it into the court histories there were likely other small-scale uprisings from *Aji* that threatened the regime but were not recorded.

With challenges from within and without, the first Shō dynasty lasted only three decades after the death of Shō Hashi, and had only seven kings, including Shō Shishō.

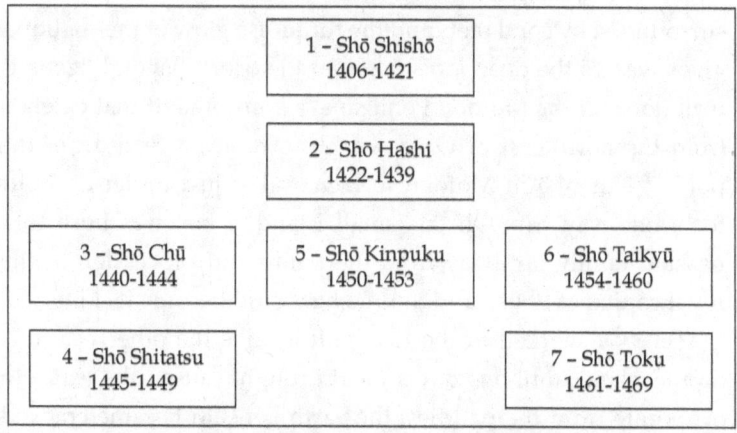

The reign of each king of the First Shō Dynasty

When Shō Toku passed away in 1469, a coup d'état erupted that would see the heirs of Shō Toku murdered, and the remnants of the royal family forced to flee. With this, the royal bloodline of Shō Hashi, the founder of the first dynasty of the Ryukyu Kingdom, was eradicated.

Despite these circumstances, in the official histories of the Ryuyku Kingdom there is little hint of bloodshed during this dynastic change. According to the *Chūzan Seifu*, Shō Toku was a corrupt ruler who would execute those who had committed no crime. It was an official in the court in charge of international trade who would come to replace him, Kanamaru (1415-1476). Does the tale of a corrupt ruler sound familiar? Indeed, it is the narrative we have seen with Shō Hashi's foes during the Three Kingdoms Period, and while what happened may differ from this account, all we have is the historical records of this Second Ryukyu dynasty that replaced the first.

Kanamaru and Creation of a Second Ryukyu Dynasty
Izena is a tiny island, no more than fifteen kilometers in area. It is surrounded by coral reefs and the turquoise glow of the shallows gives way to the deep lapis lazuli of the ocean beyond. Izena is well north of the Motobu Peninsula, a spur of land that extends from the north-east of Okinawa. Even today, a ferry from the port of Untenkō in Motobu to Izena takes just under an hour for a one-way trip. On this small island, a boy was born to a peasant family far away from the pomp and procession of the royal capital of Shuri, and in time he would become its king.

The boy worked in the rice paddies like the other peasants on the island until one day a great drought caused the water to evaporate from the paddies, the earth beneath became cracked with fissures and the specter of starvation hung in the air.

There is one paddy that miraculously escaped this fate, that of the boy Kanamaru and his family. It was not long before there were rumors that Kanamaru himself was the sole perpetrator of the islander's misfortune, that he had been sneaking out in the dead of the night and a bucket at a time carrying the water from his neighbor's paddies to his own.

The hostility in the air becomes palpable, but Kanamaru continued to toil in his paddy. One day as Kanamaru had his feet deep amongst the waterlogged mud, an old man approached him. He had long white hair and a furrowed face. Kanamaru had never seen this man before and he pauses his work to face him. The sage tells him, "Kanamaru, if you value your life you must with haste leave Izena."

Kanamaru listened intently to what the old man had to say and made up his mind to leave. With his wife and younger brother, a twenty-four-year-old Kanamaru paddled a Sabani to Kunigami, the Yanbaru jungle of northern Okinawa. Kanamaru then spent the next several years moving around Okinawa until in the year of 1441 at the age of twenty-seven he managed to gain the confidence of prince Shō Taikyū and worked as his retainer.

Kanamaru's rose further through the ranks when Shō Taikyū ascended the throne as king in 1454. Shō Taikyū promoted his right-hand man to royal treasurer and Kanamaru was granted a fief in Uchima. In 1459, now Lord of Uchima, he was entrusted with international trade and diplomacy, a further show of the king's confidence in the idea of a maritime nation built on trade.[xlv] Kanamaru worked as a loyal servant of the state pledging his life to the king, but when Shō Taikyū passed away in 1460, his son Shō Toku ascended the throne. Shō Toku was a corrupt king whose actions were against the wishes of the people. Kanamaru attempted to guide the new king to act more like his father, but the king was surrounded by corrupt officials and took no notice of his father's loyal servant.

Dejected by his lack of influence and the corruption at the heart of the land, Kanamaru retired to his fief in Uchima in 1468. Kanamaru is not the only one; other righteous officials also resigned with the corrupt only too eager to fill their places.

Suddenly at the age of twenty-nine, Shō Toku died, and a succession crisis enveloped the kingdom. The officials of the kingdom gathered in a garden within the castle walls to decide who should ascend the throne. The corrupt officials wished to see a continuation of the arrangement with Shō Toku, a young king they could easily manipulate. Amongst the bustle of officials one cried out "should not someone noble of heart like Kanamaru ascend the throne?"

This is met with a cacophony of agreement, and the corrupt officials, seeing that they are outnumbered, fled. Kanamaru was asked to become the next king of Ryukyu, but he hesitated.

"I am not one who has the worthy abilities of a king," he declared. "Since I will defile the throne, please find another suitable man."[13] Yet the other officials insisted that it could be none other than Kanamaru. So he ascended the throne, adopting the name of King Shō En and thus began the second Ryukyu dynasty.

This tale of how Shō En ascended the throne is recorded in *Chuzan Seikan* and *Chuzan Seifu*, official histories of the Ryukyu Kingdom almost two hundred years after the events supposedly took place.[14] As with many royal histories the events described are too convenient to be entirely true. There are also several peculiarities within Kanamaru's ascension story. The story is consistent with corrupt kings being disposed by noble courtiers that is written about the Three Kingdoms period such as King Bunei of Chūzan.

The old man who warned Kanamaru to flee Izena island at the beginning of the tale is also strikingly similar to the story of Shō Hashi's grandfather Samekawa.[xlvi] In the story, Samekawa flees from the island of Iheya north of Izena after the peasants there plan to murder him, much like Kanamaru. Like Kanamaru, Samekawa is also warned by an elderly sage-like figure to leave,

---

13 *Ryūkyū no Jidai: ōinaru rekishizō o Motomete*, 99-100.
14 *Ryūkyū Ōkoku to Wakō Omoro no Kataru Rekishi*, 48.

prompting him to go to Nakijin in the Kingdom of Hokuzan. At Nakijin he hears the voice of the gods, perhaps through an oracle, which encourages him to move to Sashiki in the Kingdom of Nanzan where he eventually enters influential ranks by marrying the Aji's daughter, thus setting the stage for his grandson Shō Hashi to be in a position where he can overthrow Bunei and become King of Chūzan. Such narratives are likely the product of future royal generations justifying their right to rule: a right brought about by divine providence.

But even within these myths there is surely an element of truth and we know for certain that the First Dynasty of the Ryukyu Kingdom gave way to the second with Kanamaru ascending the throne. The first Shō Dynasty was unstable and there were constant feuds for the throne and within this context, Kanamaru's rise to power is not particularly surprising.

Delving into the historical inconsistencies, Takara Kurayoshi suggests it is likely that Shō Toku was killed by poison.[15] Even in the official histories, cracks appear in the narrative. In *Chuzan Seikan* it is mentioned that the queen, the heir to the throne and wet nurse are all killed by soldiers while they hid in the most sacred place within the castle.[16] This was likely a warning to any who wanted to use relations with the first Shō dynasty to overthrow the kings of the second.

As the later court histories justify the divine right of Kanamaru and his scion, there was also a need to justify this change to China. In 1471, Kanamaru sent a mission to the Ming court in which he professed that he was the heir to Shō Toku, and that his 'father' had died. Like his 'father', Kanamaru sought to continue tributary relations with the ruling Chinese dynasty. To continue this lineage, Kanamaru adopted the name Shō En upon

---

15　*Ryūkyū No Jidai: ōinaru rekishizō o Motomete*, 102
16　*Ryūkyū Ōkoku to Wakō Omoro no Kataru Rekishi*, 50

THE RYUKYUS

his ascension to the throne, in the process claiming ties to the previous regime, just as King Shō Shishō, the father of Shō Hashi, had done when he claimed he was the successor to Bunei of the Kingdom of Chūzan.

To differentiate this new Shō dynasty, possessing no blood links to the first, historians classify the dynasty beginning with Shō En (Kanamaru) as the Second Shō Dynasty, a line of nineteen kings which ruled until its fall in the late 19th Century.

4

The Palace of One Hundred Inlets and the Conquest of Yaeyama

The Ascent of King Shō En
The most influential of the kings of the Second Shō Dynasty was the third king, Shō En (1465–1527), whose reign would see a wave of reforms that centralized power in a way that the First Shō Dynasty that had been unable to do, ultimately bringing stability to the kingdom. It was also under the reign of Shō En that the kingdom at last managed to extend its dominion to the most southern edge of the Ryukyu Archipelago: Yaeyama.

When Shō Shin's father Kanamaru passed away in July 1476, Shō Shin was just eleven years old and being too young to rule, Kanamaru's brother Shō Seni (1430-1477) ascended the throne. However, soon after his ascension Shō Seni was told by an oracle that the goddess Kimitezuri, the protector god of the Ryukyu Kingdom and ruler over the sun and seas, desired the young Shō Shin as the rightful heir to the throne, not he.[xlvii] Shō Seni subsequently abdicated, allowing for the reign of Shō Shin to begin under a regency.

Iha Fuyū (1876-1947), one of the first scholars of Okinawa (and a figure we will examine more in later chapters), suspected that while there are no records, it was probably Ogiyaka (1455-1505), the second wife of Kanamaru pulling the strings. Shō Shin ascended the throne in 1477, the same year that Shō Seni died; Ogiyaka possibly had him killed while he was king or soon after his abdication.[xlviii] Upon his ascension to the throne, Shō Shin took the title of 'heir to Chūzan'.

Shō Shin went on to rule from the age of twelve in 1477 to the age of sixty-one in 1526, bringing a heretofore unseen period of stability for the fledgling kingdom. With those around Shō Shin, including his mother, having secured power in Ryukyu, they soon sent an emissary under the name of Shō Shin to China to pay tribute, and inform the Ming court of the new king.

Chinese Envoys and the Enthronement of Kings

The following year, in 1478, the Chenghua Emperor (1447-1487) dispatched a junk fifteen meters in length, and a ceremony was likely held to mark the new heir's ascension to the throne. While nothing is recorded about Shō Shin's enthronement ceremony an outline of what took place can be gleaned from the ceremonies of later kings.

To mark the rise of a prince to a king, an envoy called the *Sappōshi*, would be dispatched from China to Ryukyu. Under the Ming and Qing dynasties, a total of twenty-three such delegations visited Ryukyu.[xlix]

The Chinese delegation would typically have about 500 members ranging from scholars to diplomats, from scribes to cooks. They would arrive in Naha after setting sail from Fujian, bringing aboard their junks the royal clothing and *Hibenkan* crown for the new king. The Chinese would be welcomed and housed in a building called the Tenshikan, built for their specific use while they sojourned in the kingdom.[l] While in Naha they would pay homage to the kings of yore at Sōgen-ji temple. Sōgen-ji was one of the most important Buddhist temples in the kingdom.

THE PALACE OF ONE HUNDRED INLETS AND THE CONQUEST OF YAEYAMA

Approaching the temple, one would first see the dense castle-like walls of white limestone, passing through these one would come to the temple itself. It was a wooden structure, raised from the ground on a stone platform, inside would be the resinous scent of wood, a companion within the hallowed halls. The gabled roof of the temple is pieced together from bright red tiles with white inflections — the quintessential tiled roofs that characterized the Ryukyu Kingdom.

When the day finally came for the enthronement ceremony, the Chinese delegation would begin an extravagant parade, marching from the port of Naha to the royal capital of Shuri.

As these dignitaries made their way, the people of Ryukyu would have been able to sense the power of the world's strongest empire and their kingdom's connection to it. The heir to the throne would meet this delegation at the castle's Shurei Gate and escort them to the palace.[li]

The palace within the castle walls, a mix of lacquered wood, red and white tiles and dragon motifs was known as 'the palace of one hundred inlets' an expression of the far-reaching rule of the Ryukyu Kingdom.[lii] Directly before this palace was the Unā courtyard, of orange and white tiles.

Running diagonally towards the palace was a path raised fifteen centimeters off the ground called the *Ukimichi* – 'the floating path'.[liii] Why the Ukimichi is at such an angle we can only speculate. One possibly theory is that the Ukimichi, which runs from the palace and Hōshin Gate that surrounds the Unā is that this is a direct line to Suimui-Utaki.[liv]

This Utaki, a religious site, can be found on the other side of the Hōshin Gate before one goes through to the Unā, a legendary place in the indigenous religion and believed to be the place that the Gods descended from the heavens to create Ryukyu. During the enthronement ceremony, the Chinese delegation would enter

THE RYUKYUS

the Unā and precious objects would be presented to the heir to the throne in a special building constructed for this purpose. A ceremony would be conducted in classical Chinese, in which it was proclaimed that the Emperor of China recognized the new king. The *Hibenkan* and *Hibenfuku* (royal clothing) would be presented and Chinese music would play throughout the ceremony.

Ryukyu Women Through the Eyes of The Chinese Delegation
These enthronement ceremonies were also a rare chance for outsiders from China to offer a glimpse into the position of women within the kingdom, about which there is not a great deal of information from the kingdom's own historical documents. During a 1663 delegation to Ryukyu, Zhang Xueli (Japanese— Chō Gakurei), described the women as Ryukyu as follows[lv]:

> "From a young age the girls tattoo black marks on the back of their fingers, these are increased year by year, and by the time they are twelve or thirteen and old enough to work these marks become the motif of a plum flower. By the time women have entered old age the back of their hands have become completely black. Their length of hair is four to five Shaku (one Shaku is equal to about 30.3 cm), and bound into a single bun, their hair is reflective like oil and jet black. Nothing is done to style their eyebrows, and they wear no hair accessories or necklaces, they do not wear makeup."[17]

The tattooing practice that Zhang Xueli describes is called *hajichi*, and it is one of more frequently noted curiosities recorded by

---

17 Okinawa Ken Kyoikuchō Bunka Zaika Shiryō Henshūhan, ed., *Okinawa Ken Shi Kakuhen Ron 8 Joseishi* (Haebaru : Okinawa ken kyōiku iinkai, 2016), 20-21.

THE PALACE OF ONE HUNDRED INLETS AND THE CONQUEST OF YAEYAMA

Chinese visitors to Ryukyu and, centuries later, Westerners. The Chinese who visited Ryukyu recorded many differences between their homeland and Ryukyu. Another member of a delegation in 1683 remarked how Ryukyu women did not partake in the custom of foot binding, as was done to upper-class women in China, but instead wore sandals like men. Common women were also worthy of record, in 1719 Xu Baoguang (Japanese Name Jo Hokō) wrote[lvi]:

"In the markets there is not a single man, all the stalls are set out by the women [...] despite coming to the market, there is no one to carry the goods, [women] pile up big and small loads and carry them on their heads."[18]

The Battle with Yaeyama's Akahachi

One of the most crucial events that happened under the reign of Shō Shin was Ryukyu's battle with Yaeyama and the eventual integration of the southern Ryukyu Islands of Miyako and Yaeyama into the Ryukyu Kingdom. While the Sakishima Islands did have interactions with the Ryukyu Kingdom and the three kingdoms that preceded it, direct control from Okinawa never extended far south.

One of the earliest records is from the court history *Kyūyō* where it is noted that in 1390 both Yaeyama and Miyako paid tribute to the Ryukyu court, while the first written details about Yaeyama are from shipwrecked sailors and recorded in the *Veritable Records of the Joseon Dynasty* in 1477.[lvii]

By the end of the 15th Century in Sakishima local chieftains were fighting amongst themselves for power, much like the *Aji* in Okinawa during the Gusuku Period. This power eventually became concentrated in the hands of Nakasone Tuyumya Genga

---

18   *Okinawa Ken Shi Kakuhen Ron 8 Joseishi*, 21.

in Miyako and Oyake Akahaci in Yaeyama (or Hongawara Akahachi).[lviii] Akahachi had come to Ōhama in Ishigaki and had gradually extended his power across the island, and then throughout Yaeyama.[lix]

According to the histories of the Ryukyu court, in 1500 Akahachi was planning to feign tribute to Ryukyu and use the opportunity to stage a coup. To prevent this, Ryukyu soon dispatched an armada to subjugate Yaeyama. A very different narrative can be found in Yaeyama, where it is recorded that it was Ryukyu's demand for taxes and disrespect for the gods of Yaeyama that led a furious Akahachi to rise up and fight for his people against the infinitely more powerful Ryukyu Kingdom.[lx]

With Ryukyu set to launch an attack, the chiefs of Miyako and Yaeyama had but two choices: submit to Ryukyu or fight against them. Nakasone chose the former while Akahachi choose the latter, and Nakasone eventually provided the Ryukyu army with support for their offensive on Yaeyama.

A monument in Shuri Castle describes how one hundred ships were sent by Shō Shin to put Akahachi in his place, and with this Yaeyama and Miyako became formally part of Ryukyu.[lxi]

Yaeyama's Integration into the Ryukyu Kingdom
Now a formal member of the kingdom, in 1524 a *Kuramoto*, a branch of the royal government, was established on Taketomi Island, which would remain the center of government in Yaeyama, until the decision was made to move the *Kuramoto* to Ishigaki, as Taketomi was small and lacked fresh water.

This first *Kuramoto* was built by the Taketomi native, Nishitō. Nishitō was a young boy during Ryukyu's battle with Akahachi and legend dictates that the Ryukyu general who led the offensive saw potential in him, spiriting him away to the royal capital of Shuri.

THE PALACE OF ONE HUNDRED INLETS AND THE CONQUEST OF YAEYAMA

At Shuri, Nishitō learned the Okinawa language and how to read and write, eventually becoming a civil engineer for the kingdom.[lxii] After many years of service at the kingdom's epicenter, he was entrusted with overseeing Yaeyama on behalf of the kingdom. Here he returned to Taketomi building the first *Kuramoto*, and Kuninaka-Utaki, the only Utaki in Yaeyama to this day that has a direct connection to Shuri.[lxiii]

One form of taxation that faraway islands such as Yaeyama and Miyako would pay to Ryukyu would be consignments of cloth, and part of the motivation for the establishment of *Kuramoto* in Sakishima was to oversee the production of the cloth. It would be officials at the *Kuramoto* who would deal with the collection, inspection and transportation of cloth, as well as giving orders on length, width, fabric and design. Various styles and types of clothes developed throughout the Ryukyu Archipelago, their emergence coincided with an increase in trade between the late 14th and 16th Centuries; many of the techniques would be imported from across South-East Asia and East Asia.

In Sakishima, the Ramie nettle was used to make cloth, and much of the cloth produced in Sakishima would go on to China and Japan as tribute.[lxiv] Throughout Ryukyu cloth was weaved from hemp, cotton and fiber banana and was generally women's work. The work of these women was highly valued within Ryukyu society, and the Historian Miyagi Eishō has argued that this, alongside their role within the Ryukyu religion, led to these women holding a less subservient status compared to their Japanese counterparts. This was also due to a lack of proliferation of the teachings of Confucianism and Buddhism at the level of the common people to the same extent as on mainland Japan.[19]

Sakishima would, however, remain on the fringes of the

---

19 *Okinawa Ken Shi Kakuhen Ron 8 Joseishi*, 109.

THE RYUKYUS

Ryukyu Kingdom and that is why the *Monchū* lineage system spread through Okinawa but remains relatively weak in Sakishima. *Monchū* is a lineage system that began to form around the 17th Century in Okinawa, as a genealogy among nobles, the *Monchū* system gradually expanded to Okinawa's outlying islands, and eventually the more sparsely populated north.[lxv]

5
Building the Kingdom

The Relocation of the Aji to the Royal Capital

Before Shō Shin conquered Yaeyama, reforms within the kingdom proper had long been underway. One such reform was the order for all *Aji* to leave their Gusuku throughout Okinawa and make Shuri their new home. There are no documents that describe whether the *Aji* peacefully accepted this, not willing to go against the unquestionably hegemony of the second Shō dynasty, or if there was resistance. With the relocation of Okinawa's warlords, the population of Shuri suddenly expanded, these warriors laid down their arms and with their movement to the royal capital they became officials who served the kingdom.

Further orders were given to each *Aji* with the introduction of sumptuary laws which saw a highly codified set of clothing to show each official's rank. This aristocratic-bureaucratic class were known as *Samurē*, showing their warrior origins, or *Yukatachu*.

This distinction amongst officials is mostly clearly seen in the turbans called *hachimachi*. Brocade *hachimachi* were only to be worn by those who were potential heirs to the throne, the princes and kings' brothers. Below this rank, but nevertheless highly ranked, officials of the kingdom were permitted to wear a purple *hachimachi*, and hold the title of *Wēkata*, such a position would extend to the highest-ranking officials in the land, the 'Council of Three'.[lxvi] Below this was the rank of *Pēchin*, middle level officials who were permitted to wear yellow *hachimachi*.[lxvii] Below this again were lower officials known as *Satunushi* and *Chikudun*, who were permitted to wear red *hachimachi*.[lxviii] At the bottom of this official system was an untitled class of officials permitted to wear blue *hachimachi*.

The ranks of the *Aji* that had become the representatives of the Ryukyu Kingdom, was likely determined based on their status within their Gusuku, with the feudal lords of these Gusuku earning the highest titles. It is also not clear from the official records whether the land these officials oversaw had any relation to their old domains or whether they were given entirely new tasks and regions.

While the *Aji* had been reorganized into the role of officials, it did not mean military power disappeared from the kingdom. Soldiers called *Hiki* were stationed throughout the Ryukyu Archipelago. There are few historical records concerning the *Hiki*, and it is not clear when this system was introduced. Two places in which *Hiki* were prominent was as guards at Shuri Castle, and the port of Naha: the center for the kingdom's overseas trade. *Hiki* would also go overseas covering Ryukyu's vast trading network in East and South-East Asia.

Hachimachi and their rank

Type of Hachimachi	Rank
Brocade	Members of the royal family, such as princes and the brother of the king
Purple	High level officials (Wēkata) including the council of Three
Yellow	High to mid-level officials (Pēchin)
Red	Lower ranking officials (Satunushi)
Blue	Lowest ranked officials

BUILDING THE KINGDOM

Administrative Divisions

Under Shō Shin the land throughout the kingdom was divided into districts called *'Shima'* which in turn were divided into smaller units called *'Magiri'*.[lxix] A *Magiri* was usually a settlement while a *Shima* was a group of settlements that were governed as one political unit. The officials who supervised the *Shima* were generally known as *Ōyakumoi* or *Yunchu*, although other names also existed for them.[lxx]

This system extended across the kingdom from Amami in the north to Yaeyama in the south. The officials who were given their position like most roles in the Ryukyu kingdom received a 'notice of appointment' document from the royal government.[lxxi]
This land system tied the fate of the common people to the Ryukyu court through a system of land taxes for each *Magiri*. This all-encompassing system even decided who the youngest members of society could marry. In Okinawa, there was a custom called *Mōashibi* in which young men and women would gather on the beaches and plains in evening and eat, dance and sing together until late at night.[lxxii] Unlike nobles, this gave the common people of Okinawa a degree of choice in selecting their partners, although they would have to seek permission from their parents when choosing a husband or wife. Under the *Shima* system the practice of *Mōashibi* continued, but it was encouraged that one's marriage was within the village as there was a land tax that each *Magiri* was obliged to pay. Although, if a common man did want to marry outside of his village, he could pay a penalty fine called an *Uedema* and move to a different *Magiri*.[lxxiii]

Women as Priestesses

Under the reign of Shō Shin, it was not only men who had their position in Ryukyu society reformed, but also women. Within

THE RYUKYUS

Ryukyu society there is a long-held belief that women possess innate spiritual powers that allow them to communicate with the spirit realm. This religion can be traced back to at least the Gusuku Period and likely has origins even earlier. This collection of beliefs can be loosely classified as *Onarigami*, although it is often referred to as Ryukyu Shintō within Japan today. The *Onarigami* belief is that sisters (*Onari*) have spiritual powers, while brothers (*Ekeri*) hold powers of protection.

Throughout the year there would be numerous religious rites often linked to agriculture where women would ask the gods for a bountiful harvest and offer the thanks of the people. The locations for communicating with these gods were the sacred groves known as *Utaki*. While the Ryukyu religion may be ancient, it was under Shō Shin that it was structurally reformed to become a national religion centered around the Ryukyu court. These changes were likely introduced at the hand of Shō Shin's mother, Ogiyaka. Under the reformed religious system, the highest rank was given to Ogiyaka's eldest daughter, the *Kikoeōkimi*.[lxxiv] The position of *Kikoeōkimi* was usually given to the king's sister, and under Shō Shin, the first *Kikoeōkimi* was his older sister, Otochitonomoikane.[lxxv]

Later *Kikoeōkimi* were the king's wife, mother or aunt, but remaining constant was the position being given to a female relative of the king. Below the *Kikoeōkimi* there were numerous high-ranking priestesses, who came under the broad title of the *Sanjūsankun*.[lxxvi] While this title has the word 'thirty-three' within its Chinese characters, it is not pointing to thirty-three specific roles, but rather is used to mean 'many'.

The priestesses of the *Sanjūsankun* would take part in royal ceremonies and usually had a blood connection to the throne, and often were based at Shuri. One example of a priestess who fitted into this rank was Shō Shin's daughter, *Manabedaru*, who held a special position called the *Sasukasa*.[lxxvii] The *Sanjūsankun* oversaw the rest of the priestesses throughout the kingdom.

This included the *Noro* at the lowest village level, and the *Ōamo* who oversaw regions of *Noro*.[lxxviii] The *Noro* were regional priestesses (although they were called *Tsukasa* in Sakishima), and just as with the *Samurē* at Shuri they received their titles through notice of appointment documents. Again, like the *Samurē*, the *Noro* were chosen for their bloodline, and they would be given land and a residency that was tied to her role.[lxxix] As with the *Ōyakumoi* (*Yunchu*) who oversaw the administration of *Magiri*, this land could be used by *Noro*, which sometimes would even come with servants, as a source of income.

Supervising the *Noro* were the *Ōamo*, who also received land and were appointed through a notice of appointment document. On set occasions, *Ōamo* had the privilege of meeting with the King a chance that was unlikely to be given to an ordinary *Noro*. What separated the *Ōamo* from the *Noro* was their larger regional power.[lxxx] There were three positions above the *Ōamo* that oversaw all these regional *Kaminchu* (priestesses): the *Mihira-no-Ōamoshirare*, the *Makabe-no-Ōamoshirare* and the *Gibo-no-Ōamoshirare*.[lxxxi] The religious system in Ryukyu with women at its center thus offered women ranked positions in society, similar to that of their male counterparts. Both received land and were appointed by the royal government.

Kikoeōkimi (The high priestess with royal blood) > Ōamoshirare (three high priestesses who oversaw parts of the kingdom) > Ōamo (mid-level priestesses) > *Noro* (regional priestesses)
Simplified structure of the Ryukyu priestess system

The Royal Mausoleum

With the creation of Okinawa Prefecture in 1879, many of the reforms that occurred under Shō Shin were replaced with a more modern system of governance. While the echo of these reforms can still be felt in Okinawa today, far more noticeable is the architectural and infrastructural projects that began to be carried out under Shō Shin and were continued by his successors, many of which remain standing to this day. Central to the royal family and the legacy of the second Shō dynasty, was the creation of a royal mausoleum, called Tamaudun.[lxxxii]

The construction of Tamaudun was completed in 1501 and the first remains to be entombed there were those of Shō Shin's father, Shō En (Kanamaru). From then on until the fall of the Ryukyu Kingdom, members of the royal family would be entombed in Tamaudun. Tamaudun is 2,442 square meters in size and is divided into three chambers. Interred in the central camber are the bones of the king, and later the queen, where they were ceremoniously washed.

In the traditional Okinawan burial style, the body of the deceased would be kept in the coffin (or even places such as caves for some of the poorer common people) for a few years until only the bones remained. These bones were then washed and placed in an urn which would then be moved to the family tomb. To the east of the central room was a second chamber, the first part of Tamaudun to be constructed, which was for the entombment of the king and queens' bones after they had been washed. The western room of Tamaudun was constructed for other high-ranking members of the royal family.[lxxxiii]

Shuri Castle

The most recognizable architectural feature of the Ryukyu Kingdom is of course Shuri Castle, with its contrast of red and white, so very different from the castles of Japan. However, this was not always the appearance of the castle.

Earlier incarnations of Shuri Castle were similar to Tamaudun, a large stone structure with a shingle roof. Shuri Castle would not begin to resemble its current form until numerous fires and much rebuilding led to an evolution in style. A fire in 1660 destroyed the palace, and when it was rebuilt tiles were used instead of shingle; however, archaeological surveys show that this version of Shuri Castle had grey tiles instead of the iconic red. Shuri Castle would again go up in flames in 1715 and it was during the following reconstruction that the tiles became red.

Kuba Mayumi of the Okinawa Churashima Foundation, has proposed that this change in tile color is directly related to the population of Ryukyu which had increased by many thousands of the course of a few hundred years. By the 18th Century, the royal government was making efforts to preserve wood, and since grey tiles required high levels of heat during the firing process, the less heat-intensive red tiles began to be produced instead. The change in something as small as the color of Shuri Castle's tiles shows how the Ryukyu Kingdom understood the balance between natural resources and the population.[lxxxiv]

Under Shō Shin, architectural projects at Shuri Castle would signal the greatness of the new dynasty. Such as an inscription within the palace at Shuri Castle that chronicled Shō Shin's great accomplishments, including the conquest of Yaeyama and the relocation of the *Aji*. To build this monument, as well as erect dragon statues flanking the palace, dolerite was bought from Fujian China and intricately carved in 1509.[lxxxv] The dragon pillars remain one of the most iconic architectural features of Shuri Castle. As if protecting the palace, the dragons stand guard, their bulbous eyes looking out at all who approach. The dragon on the left has its mouth closed, but the one on the right has its mouth agape, bearing its fangs. This may have similarities to the Shisa lion in which the male has its mouth open to scare away evil spirits (*Majimun*) while the female has its mouth closed prevent good fortune escaping. The exact positioning of the dragon pillars remains a point of contention, with some believing the dragons faced each other as you will see if you visit Shuri Castle today while others believe they looked out onto the courtyard.

Shō Shin's successors would also develop the seat of royal power. Another prominent feature at the palace were the numerous dragon motifs (33 in total). Most conspicuous are the multi-coloured dragon tiles that cap opposing ends of the three-meter-long roof that were first installed in 1682. Like the dragon pillars below these rooftop dragons are protectors of the palace.

The Development of Utaki

New architectural projects were also present at *Utaki* that held particular significance to the royal family. Such as Bendgadake-Utaki, and Sonohyan-Utaki, both of which were close to Shuri. Under Shō Shin in 1519, a stone gate was constructed at Bengadake-Utaki, this would be further developed under the fourth king of the second Shō dynasty, Shō Sei (1497-1555) who would construct a path for pilgrimage to the site from Shuri Castle in 1543.

At Sonohyan-Utaki a stone gate was constructed that was a mix of Japanese and Chinese architectural styles. The gate's tall roof with its gentle curve is reminiscent of Japanese temples, complete with *Shachi* (mythical carp with the body of a fish and a head of a lion), on its right and left edge. The gate is found along the path after passing through the Shurei Gate.

Religious architectural projects were not limited to the indigenous Ryukyu religion. In 1494 the Buddhist temple, Enkaku-Ji was built neighboring Shuri Castle, quickly becoming the center of Buddhism within the kingdom.

Ryukyu had also received Buddhist scripture from Korea, and the Benzaiten-Dō was built in the center of the Enkanchi Pond within the walls of Shuri Castle to house them. The Enkanchi was created in 1502 and was created so that spring and rain water from Shuri Castle and Enkaku-Ji would drain into it.[lxxxvi] The Benzaiten-Dō at the center was also where Ryukyu sailors would pray to Benzaiten, the goddess of water, among many other things, for safe voyages across the sea.[lxxxvii]

The Pearl Path and other Architectural Feats

Other architectural feats would be tied to the military and infrastructure of Okinawa, such as the Madamamichi, 'The Pearl Path' which connected Shuri to the port of Naha.[lxxxviii] The Madamamichi provided quick access for the *Hiki*, the Ryukyu soldiers, to move to Naha and defend the kingdom's central port if the need arose. The path was also opened to the average citizen decreasing the journey time between Naha and Shuri.

The Madamamichi was lined with the coral limestone and lined with pine trees.

Shō Shin's descendants would continue the infrastructural reforms that he had begun, such as under Shō Sei (1497-1555) Mii Gusuku was created as a floating fortress against the Wakō pirates. Mii Gusuku was built on the northern banks of Naha and had similarities with its sibling Yaragimori Gusuku, built on Naha's southern banks. By the end of the 16th Century, a chain could be extended between these two Gusuku to block ships entering the harbor, much like the Great Chain across the Golden Horn in Constantinople.

Both of these Gusuku were lined with cannons and served as one of the first lines of defence, should Naha be attacked from the sea. While Mii Gusuku, for the most part no longer stands,

THE RYUKYUS

its image was captured by the Japanese woodblock printer, Katsushika Hokusai (1760-1849) who captured this fort in his *'Eight views of Ryukyu'* series, as a long serpentine platform that stretches out to sea.[lxxxix]

Other architectural projects that had been completed under the First Ryukyu Dynasty were maintained by the Second, most notable: the Chōkōtei.[xc] This was a long bridge stretching about a kilometer in length across Naha, with seven water gates constructed under the reign of King Shō Kinpuku (reign 1450-1453). During this era, the geography of Naha was considerably different to today, with numerous rivers draining out into the ocean creating numerous river islands. The Chōkōtei was constructed across these islands where fresh water met salt water, improving the cities infrastructure. As with Mii Gusuku the Chōkotei was captured in the woodblock prints of Hokusai.

While the architectural projects under Shō Shin were a symbol of the new stability and power of the second Shō dynasty, perhaps Shō Shin's biggest legacy for Ryukyu was his ability to persuade China, despite numerous rebuffs, to increase Ryukyu's tribute from once every two years, to once a year by 1507. With this, the Golden Era of trade would begin in which Ryukyu sailors would sail throughout East and South-East Asia, spending time in countries ruled by other rulers, unlike their own King in Ryukyu, with different religions, habits and food. Through this trade, Ryukyu would become a center of international trade in Asia, and through these interactions with other nations, culture in the Ryukyu Archipelago would in turn be shaped and transformed, a legacy that we will see in the following chapters.

6

THE BRIDGE OF NATIONS

The Bridge of Nations Bell

In the 15th Century, a 721 kilogram bell, 155 centimeters in height and with a caliber of ninety-three centimeters and six hundred kilograms in weight was hung from the palace of Shuri Castle. On this bell was the following inscription for all to see:

> "Our Kingdom of Ryukyu occupies an outstanding location amongst the Southern Seas, learning from the culture of Korea, holding an indivisible relationship with China, and a close affiliation with Japan. These countries come across the seas, to a place that rises up from the ocean like the island of Penglai.[xci] Through our trade ships the kingdom forms a bridge between nations, filling our land with precious goods from all over the world."[20]

This was the Bridge of Nations Bell forged in 1458 under the reign of Shō Taikyū (1415-1460). The bell was a symbol of the mercantilism that transcended oceans characteristic of the Ryukyu Kingdom.[xcii] Ryukyu's vast trade network was one that would take junks piled with goods from nation to nation and

---

20 Hiroyuki Torigoe, *Ryūkyūkoku No metsubō to Hawai Imin* (Yoshikawa Kōbunkan, 2013), 41.

was made possible through the kingdom's tributary relationship with China. After returning from a tributary mission, the Ryukyu junks would be brimming with Chinese curios, an amount far more than the ten-thousand or so population of the time could make use of.

These goods would be used to trade alongside goods from Ryukyu and they were carried throughout Asia, from the Korean Peninsula to the straits of Malacca, creating a network of exchange with Ryukyu at its center.

The echoes of this trade can be found within Okinawa and wider Asia. Within Shuri Castle's holy site of the *Kyō-no-Uchi* over 500 pieces of porcelain have been excavated, three-fourths of which originated from China in the 14th and 15th Centuries, along with porcelain from as far away as Vietnam and Thailand also discovered on the site.[xciii]

Chinese porcelain can also be found throughout the museums of Southeast Asia, with Ryukyu playing a part in this transportation. Such porcelain can be seen in the Chao Sam Phraya Museum (the national museum of Thailand in Bangkok), in Indonesia's national museum in Jakarta and the Sarawak State Museum in Borneo. This highly coveted porcelain with its iridescent glow and lustrous sheen would remain in these kingdoms and sultanates of Southeast Asia. Other pieces would be carried further afield still, going as far as India and the Arabian Peninsula.

The Ryukyu sailors who bought this porcelain thus played an important role in the Silk Road. For over four hundred years, Ryukyu sailors would travel routes that would take them as far north as Sakai and Hakata in Japan, Busan in Korea, and as far south as Java in Southeast Asia. Through their journeys, these sailors would come into contact with Theravada Buddhist, Hindu and Muslim rulers very different to those of their homeland, and these cultural influences would influence not just those who braved the voyages overseas but the common people of Ryukyu as well.

Ryukyu's Golden Age of Trade developed at an exceptional time for East and Southeast Asia in which regime change was frequent, and long periods of stability a rarity.

A Shifting Asia

Ryukyu's tributary relationship with China began after the Ming Dynasty overthrew the Mongol Dynasty in 1372. Tribute, in the records at least, first began with the kingdom of Chūzan, and this system would continue beyond into the formation of the Ryukyu Kingdom, and even after the Ming dynasty was replaced with the Qing Dynasty in 1644, with Ryukyu's trade routes directly overlapped with other tributary states to China.

At a similar time to the formation of the Ming dynasty in the mainland in China, the Goryeo dynasty was overthrown in the Korean peninsula in 1392, with General Yi Seong-gye (1335-1408) founding the Joseon dynasty in its place (1392-1897). By the time of the Goryeo dynasties demise, it was facing subjugation from the Mongols of Yuan China, with the legitimacy of the Goryeo court being called into question due to intermarriage with the Mongols.

Another nuisance for Goryeo, as with Ming China, was the *Wakō* pirates who had continued to raid and pillage settlements throughout the peninsula. With the foundation of the Joseon dynasty the capital was moved from Kaesong (currently North Korea) to Seoul, the Joseon Kingdom's border now extended north to the Yalu and Tumen rivers and the dynasty went on to become the longest lasting in Korean history.

A tumultuous period of change was also taking place in Japan. Towards the end of the Heian period (794-1185) power began to shift away from the royal family as samurai who had worked for nobles began to seize an increasing amount of political influence. By the 12th Century, some of these samurai had even managed to enter the imperial court. This eventually led to a dynastic battle between the Genji and Heike samurai families, which culminated in Minamoto Yoritomo (1147-1199), the head of the Genji, triumphing and establishing the countries first samurai government in the form of the Kamakura Shogunate in the 12th Century.

As with China and Korea, any stability that was created by one regime was not to last. By the 14th Century, the Emperor attempted to retake power back from the samurai, with Emperor Go-Daigo (1288-1339) declaring a new capital in Yoshino, which stood in opposition to the northern court in Kyoto controlled by the Shogun, Ashikaga Takauji (1305-1358).

This period of two imperial courts in which both claimed legitimacy lasted for fifty years. Takauji had first fought on the side of the Emperor to overthrow the Kamakura Shogunate and restore imperial rule. The split into two courts occurred when Takauji, who was the first Shogun of the Muromachi Period, captured Kyoto from the Kamakura Shogunate in 1333.[xciv]

Following this Go-Daigo was restored to the chrysanthemum throne and much to the distaste of the samurai began attempting to turn back the clock to the Heian period in which the imperial family reigned supreme, but this was a step too far for the samurai.

This period of reform is known as the Kenmu Restoration, and lasted from 1333 to 1336.

While Takauji had initially helped restore Emperor Go-Daigo, he was not about to let his class lose power, and in 1336 Takauji drove the Emperor out of Kyoto who fled to Nara. Takauji then formed the Ashikaga (or Muromachi) Shogunate and installed a relative of the emperor he deemed legitimate. In the south, Go-Daigo claimed that only he and his scion in the southern court were the true rulers of Japan.

Under the third Ashikaga Shogun, Ashikaga Yoshimitsu (1368-1395) a compromise was at last negotiated between the southern and northern courts in which the lineage of both courts would take turns ascending the throne in Kyoto under the Muromachi Shogunate, and this return to stability opened Japan up once again to Ryukyu vessels.

Around the same time in Southeast Asia, the Ayutthaya Kingdom (1350 – 1767) was solidifying its power in present-day Thailand, while the Majapahit Empire (1293 – 1527) in Sumatra and Java had already passed its golden age and was beginning to decline. Alongside the Hindu empire of Majapahit in decline, Islam was making inroads on the Malayan peninsula, north and east Sumatra and Java, brought by Indian and Arabian merchants who rode seasonal winds to this corner of the world, they would eventually bring about Islamic states in Southeast Asia such as the Sultanate of Malacca (1400 – 1511). These merchants from the west would also be a piece in a larger network of trade routes that connected much of Eurasia, creating a network of trade from East Asia extending through India, the Middle East and eventually Europe. The formation of the Ryukyu Kingdom came at an ideal time when stable states were coming into formation in both East and Southeast Asia. The fledgling kingdom would use this degree of domestic stability to become 'The Bridge of Nations'.

7

Tribute to China

The Heart of the Tributary System
Since China was the nexus of this trade network, let us begin with a look at Ryukyu's tributary role with China. During this period China was the biggest producer of goods in the world.

China was the superpower of the era and this can be seen in Admiral Zheng He's fleet, which even today remain the largest wooden ships that have ever been built. Zheng's numerous expeditions were a display of Chinese power and even led to tribute from areas far from Asia. In Bengal, Zheng met with envoys from Malindi (present day Kenya), who gave him giraffes which were then taken to the Ming court, causing quite a stir, while at the same time showing the reach of China.

In Okinawa, tribute from China was so central to maintaining the king's position and influence that tribute would come at least once a year, sometimes even twice. This was until 1470 when China restricted it to once every two years, but by 1507 King Shō Shin succeeded in persuading China to increase this to once every year.

The Okinawan historian Takara Kurayoshi estimates that by the 19th Century Ryukyu had paid tribute to China 171 times, dwarfing what is now Vietnam, the second highest which paid tribute 89 times over roughly the same period. Japan in contrast only paid tribute a mere 19 times. Japan evidently lacked the zeal

TRIBUTE TO CHINA

for a such a close relationship with China as that coveted by the Ryukyu Kingdom.[21]

For Ryukyu paying tribute to China was much more important than just obtaining rare goods such as silk. This relationship opened up a network of Chinese tributary states for the Ryukyu to trade in. Alongside the formality of paying tribute, Ryukyu delegations to China would also be able to trade with merchants who had been designated by the Ming, another means to obtain Chinese goods which could then be traded throughout Asia. After completing their tributary mission to China, they would ride seasonal winds back to Ryukyu.

The Historian Akiyama Kenzō has estimated that as many as 77,000 Ryukyuans traveled to China as sailors, diplomats and students over the centuries in which this tributary relationship was maintained.[22] The Ryukyu delegations to China would usually consist of between two to four junks, which would carry warriors, should the need to fight of any *Wakō* pirates arise, translators and emissaries. Their destination, for most of this tributary relationship, would be the port city of Fuzhou in Fujian.

Each tributary state to China was given its own designated port and would only be in this specific port permission to dock was bestowed. Ryukyu's first designated port in China was Quanzhou in Fujian, this was then moved to Fuzhou also in Fujian by the late 15th Century. For Japan the designated port was Ningbo in Zhejiang, and for Southeast Asian countries, Guangzhou in Guangdong. In each of these ports a government office and lodgings were constructed to meet the needs of the delegations paying tribute.

Ships from Ryukyu would cross the East China sea and enter the mouth of the Min River. Here they would slowly battle

---

21 Torigoe, *Ryūkyūkoku No metsubō to Hawai Imin*, 40.
22 Takara, *Ryūkyū No Jidai: ōinaru rekishizō o Motomete*, 118.

against the currents, making their way upstream to Fuzhou. According to *The Collected Statutes of the Ming Dynasty*, a collection of procedures and regulations compiled in 1509, goods bought to China from Ryukyu included; shells, textiles, leather and sulfur.[xcv]

The shells that Ryukyu provided were the main ingredient used in mother of pearl, while the horses made excellent pack animals and as many as nine hundred could cross the sea in a single year. These horses were indispensable to the Ming's fight with Mongols north of the Great Wall and there are also examples of Chinese officials being required to go to Ryukyu to get more horses under the order of the Emperor.[xcvi]

Another item of particular note is sulfur which is a component of gunpowder. Ryukyu's sulfur came from the relatively small, 55-square kilometer island of Iōtorishima, which is 65 kilometers west of Tokunoshima. Today Iōtorishima is the most northern island within Okinawa Prefecture, and the prefecture's only active volcano. It is not clear from when the people of the Ryukyu Archipelago discovered that sulfur could be mined on Iōtorishima, but it is possible it coincided with the genesis of the Ryukyu Kingdom, and it could be no earlier than the Gusuku Period, as iron tools would be required to mine. Iōtorishima itself is only one kilometer wide, but despite this small size of the island it is home to two volcanoes, the Iōdake Volcano on the northern side of the island has a five-hundred-meter caldera, which was formed by lava slowing oozing onto the surface over hundreds of years. A plateau separates the two volcanoes, to the south of Iōdake is the Gusuku Volcano which also a caldera the roughly the same width.

Those coming to Iōtorishima to collect sulfur during the age of the Ryukyu Kingdom would be met with fumaroles bellowing smoke from beneath the earth and would have little protection from these gasses. But this was a precious substance that was worth any risks involved, to the kingdom at least if not for those who were ordered to carry out the work.[xcvii]

Although the Ming had driven the Mongols north, they remained a constant threat pushing on the northern limits of the empire. Even half a decade into the dynasty it took constant vigilance to keep the Mongols at bay. Without gunpowder the Ming's power was fragile and difficult to maintain.

The Ming's unsteady position can be seen particularly during the Tumu crisis in which the Mongol Esen Taishi of the Oirat Tribe invaded, dealt numerous defeats and eventually captured Emperor Yingzong (1427-1464) on September 1, 1449. The loss of this battle was an embarrassment for the Ming dynasty which had a far larger army than the Mongols and had extended the Great Wall precisely to keep them out. This event is just one example of why sulfur provided by Ryukyu was so valuable to the Chinese.

Yet, goods indigenous to Ryukyu alone were not satisfactory tribute for China. It is also recorded that Ryukyu ships carried goods from Japan such as gilded fans and swords, from Southeast Asia ivory, palm trees and spices as well as wares from the Korean Peninsula. This is also recorded on the Ryukyu side, with the *Rekidaihōan*, a compilation of around 250 diplomatic documents collected between 1424 and 1867 recording how on numerous occasions that it was necessary for the Ryukyu Kingdom to send ships to other countries throughout Asia in order to meet an acceptable level of tribute for China.[xcviii] This exchange of goods would continue with the items Ryukyu received from China, in which these Chinese goods were traded in Japan, Korea and Southeast Asia.

In the Ryukyu Kingdom there were no private merchants and all trade between Ryukyu and any other nations was overseen

THE RYUKYUS

by the royal government. The tributary process within China was also highly formalized, and Ryukyu would have designated 'stations' built for them in Fujian.[xcix]

Fujian

Until 1472, those from the Ryukyu Kingdom would arrive in Quanzhou were a special building for the Ryukyu delegation, 'Laiyuan Station' was built for the party, this building was also known as the Ryukyu Hall. It was here that the emissaries of the Ryukyu Kingdom would wait while a select number made the journey to the imperial capital to formally make tribute.[c] During this time those who were left in Quanzhou would trade with designated Chinese officials who were also well versed in the Okinawan language.[ci]

Quanzhou was one of the world centers of economic activity during this period. From as early as the Tang Dynasty (618-907) Muslim merchants gathered in this city and established settlements. From the Song Dynasty onwards, Quanzhou's population boomed, going over 50,000. Quanzhou was known far and wide and is mentioned in both the writings of Marco Polo (1254−1324) and Ibn Battuta (1304−1368). Polo called Quanzhou 'the most noble Port of Zai-tun' and the sheer scale left quite an impression on him:

> "A noble port, where all the ships of India arrive, and for one laden with pepper which comes from Alexandria to be sold throughout Christendom, there go to that city a hundred. It is one of the two best ports in the world, and the most frequeneted by merchants."[23]

Quanzhou was a walled city famous for its Deigo Trees (also

---

23   Marco Polo, The Travels of Marco Polo (Oliver & Boyd, 1845), 202.

called Erythrina or coral trees) and the city held the moniker 'the Deigo castle'. The Quanzhou Ryukyu Hall was located outside of the cities southern gate along a subsidiary of the Jin River. In 1472, the official tribute reception location for Ryukyu in China was moved from Quanzhou to Fuzhou. This was a result of sediment building up over the centuries which had made the Jin River increasingly shallow and no longer suitable for large ships.[cii]

At Fuzhou the 'Rou Yuan Station' (the characters in the station name signify a place where guests from far away can rest) was provided for Ryukyu. This Ryukyu Hall was about 200 kilometers from Quanzhou, and this would remain the base for tribute from Ryukyu until the 19th Century.[ciii]

Ryukyu junks would enter Fuzhou by going along the Min River, a waterway over 500 kilometers long that drains into the East China Sea. As the Ryukyu junks made their way inland, they would pass natural formations that became landmarks for them. One notable landmark was the 'Gate of Five Tigers', a formation of granite rock clusters, which having been eroded by the wind and snow over hundreds of generations resemble five sitting tigers.[civ]

The junks continued further upstream on past the Gate of Five Tigers, passing by two reefs, dubbed the 'northern turtle' and the 'southern turtle'. In the traditional folk beliefs of Fujian these animals are protectors of the Min River. However, they also made the Min a difficult course to navigate. The Ryukyu junks would successfully have to maneuver past these obstacles while fighting against the current to eventually make their way to Fuzhou on the river's northern banks.

Once the Ryukyu delegation had arrived in Fuzhou they would follow a canal that took them to the Ryukyu Hall and would use small boats to unload goods from their larger junks.

THE RYUKYUS

Like Quanzhou before it, Fuzhou was a walled city, and in historical texts has been revered to as the 'Banyan Tree Castle'. Banyan Trees, or *Gajumaru* as they are known in Japanese (from an Okinawan loan word) are also prevalent throughout the Ryukyu Archipelago and their abundance would have been one of the points that reminded them of home while in this foreign land.

The Ryukyu Hall itself was located outside of the city's walls, near the southern gate. In its heyday, the Ryukyu Hall was about 5,600 square meters, and was surrounded by walls and a gate with the characters 海不揚波 (safe travels on the sea) engraved in large characters.[cv] Through the gate were building of numerous stories complete with thatched roofs. These buildings provided lodgings for the Ryukyu sailors, as well as being a designated point for Chinese merchants.

The Ryukyu Hall thus served a commercial as well as diplomatic function, and was furnished with guards, translators and helpers.[cvi] While those in the Ryukyu Hall were permitted freedom of movement throughout the day, they were not permitted to leave the premises after nightfall.

Journey to Beijing

Only a chosen ten to twenty or so of the Ryukuans who crossed the sea would make the journey to Beijing to pay homage to the Emperor, with the majority of the delegation staying behind at Fuzhou to trade. An even smaller group stayed in Fuzhou for a period of three years. The journey to Beijing would be made during winter to make it in time for the imperial capital's lunar New Year celebrations.

The winter trek made this treacherous journey all the more difficult, the journey only one way would take two months. With the long and frigid weather, many Ryukyuans would fall in the mountain passes, forests and roads between Fuzhou and Beijing. By 1691 in the Ryukyu Hall there was a small shrine where those who Ryukyuans who had passed away in China could be enshrined and prayed for.[cvii] When the historian Kobata Atsushi visited the Fujian Ryukyu Hall in 1937, he recorded that over 5,000 mortuary tablets were enshrined here.[24]

The route to Beijing involved going further upstream the Min River, then they would leave their boats at the base of the Wuyi Mountains and proceed on foot, crossing over into the Tiantai Mountains. These mountains are crossed by a number of passes, with thick forests and a sparse population, and have long been associated as sanctuaries for Daoism and Buddhism.

After passing through the mountains they would board small boats and use the currents of the Fuchun River, which flows into the much larger Qiantang River. The Qiantang River would take the Ryukyu delegation to the city at the heart of Zhejiang, Hangzhou. From here on, the journey to Beijing would ease, and the Ryukyuans could make use of the Jing-Hang Grand Canal.

This is a series of waterways that connected Hangzhou to Beijing stretching over 1,000 miles in length, it is the world's longest man-made waterway. At the final point of Grand Canal they would leave their boats and make the last leg of their journey on foot, to what was the biggest city in the world, Beijing.

In the imperial capital, they would stay in a special lodging built for foreign dignitaries.[cviii] As in Fuzhou, the delegation was given a chance to sell wares to designated merchants who would pay a hefty price in return. Having arrived in Beijing during the New Year celebrations they would attend a ceremony and finally present their items of tribute and a letter from the king of Ryukyu to the Emperor. The Ryukyu delegation would spend about fifty

---

24 Mamoru Akamine, *Ryūkyū ōkoku: Higashiajia No kōnāsutōn* (Kōdansha, 2004), Chapter 6.

THE RYUKYUS

days in the imperial capital, and then during the dead of winter they would begin the journey back when many of the canals were frozen. They would trace the same route back in their trek to Fujian, arriving in the early spring. By the time they reached Fuzhou they had traveled over 6,000 kilometers.[25]

While Ryukyu's tributary relationship with China lasted for over 400 years, the Ming dynasty itself would not. In 1636, the Manchus from what is now the northeastern part of China invaded and established the Qing Dynasty. But the Manchus adopted the Ming form of governance and, employing Chinese officials in the Qing court, the dynasty lasted for a two and a half centuries and pushed the borders of China as far as present-day India, Nepal and Afghanistan.

Ryukyu's tributary relationship with China continued after this regime change from the Ming to the Qing, and in March of 1654, King Shō Shitsu (1629-1668) sent an emissary to China to return the seal the Ming had provided and in turn was given a new seal complete with Chinese and Manchu script.[cix]

---

25   *Ryūkyū ōkoku: Higashiajia No kōnāsutōn*, Chapter 6.

8

CHINA'S CULTURAL LEGACY IN RYUKYU

Kuninda and the Chinese in Ryukyu

During the existence of the Ryukyu Kingdom, between 200 to 500 Chinese officials visited the Ryukyu Kingdom on official business.[26] The history of the Chinese in Ryukyu goes back long before this at least as far back as the Shell Mound Period. From the official records, we know that some Chinese had begun moving to Ryukyu at least as early as the reign of King Satto of Chūzan establishing a settlement called Kuninda in 1392, which is in Naha today and is also known as Kume.

In the historical record these Chinese are described as being 'thirty-six', although this was more an auspicious number in Feng Shui then an actual recording.[cx] The social anthropologist, Higa Masao has pointed out that even before the record of this first 'thirty-six' there were already Chinese who had settled in Ryukyu conducting private trade without the emperor's permission.[27] These Ryukyuans of Chinese descent played a vital role in the kingdom's maritime voyages, as navigators, translators and diplomats.[cxi]

There were certainly Chinese in Ryukyu even before this official event in 1392. As early as 960 AD during the Song Dynasty, Chinese merchants had proactively pursued trade,

---

26 Takara, *Ryūkyū No Jidai: ōinaru rekishizō o Motomete*. Chikuma Shobō, 118.
27 Masao Higa, *Okinawa Kara Ajia Ga Mieru* (Iwanami Shoten , 1999), 77.

and the emperor himself was more than happy to allow this to boost the empire's income. Some of the goods carried by Chinese merchants of this era include ivory and spices from Southeast Asia, just as Chinese communities there were developing. It was under the Song Dynasty that Chinese cities began to rapidly expand thanks to this foreign trade.

The Song also possessed advanced technology which alllowed for their naval exploits. The *Records of Foreign Peoples* records the use of compasses and junks of over thirty meters in length and over ten meters in width. Chinese can also be seen to during the early days of the Ryukyu Kingdom. The *Ming Shilu* records that in 1411 a loyal retainer of King Satto of Chūzan in what is now Jiangxi Province had served his king for more than forty years, and now in old age wished to return to China. The *Rekidaihōan* also records that in 1431, the captain of one of Shō Hashi's tributary ships had entered his eighties, and was now no longer confident that he could lead tributary ships as requested to return to his native Fujian.

Before the Ming dynasty issued its maritime ban, there were also Chinese merchants throughout wider Asia. Many of them took up roles under the local regimes as diplomats, merchants, ship builders and translators. An example of one such Chinese settlement is in Palembang (Sumatra) that had some similarities to Kuninda. In the *Rekidaihōan* it is recorded that diplomatic relations between Palembang and Ryukyu were established under the reign of Shō Hashi, but what is more likely is that these two Chinese communities already existed, and it was these links that were made use of by the Ryukyu Kingdom's founder.

In the same year of 1392, that the 'thirty-six' Chinese were sent across the ocean to the kingdom in the east, Ryukyu students were sent to study in China to the west. Here they would embark on a 3,000 kilometer walk from Tianjin to Beijing. The first one hundred or so of these Ryukyu students who made their way to China were the sons of princes and high-level bureaucrats. Ryukyu students would continue being dispatched to learn in China until 1868, a 476-year period.[28]

Under Shō Shin this privilege was extended to those from Kuninda, and by the end of the 18th Century during the reign of King Shō On (1795-1802) this was further extended to nobles from the royal capital of Shuri and central trade port of Naha. The students who ventured to China attended the imperial university, Guozijian, where they would spend six to seven years studying the Chinese classics; *The Book of Rites* which was a collection of texts describing the social reforms, administration and ceremonial rites of the Zhou dynasty (BCE 1046−256), *The Analects*, a collection of sayings and ideas attributed to Confucius, The Four Books and Five Classics, which were the authoritative texts on Confucianism written before 300 BCE. At Guozijian, the Ryukyu students brushed shoulders with Chinese royals and nobles, as well as those from further afield such as the Korean Peninsula. After completing their studies in China, the students would return to Ryukyu where they would take up government posts.

Those who were from Kuninda referred to themselves with the characters 唐 (China) and 栄 (Prosperity).[cxii] This was an expression of the pride they held in their expertise and as channels between the Kingdom and China who were vital to the prosperity of the Ryukyu Kingdom.

It was thanks to those in Kuninda that it is even possible to know much of the history of the Ryukyu Kingdom that can be known today. Documents and letters written under the Ryukyu Kingdom, for the most part, were written in Chinese, and this

---

28   *Okinawa Kara Ajia Ga Mieru*, 86.

extended to the letters written to the heads of state of Ryukyu's trading partners, and their replies. What made Kuninda different from other Chinese communities throughout Asia was that these individuals were not just merchants, but also official representatives of China within the kingdom.

Many influential figures from the Ryuyku Kingdom's history have their roots in Kuninda, such as the statesman Sai On (1682-1761), who was a member of the king's closest advisors, The Council of Three and carried out agricultural and forestry reform across the kingdom. We will see more of him in later chapters.[cxiii] Those from Kuninda also brought technological innovations such as, Gishitetsu (1653-1738) who carried out the first surgery under anesthesia around one hundred years before any such procedure was carried out in mainland Japan.[cxiv]

Chinese Influences on Ryukyu

Ryukyu's long connections with China would have a profound effect on the culture of the archipelago, and continue to shape the islands to this day. Totems that offered protection can be found throughout the archipelago. One such example is the *Ishigandō*, a stone with the characters 石敢當 engraved or painted on it. The *Ishigandō* can be found outside of houses, along stone walls and even in front of department stores and hotels.[cxv] There are over ten thousand *Ishigandō* in Okinawa alone. *Ishigandō* are said to prevent bad luck, and be particularly effective against *Majimun* (evil spirits).

Ishigandō are often found at places such as crossroads as it is thought that this prevents the *Majimun* from going straight down the road into the individual houses. Throughout Okinawa, *Ishigandō* are on average around fifteen centimeters in height, but there are also gigantic Ishigandō made from boulders.

The origins of *Ishigandō* are not entirely clear, but there are theories that the first *Ishigandō* were placed in the ninth century in Fujian, from where the idea would have been transmitted to Ryukyu. The *Ishigandō* of the kingdom were something that was mentioned by Chinese delegations to Ryukyu, including a delegation in 1756 under the reign of Shō Boku (1739–1794), which noted the presence of *Ishigandō*. One of the oldest known Ishigandō can be found on Kumejima, the almost Africa-shaped island at the most western reaches of the Okinawa group. This weathered *Ishigandō* about 1.2 meters in height dates to 1733. It has the characters for Mount Tai, one of China's five holy mountains, carved deep into the rock. *Ishigandō* like this, while more common in China, can also be found throughout the Ryukyu Archipelago.[cxvi]

Ishigandō would also be taken wherever Okinawans migrated around the world and can be found today in mainland Japan, and as far as Brazil.[cxvii] Other pieces of cultural transmission from China that continue to dot the Okinawan landscape are the *Hinpun* walls, which can be seen at traditional and modern houses. The *Hinpun* walls are erected between the gateway into a household and the main building, and as with the *Ishigandō* their purpose is to ward off misfortune.

Another import from China which cannot be missed across the archipelago's landscape are the Turtleback Tombs which have been given this moniker due to their resemblance to gargantuan turtle shells. While these tombs may have their origins in China, their construction in Ryukyu is unique to the archipelago. The tombs themselves can be thought of as a miniature version of Tamaudun, the royal mausoleum. The tombs vary in size and shape, with those of noble lineage having vast tombs that are elegantly shaped. But even the more turtleback tombs of more common families are still larger than anything that can be seen in Japan or Western Europe, and their use is a custom that continues in Okinawa today.

THE RYUKYUS

The graves are so large in size that when Commodore Matthew Perry (1794–1858) arrived in the Ryukyu Kingdom en route to Japan in the 19th Century, members of the crew at first mistook them for the houses of the people in Okinawa. As in China, there is an annual tomb sweeping festival in early April called *Shiimii* in Okinawa. During this festival, people clean the graves of their ancestors, place incense and offerings and even have picnics with their family in the tomb's courtyard.[cxviii] Similar customs can be seen throughout Chinese communities in Asia as well such as in Manila and Singapore.

Another example of something that was borrowed from China and then adopted, is the iconic *Shisa* lions. Unlike in China, these *Shisa* are placed everywhere, at the entrance to villages, on the top of graves, and even on the roofs of houses. If one is anywhere where there is a building in Okinawa Prefecture today, one is sure to be close to at least a few *Shisa*.

In the era of the Ryukyu Kingdom the most significant import was the great Chinese junks. The first junks that the kingdom was provided with are recorded in the *Ming Shilu*. This was from the very early days of the kingdom with even thirty junks in the days of Shō Hashi.

When these junks inevitably became worn down, China would provide replacement vessels. While the *Ming Shilu* does not record the size of the junks given to Ryukyu, by the 16th Century these junks were about forty meters in length, ten meters in width and had a height of about five meters. The main mast of the ship towered at thirty meters, and in addition to this the ships had two supporting masts. The ships would weigh between 2,000 to 3,000 tons and could support a crew up to 300 as well as at least ten horses.[29]

---

29 Kurayoshi Takara, *Ajia No Naka No ryūkyū ōkoku* (Yoshikawako bunkan, 1998), 85-86.

CHINA'S CULTURAL LEGACY IN RYUKYU

The keel of the junks was constructed from pine, with numerous divisions below deck which meant that the gunwale when damaged would allow water to enter just one of these many divisions rather than the entire ship.

The only ships that were comparable to the Chinese junks were the Dhow ships used by Muslim merchants to cross the Arabian and Indian oceans.

But as the centuries progressed and the power of China began to gradually decline, the number of ships given to the Ryukyu Kingdom decreased and by the mid-15th Century the kingdom had begun to build its own Chinese junks, which while slightly smaller contained all the technological innovations which allowed these formidable ships to cross oceans.

Ceremony was an important part of the creation and sending off of these tributary ships. The kingdom bestowed each ship with a name, and the honorific suffix 'Tomi'. Examples of ship names under the Ryukyu Kingdom are Sedaka-tomi, Ukimi-tomi and Sejiara-tomi, these names were bestowed upon the ships by the *Kaminchui* priestesses, one of the many ways the act of tribute was integrated into the Ryukyu religion.[cxix] To bless ships for safe passage, a celebratory event was held at Shuri Castle, attended by the King himself and the Council of Three. During this ceremony, the sailors would create a rope and lay it on the *Ukimichi* (the 'floating path') and a banquet was held in which *Omoros* were sung.

Ryukyu's Central Ports

Under the Ryukyu Kingdom, there were two main ports in Okinawa. The first was the central port of Naha from which ships would go to China, stopping off in the Kerama Islands on their way. The nearby port of Tomari acted as a supplementary port with ships going further west to Kumejima and then onto

China, Naha itself is about 800 kilometers from Fujian on the China coast.

If ships were not granted favorable winds they would wait in Agonoura Bay at the island of Zamami, and once the conditions had settled leave for China. Further west in Kumejima, the port of Kanegusuku served a similar purpose.

One of the main differences between Ryukyu merchants and Chinese merchants throughout Asia was that the former never established foreign settlements overseas, as any trade carried out by the Ryukyu Kingdom was officially at least a form of diplomacy rather than capital accumulation. This did not mean, however, that the Ryukyu sailors were always well-behaved. In 1470, the leader of the Ryukyu delegation to China was caught making illegal deals with a Chinese bureaucrat and in the same year the Sultan of Malacca complained of a rowdy individual amongst the Ryukyu delegation. Such problems likely occurred every now and again, but there are no records of any major incidents. In response to the Sultan of Malacca, King Shō En apologized, promising that there would be no recurrence and that said individual would be duly punished.

Through its relationship with China, Okinawans took elements of Chinese culture and adapted and modified them in their own ways, creating something distinctly Okinawan, and this legacy can very much be felt in the islands to this day.

9

KOREA AND JAPAN

Ryukyu and Korea

The Ryukyu Kingdom's other important trading partners in East Asia were Korea and Japan. Since Ryukyu and Korea both paid regular tribute to China, the two nations had a special relationship. The first recorded contact with Korea was under King Satto of Chūzan, who returned Koreans who had been captives of *Wakō* pirates.

As with China, it is likely that Ryukyu's relationship with the Korean Peninsula dates back further than the historical records. Yoshinari Naoki has proposed that the three Tomoe marks which are the symbol of the martial god Hachiman, and appear on the Ryukyu Kingdom's royal crest are one such sign of this with Yoshinari proposing that the origins of Hachiman are in the Korean Peninsula and this subsequently spread to the Ryukyu Archipelago and Japan.[30]

Wakō pirates did view Hachiman as a guardian deity and were active off the coasts of the archipelago even during the Three Kingdoms Period.[cxx] Hachiman was so prevalent that even as far north as Hokkaido, Hachiman Shrines established by mainland Japanese in outpost settlements prompted the indigenous Ainu to incorporate the design into their necklaces called *Shitoki*.

---

30 *Ryūkyū Ōkoku to Wakō Omoro No Kataru Rekishi*, 139.

THE RYUKYUS

It was in 1389, that King Satto sent Koreans back to what was the Kingdom of Goryeo, and he used this opportunity to trade, sending sulfur, pepper and palm trees to the Ryukyu delegation to Goryeo. In 1392, a Korean representative was sent to the Ryukyu Kingdom to express thanks. The same year, the Goryeo dynasty came to an end and was replaced with the Joseon, but as with dynastic change in China, the Ryukyu Kingdom's relationship would smoothly transition with the new regime.

Ryukyu junks making their way to Korea would head north, past Amami Ōshima, Kagoshima's Bōnotsu along the west coast of Kyushu, and sail further still past the island of Tsushima, which lies almost directly between the Korean Peninsula and Kyushu. The destination of the Ryukyu junks was Busan, and this was a treacherous journey in *Wakō* pirate infested waters. Both ships from Korea and Ryukyu could be the target of these pirates.

It is likely that Koreans who had become the victim of *Wakō* pirates had long made their home in Okinawa, even before King Satto's mission. The *Annals of the Joseon Dynasty* records that in 1453 there were at least sixty of their countrymen living in Ryukyu, probably in Naha, although it is not clear exactly where. These Koreans had married Ryukyuans, and their families were well off. What's more, fifty of these Koreans were elderly and had likely spent decades in their adopted home.

Since Ryukyu items alone were not sufficient as a tributary offering to China, the kingdom proactively sought to establish tributary relationships with the peninsula as it needed a market to sell Chinese and Southeast Asian goods as well as to buy Korean goods to trade with other nations.

In contrast, Korea's relationship with Ryukyu was rather more passive. Korea's reluctance to send ships to Ryukyu was probably because of the *Wakō* pirates, although when Ryukyu ships did arrive on Korean shores they would be well furnished. One such priceless item provided to Ryukyu by Korea was a print of the *Tripiṭaka Koreana*, a collection of Buddhist scriptures compiled in the 13th Century.[cxxi] This text was proudly carried to Okinawa, and under Shō Shin (reign 1477–1527) was enshrined in the Benzaiten-Dō, in the royal capital of Shuri.[cxxii]

The Ryukyu Kingdom would also leave its own legacy on the Korean Peninsula. In 1433 two Ryukyuan ship builders were sent to Korea, Ufuyaku and Saburō to create a model ship. During their sojourn in Korea, Ufuyaku fell in love with a Korean woman, but under the Joseon Kingdom it was forbidden to marry an individual from overseas. Ufuyaku decided to renounce his rights as a citizen of Ryukyu so that he could stay. Less than a year later, Ufuyaku built a splendid Ryukyu ship to take on the *Wakō* pirates, and the king of Joseon ordered that its speed be put to the test against a Korean ship. The Ryukyuan ship was considerably faster than its Korean brother, and thus Ufuyaku was able to contribute his own ship building expertise to the Joseon navy.

Lying in *Wakō* pirate infested waters, the journey to Korea was particularly dangerous, and to decrease this risk from the middle of the 15th Century onwards Ryukyu began to increasingly trade Korean goods either through merchants in Tsushima an island almost directly between Korea and Japan, or in Kyushu, through middlemen Japanese merchants from Sakai or Hakata.

The waters around the Korean Peninsula became all the more dangerous with the outbreak of the Ōnin War (1467-1477) as a succession dispute erupted within the Ashikaga Shogunate which would lead to the samurai of Japan fighting amongst each other for the next century and a half. Thus Korea's sibling nation Ryukyu was pushed further away.

THE RYUKYUS

Ryukyu and Japan

This loss for Korea, was a gain for Japan. The *Omorosaushi* refers to the event of going to Japan as '*Yamato Tabi*' (journey to Yamato) and the word 'Yamato' remains one of the words that is still used to refer to mainland Japan in Okinawa today.

By the 15th Century, the Ryukyu Kingdom had already sent a letter to the Ashikaga Shogun to which he had recognized the 'ruler of Ryukyu' in turn. Tribute was sent to Japan even before a unified kingdom was formed in Okinawa. In 1414 under the 4th Ashikaga Shogun, Ashikaga Yoshimochi (1394-1423).

A delegation to Japan was even sent before the formation of the Ryukyu Kingdom with Shō Shishō, the father of the Ryukyu Kingdom's founder Shō Hashi, sending a delegation. Another notable tributary event was in 1466 when a delegation was sent by King Shō Toku (1441–1469). During the proceedings, in celebration the Shogunate set off a volley of gun fire outside Kyoto's main gate, startling the cities' denizens.

Trade from Ryukyu was of equal importance to Japan and under the Ashikaga Shogunate a magistrate was constructed to receive and manage trade from Ryukyu at Hyōgo on the inland sea.

This exchange was not limited to official channels either, merchants from Hakata and Sakai in particular traded with sailors from Ryukyu, allowing a flow of Southeast Asian and Chinese goods into Japan.

Just as the Ōnin War destabilized the waters around Korea, the Japanese archipelago at the center of the conflict became increasingly unappealing, with areas such as the inland sea around Hyōgo now a war zone and the *Wakō* pirates remaining a problem as ever, Ryukyu ships began to decrease.

Yet, this decrease in the number of Ryukyu ships in Japan did not hamper Japanese merchants' desires for trade with Ryukyu, and merchants from Hakata and Sakai began to increasingly venture south to Naha. These merchants would ride seasonal winds, staying in the Ryukyu Kingdom until they could ride the returning winds back home. As with Koreans and Chinese in Okinawa, it is of course likely that there was already a degree of Japanese settlement before they are first mentioned in the historical records.

These Japanese bought with them Shintō, Japan's indigenous religion and in, particularly Kumano shrines, who the Japanese merchants would pray to during their crossings of the rough seas. In the years after the Ōnin War, monks also made their way to Ryukyu, mostly with plans of going on to visit China, although some became permanent residents of Ryukyu instead.

These monks bought with them Mahāyāna Buddhism, the form of Buddhism most prominent in East Asia. One such example is the monk Raijyū who turned one of the most important religious sites in the Ryukyu Kingdom into a temple to protect the nation, what is now Nami-no-ue shrine.[cxxiii]

Other examples of Japanese monks bringing Buddhism and Shintō with them is Kaiin Shōko who came and spread the Rinzai school of Zen Buddhism in Ryukyu, and Nishū Shōnin (1503-1577) who built the Kinkannon-Ji temple in northern Okinawa.[cxxiv]

Burial at Sea

At the base of the Kii Mountains there is a temple.[cxxv] The monks in this temple are believers of a pure land overseen by the Bodhisattva Kannon, the realm of Fudaraku.[cxxvi] Not far from the temple in the bay of Nachi monks gather around the sandy beach on an overcast November afternoon. They are looking out to a small boat anchored to the land with a white rope as it is pushed back and forth by the waves. There is a small thatched

THE RYUKYUS

house on the boat surrounded by four miniature Torii gates, lacquered in an iridescent red. From the vessel stands a mast with a lone white sailcloth fluttering back and forth as it is caressed by the wind. There is a man sealed within this house, before he was entombed within he had prayed to the Thousand Arm Kannon within the temple, the other monks had supplied a months' worth of food and water and then he was sealed within. This monk by the name of Nisshu is going to the heavenly realm of Fudaraku.

It is from the temple of Fudaraku-Ji that more than half of such vessels were sacrificed to the Pacific. The monks believe that by praying as the boat drifts south they will be reborn in this pure land.[cxxvii]

This is a burial at sea, and all are aware. On parallel sides of the boat there are two torii gates, and two larger one's perpendicular symbolic of the four gates the dead are expected to pass through to reach the pure land.[cxxviii]

After chanting from the sutras the monks on the beach cut the white rope, and the Fudaraku boat is carried south by the boreal wind. As the days pass, Nisshu spends his time confined in the darkness reading from the sutras in the flickering candle light and praying for his rebirth in Fudaraku.

From within this atramentous womb, Nisshu can feel the vessel being thrown back and forth by the waves. Like Odysseus's raft, Nisshu's boat is hurled by the wind, 'the South Wind hurls it, then the North Wind grabs it, then the East Wind yields and lets the West Wind drive it.'[31] Unlike Odysseus, Nisshu is not rescued by a goddess, but instead washes ashore on the white limestone of the northern Magiri of Kin on the island of Okinawa.

---

31 Homer and Emily R. Wilson, *The Odyssey* (W.W. Norton & Company, 2018), 191.

KOREA AND JAPAN

When early dawn appears and lights up the sky with blossom, a young boy from the village discovers a warped boat washed up on the shore. The mast has been cleaved in two, most of it likely somewhere amidst the waves, and the brow of the boat has been beaten beyond recognition. Most curious of all is the box like structure at the boats center, and the boy from Kin's heart swells in anticipation for what forgotten treasure he will discover inside.

He pulls apart the waterlogged wood with his bare hands, and finds inside a monk breathing a faint wheeze. The boy from Kin is taken aback, but after he has composed himself he rushes to the village and brings hot gruel back to the monk.

Having been revived from the hearty meal, Nisshu thanks for boy and introduces himself and is taken to a spring where after taking a drink from the crystal waters remarks "this is indeed good water". Nisshu washes the brine from his body in the spring and after this is taken to the village of Kin.

A calamity has been plaguing the people here, an antediluvian beast. When the villagers met the monk that the boy has bought back they are quick to ask for his aid, a gigantic snake has been terrorizing them, the first incident was when a girl was collecting water from a river, the beast rose up, dragged her to its lair and devoured her. The villagers had become so afraid that no one dared go to collect water and without rain their crops would soon fail. "Monk, will you not aid us and purge this infliction from the land?" Nisshu is asked.

Realizing that it is not yet time for him to go onto the pure land, there are people in these islands who he can save from the endless cycles of suffering and rebirth, he replies "take me to the beast's lair".

The able-bodied men of the Kin lead the monk to a cave in which the serpent makes its home. While the men hold their distance, Nisshu walks towards the mouth of the hollow. Nisshu can hear something like the meeting of wave dashing against cliffs, the ghastly hissing of the serpent. As his eyes adjust, the bulk of the beast comes into vision. It is as thick as a tree trunk, its hide a dark green with white inflections. Its eyes an acidic yellow, the pupils a thin black line. As Nisshu meets the gaze of the snake it opens its mouth, baring its venom laced fangs and an awful hiss.

Some of the villagers faint in horror at the sight, but Nisshu composes himself. He sits down on the cold rock of the cave and begins chanting sutras.

As he chants the sky suddenly clouds over and becomes dark, heavy rain lashes the earth and thunder reverberates across the land. The serpent cannot move, and as another clap of thunder rips through the sky, the beast is sealed within the stone walls, never to torment Kin again.

Nearby the cave Nisshu constructs a Buddhist temple, Kinkannon-Ji so that these people may learn of the Four Noble Truths and be reborn in Nirvana.

News of Nisshu's miracle soon spreads to the neighboring Magiri, and eventually makes its way to the King of Ryukyu, Shō Shin. The king is intrigued by the priest's teachings and sends a retainer to Kin inviting him to the royal palace in Shuri. Having saved the people of Kin not only for this life but hopefully the next, Nisshu is satisfied and agrees to make the journey south.

In the Palace of One Hundred Inlets Nisshu enters an environment of golden dragons, and elegant masonry, a very different world from his life as a monk in the temple far across the fathoms, even further from the Fudaraku boat he had boarded to end his life.

Shō Shin urges Nisshu to take up an official role as a Buddhist priest within the Ryukyu court, being given the opportunity to free even more from the endless cycle of rebirth and death, Nisshu accepts.

Nisshu's accomplishments across the kingdom are numerous. At Naha port he erects a temple, Gokoku-Ji to safeguard the kingdom and enshrined there the Bodhisattvas Kannon, Amitabha and Pindola, the healing Buddha.

Neither did Nisshu's encounters with the occult end at Kin. On one occasions Nisshu comes across talk of a spectral being, a Yōkai (ghost) haunting people on the road between Urasoe and Shuri.

The nucleus of these incidents was a hill covered in a thick forest of pine. When Nisshu ventured to the haunted knoll he buried in the earth a stone onto which was carved verses of the Diamond Sutra.[cxxix] The people henceforth called the place 'Sutra Hill' and no longer had to worry about the Yōkai.

As with the temples, the sacred hill would carry a legacy for centuries. On one occasion a man traveling the roads decides to rest under the shade of a pine tree, and was awoken from his slumber when he heard a commotion from people in the town below. He ventures down and is told 'There was just a huge earthquake, how can you not know?' and from that day forth the people of Okinawa would chant the name of Sutra Hill for its protection during an earthquake.

———∞———

Nisshu's mythical story of how he came to propagate Buddhism in Okinawa tells us much about how the people associated the religion with not just a means of being reborn as a higher being in the next life, but as a force that could solve the problems of today. As with the some of the fantastical stories of the Ryukyu Kings in the official histories, we can be sure that there was a monk called Nisshu who founded the temples of Kinkannon-Ji and Gokoku-

THE RYUKYUS

Ji, and that such stories have at least some basis in history. Nisshu's story tells us much about how monks from Japan had a cultural and religious influence on the islands of Okinawa, long before the kings of Ryukyu were forced to prostate themselves before the samurai in the 17th Century.

10

TRIBUTE TO SOUTHEAST ASIA

The Silkroad of the Sea
While trade with Korea and Japan was undoubtedly important the Ryukyu Kingdom relied more on other tributary states to China throughout Southeast Asia. Exactly when the peoples of the Ryukyu Archipelago began trading with those in Southeast Asia is not clear. It is possible that Miyako islanders set out to trade with what is today Singapore as early as 1317, and when King Satto of Chūzan first sent a delegation to China they bought goods from Southeast Asia such as pepper with them.

It is also known that Southeast Asian ships could make their way as far as East Asia by the 14th Century, with ships from Siam being spotted off the coast of Japan and Korea. In the *Ming Shilu* it is recorded that in 1404 a boat from Siam ran adrift at Fuzhou. When Ming officials questioned them, the crew replied that they were on a diplomatic mission to the Ryukyu Kingdom. They were subsequently furnished with supplies, had their boat repaired and were sent on their way to Ryukyu.

Taking goods from East Asia further south to trade with the nations of Southeast Asia, Ryukyu was in a prime location both geographically and politically for international trade. Those in Ryukyu called Southeast Asia *'Naban'* or *'Manaban'*.[cxxx] While the characters of this word literally mean 'southern barbarians' this is not to say that Ryukyu looked down on the nations of Southeast

THE RYUKYUS

Asia as baser than themselves. Rather this term comes from the Sino-barbarian dichotomy, which saw all foreigners outside of Ming-centered China as either a northern, southern, western or eastern 'barbarians'. Despite this term being Sino-centric, the Ming paid respect to its tributary states, and the kings of the Ryukyu Kingdom treated their counterparts in Southeast Asia as equals and with the utmost respect.

Takara Kurayoshi, who has written extensively on the Ryukyu Kingdom's overseas ventures, has estimated that to the Buddhist nations in the Ayutthaya Kingdom (Siam/Thailand) Ryukyu sent up to sixty or more delegations. Under the Hindu Majahapit Empire Ryukyu sent four delegations to Palembang, and six to Java (Indonesia). To the Sultanate of Malacca (Malaysia) at least twenty delegations, eleven to the Sultanate of Patani (parts of Thailand and northern Malaysia), and at least three to the Aceh Sultanate in Sumatra (Indonesia).[32]

The visits to these places and beyond are recorded in the *Rekidaihōan*. There are also theories that, while it was never recorded, Ryukyu sailors also ventured to present-day Cambodia, and as far as the Philippines and northern Borneo.

The Ayutthaya Kingdom (Thailand)

Since the Ryukyu Kingdom's biggest trade partner was the Ayutthaya Kingdom, it is with that we shall begin. Ayutthaya was a Siamese kingdom that existed from around 1350 to 1767. Between 1425 and 1570, the Ryukyu Kingdom sent tributary delegations close to sixty times. Ayutthaya also sent delegations to Ryukyu such as when in 1479 a Ryukyu junk caught fire near the Siamese Kingdom, Ayutthaya sent the delegates back on a boat in the following year, which also bore a diplomatic letter

---

32 *Ryūkyū No Jidai: ōinaru rekishizō o Motomete*, 164.

from one king to another as well as tribute.

The capital of this Siamese kingdom was the great city of Ayutthaya, located upstream on the Chao Phraya River. This is the main river that flows through Thailand for more than 365 kilometers before it drains out into the Gulf of Thailand. During the age in which Ryukyu paid tribute in Siam, the modern capital of Thailand, Bangkok had yet to be established; the capital of Ayutthaya was located further north along the Chao Phraya than Bangkok which can be found downstream.

Ryukyu junks would navigate this river upstream until they arrived at Ayutthaya. The city itself was in a delta region, surrounded by the Chao Phraya River, the Lopburi River and the Pasak River, the royal city was thus surrounded by waterways. In addition to the natural barriers provided by the rivers, the city was also complete with towering city walls, palaces, temples, and mansions far outstripping anything that could have been seen in Ryukyu. This glorious city was hardly ever seen by ordinary Siamese who were not permitted to enter the royal capital, and the same was true for most foreigners.

In this nexus where east and west met, merchants from as far as the Gulf of Bengal and the Malaysian Peninsula came to the royal capital and the city would be Ryukyu's longest point of trade in Southeast Asia throughout the Golden Age of Trade.

The Ryukyu Kingdom would send a delegation to the Ayutthaya Kingdom on average at least once every two to four years. When Ryukyu junks arrived, they would head to a customs office at the entrance of the city. Here their goods would be inspected by beady-eyed officials and from then on they would be allowed to take their tributary items along with a personal letter from the King of Ryukyu for an audience with the Ayutthayan King.

Yet, no matter how empowering the Ayutthaya was during

THE RYUKYUS

its height, it as all kingdoms do would eventually fall. For the Ayutthaya this devastation began in the 16th Century close to home. In 1569, an attack was launched on Ayutthaya from Burma and a fifteen-year occupation followed. Ryukyu, which paid particular attention to avoid any region that was politically unstable, sent its last tributary ships to Ayutthaya in the following year of 1570.

The demise of Ryukyu's greatest trading partner in Southeast Asia would come some two hundred years later. In Burma, the third king of the Konbaung Dynasty, Hsinbyushin pursued an expansionist policy, amd in 1764 he sent his armies eastwards eventually invading the Chao Phraya River valley. In April of 1767, Hsinbyushin had captured Ayutthaya and in the fall of the royal capital's wake he deported thousands of prisoners to Burma.

But the Burmese control of Siam was brief. The Siamese General Taksin drove the Burmese out, and Taksin founded the short-lived Thonburi Kingdom (1767-1782) in place of the Ayutthaya with its capital south Thonburi south of Ayutthaya along the Chao Phraya. Once in power, Taksin convinced himself that he was well on his way towards enlightenment and would soon become a Buddha. In his hubris Taksin forced the Buddhist monks of Siam to accept his religious convictions, instead officials rose up in rebellion. The chief of these generals then succeeded to the throne, crowning himself Rama I (1736-1809) and establishing the Rattanakosin Kingdom. Under King Rama I, a new capital, present-day Bangkok was established on the opposite side of the river with Bangkok absorbing Thonburi in 1971.

The remains of Ryukyu's great Southeast Asian trading partner can be seen in the city today, making it possible for contemporaries to catch a glimpse of some of the sights that would have been familiar to the Ryukyu sailors of yore such as some of the great stone temples and Buddha statues that stand to this day.

While long gone, the cultural legacy of Ayutthaya on the Ryukyu Archipelago can still be felt in Okinawa today, most clearly in Okinawa's most symbolic alcoholic drink, Awamori. This quintessential Okinawan drink has a vital ingredient that cannot be found in East Asia, jasmine rice from Thailand. Awamori has its origins in the Ayutthaya Kingdom and this is why it has a different brewing method as well as a different type of rice compared to Japanese Sake.

From its adoption, Awamori soon became one of the many tributary items to that Ryukyu sailors would take to China and Japan. The popularity of Awamori has not died down in the hundreds of years since either. It can still be found throughout Okinawan bars, homes, and even in the shops that line the main street of Kokusai-Dori, Naha's main street, where large jars of Awamori some complete with coiled vipers with their fangs bear at the bottom of the glass.

The Majapahit Empire (Indonesia)

Ryukyu ships also went even further south towards the equator, to another powerhouse of the era, the Majapahit Empire (1293-1527) in Sumatra and Java.[cxxxi] The island of Sumatra would have been a very different world to the Ryukyu sailors, the thick and vast rainforests of the island making the northern Okinawan forest of Yanbaru look all the more puny. There were also many unfamiliar creatures, including orangutans, elephants, tigers and rhinos lurking in the forest.

The Majapahit Empire came to be in 1293, when 20,000 Mongol soldiers and one thousand Mongol battleships invaded Java. It was Raden Wijaya (reign 1293-1309) that led the forces against them, laying the foundations for the Majapahit regime.

THE RYUKYUS

Despite founding the empire, internal strife continued until the mid-14th Century when the military leader Gajah Mada (1290-1365) succeeded in stabilizing the regime. The Majapahit Empire saw its golden age under Hayam Wuruku (1334-1389) with the empire expanding from Java to Bali to Madura off Java's northeastern coast.

The Majapahit Empire now stretched from Sumatra and the Malayan Peninsula to much of modern-day Indonesia. The island of Java was the birthplace of the Majapahit, and while it is known that Ryukyu junks visited Java and the *Rekidaihōan* records that the first ships to visit were in 1430, it cannot be said with absolute certainty where in Java this was.

One of the pioneers of Okinawan studies, Higashiona Kanjun (1882-1963) has suggested that it was probably what is present day Jakarta, since in the *Omorosaushi* there is a reference to 'Kawara Naban'.[33] This 'Kawara' is likely an accented version of 'Kelapa' the Malay word for palm tree and is a place name in the city of Jakarta today.

What made Jakarta different from Fuzhou or Ayutthaya was that unlike these cities, which were located on the banks of large rivers, Jakarta was a port city facing the sea. The Portuguese apothecary Tomé Pires described the port in the *Suma Oriental*, written between 1512-1515 thus:

> "The port of Calapa is a magnificent port. It is the most important and best of all. This is where the trade is greatest and whither they all sail from Sumatra, and Palembang, Laue, Tamjompura, Malacca, Macassar, Java and Madura and many other places."[34]

---

33   *Ryūkyū No Jidai: ōinaru rekishizō o Motomete*, 151.
34   *Ryūkyū No Jidai: ōinaru rekishizō o Motomete*, 151.

TRIBUTE TO SOUTHEAST ASIA

The other port of the Majapahit Empire that Ryukyu would call on was Palembang in Sumatra, a port city situated on the Musi River that drains out into the Sea of Java. According to the *Rekidaihōan*, Ryukyu's formal relationship with Palembang began when twenty individuals from Palembang washed up on the shores of Japan. Since the Ryukyu Kingdom regularly sent ships to Southeast Asia, Japan requested that Ryukyu return those who had been shipwrecked. They were subsequently put on a Ryukyu junk to Ayutthaya, and then sent from Ayutthaya to Palembang.

It was six to seven years after this that the first Ryukyu ship docked in Palembang in 1428. The delegation carried with them a letter from founder King Shō Hashi requesting the opening of trade relations.

The Ryukyu Kingdom would send further ships to Palembang in 1430, 1438 and 1440 and beyond. However, by the time Ryukyu sailors began visiting Palembang, the Majapahit Empire was already waning. This was coupled with the arrival of Indian merchants who began to increasingly appear, bringing with them Islam. Palembang was not the only port Ryukyu ships would enter during this period, and the influx of this new religion did not put a halt on Ryukyu's trade.

While there is no record in the *Rekidaihōan*, it is likely that Ryukyu ships would also call at the ports of the Aceh Sultanate (1496-1903) in northern Sumatra. The origins of the Aceh Sultanate begin in the late 13th century, with the monarch of the Samudra Kingdom converting to Islam. The sultanate would remain in power until the end of the 18th Century when the sultanate lost control of parts of the Malay Peninsula to the British. As with the Ayutthaya Kingdom, a cultural legacy has been left by Ryukyu's contact with Indonesia throughout the Golden Age of Trade. This can be seen in particular in traditional Okinawan folk songs, which are almost always sung with the accompanying instrument the *Sanshin*, a banjo shaped instrument with a snake skin body, a long neck and three strings.[cxxxii]

This, like Ryukyu's other relationships, can still be felt in Okinawa today. When Higa Masao, a professor at the University of Ryukyu, was guiding a visiting Indonesian professor, there was an occasion when they were walking through a northern Okinawan village in the evening, when the visiting professor abruptly stood still. Higa asked him what was wrong, and he replied, "I can hear Indonesian music". What he was actually hearing was a children's song written by Asa Hiroshi (1934-2007).[35] According to Higa, the similarities between the music comes from the singing of Okinawa folk songs having a similarity to the singing that accompanies the Indonesian gamelan gong and this is why the professor thought he heard Indonesian music.

The Sultanate of Malacca (Malaysia)
The most important of the Islamic states in the region for the Ryukyu Kingdom was the Sultanate of Malacca (circa 1400-1511). The Sultanate Malacca was situated in between the two great powers of the era, the Ayutthaya to the north and the Majapahit to the south. The founder of the sultanate was Paramesvara, a Sumatran prince who had fled from his home of Palembang during a Javanese attack. Paramesvara briefly went to what is now Singapore, before settling in Malacca in either the last few years of the 14th Century or the early 15th Century.[cxxxiii]

Once Paramesvara converted to Islam, he took the title Sultan Iskandar Shah in 1414, and soon established a tributary relationship with Ming China, benefiting greatly from the trade

---

35 *Okinawa Kara Ajia Ga Mieru*, 110.

that came to Malacca from Arabia and India.[cxxxiv] Since Malacca was an Islamic nation it's official history, the *Sejarah Melayu* (Malay annals) was written in Arabic and the inscriptions on the king's graves were written with Arabic calligraphy.

By the 1430s, the city of Malacca had become one of the most cosmopolitan in the world and had a mix of peoples from Arabia, Persia, India, China, Southeast Asia, and of course Ryukyu, visiting its shores. As with the Ryukyu Kingdom, by becoming a tributary state to China, the Sultanate of Malacca befitted from China's trade networks. What's more, by establishing relations with China, Malacca was able to free itself of control from Ayutthaya to which it had to pay tax and could increasingly establish its own independence. Malacca faced numerous Siamese invasions from the north. In 1431 and in 1445 invasions were launched on the Sultanate but these were successfully repulsed. Malacca's first tributary delegation to China took place in 1405, and there was such a level of enthusiasm in the country, that the sultan himself went with an entourage of over 500 to China in 1411.

The Ryukyu Kingdom established relations with the Sultanate of Malacca just as the nation had succeeded in repelling foreign attacks and solidifying its power over the Malacca straits, and this is exactly what the Ryukyu Kingdom looked for in its trading partners, a degree of stability. The city of Malacca itself was situated on a river considerably smaller than those in Fuzhou or Ayutthaya, but Malacca had something else that would create its wealth, the Strait of Malacca. The Strait of Malacca is a narrow stretch of water between the Malay Peninsula and Sumatra. Even today, it remains one of the most important shipping lanes in the world and this 580-mile waterway connects the Indian Ocean to the Pacific. During the time of the Ryukyu Kingdom, it was the Sultanate of Malacca that oversaw all trade that passed through the strait, making it one of the most international locations throughout all of Asia.

Through this relatively tiny body of water ships would pass East Asia going west and trade from Arabia and India going east. Malacca was thus the crossroads of Southeast Asia, at a location under which almost all trade by ocean must pass through.

The trade routes that flowed through the strait were enormous, covering the Indian Ocean, Arabian Ocean, and even as far as the Mediterranean to the west, while to the east were the many East Asian and Southeast Asian countries. In March, the north-eastern monsoon winds would bring merchants from as far as the Arabian Peninsula to Malacca, then these same merchants would ride south-western winds back home around May of the same year. The trade winds would bring people from all over the world to the Sultanate of Malacca. The Indian merchants who visited these shores were from the Coromandel Coast, the Malabar Coast, and Bengal. Most of these merchants had converted to Islam, and they bought their religion with them to Southeast Asia.

The trade goods that these Indian and Arabian merchants took back west with them would make it to the bazaars of Istanbul and from there to the Mediterranean. Boats from Java would also arrive in Malacca in the summer, bringing with them spices, making their return journey in the winter. Ryukyu junks would arrive in Malacca during the winter, bringing things such as maritime products from the South China Sea. The Ryukyu junks would then head north in the early summer of the following year. While the Ryukyu sailors sojourned in the Sultanate, they would have had the chance to trade with the Indian and Arabian merchants there, allowing them to more fully diversify their wares. Unfortunately we do not have any records of what the average Ryukyu sailors thought of the Arab and

TRIBUTE TO SOUTHEAST ASIA

Indian merchants they met in Malacca nor the Arab and Indian merchants impressions on those from Ryukyu. Perhaps they were met with a degree of fascination coming from a faraway and little known land.

While Ryukyu ships likely visited Malacca long before this, the first official record is in 1463, when a delegation of 100 or more to Malacca, led by the diplomat Gushiken who presented an official letter to the Sultan Mansur Shah (reign 1459-1477).[cxxxv]

Gushiken presented porcelain and silk from China and swords from Japan. This tribute from the King of Ryukyu to the Sultan of Malacca would have taken place in the Sultan's palace on Bukit Malacca (Hill of Malacca). The Sultan's palace was not as ostentatious as Shuri Castle. In contrast to the lacquered red and gold of Okinawa the Sultan's palace was a long wooden structure with numerous pointed eves. Religion also played a central role in palace life and just as how there *Utaki* within the grounds of Shuri so too was there a mosque within the palace walls at Malacca.[cxxxvi]

The Sultan would also pay tribute to the Ryukyu Kingdom sending at least six delegations to Ryukyu. Each of these delegations would bear a letter from the Sultan to the King in addition to gifts.

The Ryukyuan presence in Malacca also gave Europeans one of the first chance to catch a glimpse of the people of the Ryukyu Kingdom. In the *Suma Oriental*, Pires records that

> "They hold an integrity they do not buy slaves and would not sell their brethren for the world. This is a matter they are willing to go as far as to bet their lives on. They are a people of pale skin, and wear clothes of superior quality to the Chinese, they are a proud people. To the Malays, there is not much difference

THE RYUKYUS

between the Ryukyuans and Portuguese, except that the Portuguese will pay for women, something that the Ryukyuans will not do. The Ryukyuans sell their wares freely, if someone tries to deceive them, they will draw their swords and demand their due. They are more honest than the Chinese, and more feared. They are talked about in a similar way as we Europeans talk of the Milano's by the people of Malacca."[cxxxvii]

It was this Portuguese presence in Malacca that eventually led to the Ryukyu Kingdom abandoning their visits when in 1511 the governor of Portugese India, Afonso de Albuquerque (1453–1515) captured the city on the strait. After the fall of the sultanate, Ryukyu ships would call at the much smaller Sultanate of Patani, further north in the Malay Peninsula, although this was never on the frequency in which Ryukyu junks had visited the Sultanate of Malacca, as Patani lacked the strategic position of Malacca.[cxxxviii]

The End of the Golden Age
While Ryukyu had prospered through the China's tributary states, this network was dealt a blow when Europeans began advancing into Asia. In December of 1496, Vasco da Gama (1460-1524) led a fleet of four ships around the Cape of Good Hope, and onto the west coast of India, arriving in Calicut. Da Gama's arrival marked the first of numerous European pushes east. A mere two years after the Portuguese had arrived in India, they were forced to realize that they would not be met with open arms. The Muslim merchants did not appreciate these commercial competitors and incited attacks on Portuguese ships. This reached a peak in 1500, when tensions between Arab and Portuguese merchants in Calicut exploded into riots, which saw the destruction of Portuguese ships and many dead. This tension

TRIBUTE TO SOUTHEAST ASIA

was a sign to the Portuguese that the only way they could strengthen and grow trade routes throughout Asia, Africa and beyond was through colonization. In response to the Massacre of Calicut, King Manuel I of Portugal (1469-1521) ordered Francisco de Almedia (1450-1510) who led a fleet of thirty ships into the Indian Ocean seeking retribution. The Muslim merchants in India, who were unable to stop the Portuguese sent an envoy to the Mamluk Sultanate of Egypt (1250-1517) asking for aid.[cxxxix] This culminated in the February 1509 Battle of Diu, in which a naval battle between the Sultanate of Gujarat (1407-1573), the Zamorin of Calicut and the Mamluk Sultanate, with the aid of the Venetians, faced off against Portugal. Despite the later alliance, it was the Portuguese who triumphed.

This victory at the Battle of Diu, in the far away Arabian Sea would have devastating consequences for the Ryukyu Kingdom. Following the Battle of Diu, Afonso de Albuquerque (1453-1515) succeeded in conquering Goa on India's west coast in 1510, and having secured the Indian Ocean, made his way further east. The following year, in July 1511, Albuquerque led a fleet of sixteen ships and launched an assault on Malacca, overthrowing the Sultanate in the process. Following their success at the Strait of Malacca, the Portuguese entered the Gulf of Siam, and proceeded to attack the Ayutthaya Kingdom. Within a few decades, the Portuguese had succeeded in doing the unthinkable, capturing a piece of not a tributary state but China itself, with the establishment of a base in Macao in 1557. It was under the reign of Shō Shin, that Malacca fell, and Ryukyu stopped trade there after this. The last record of tribute was in 1570, likely ended as a result of the Portuguese violence and mercantilism. With this, the people of Kuninda, who were officially representatives of China, became all the more Okinawan over the coming generations, now that they would have less direct contact with China, and

THE RYUKYUS

other overseas Chinese communities.

Around the same time Europeans were making roads in East Asia, the Ming's power was weakening within China. Chinese merchants increasingly flouted the maritime ban rules. By 1567 there was also less need for the maritime ban, with continued Ming efforts to purge the pirates from the high seas, and in 1588 the Japanese Shogun Toyotomi Hideyoshi gave orders for all piracy around Japanese waters to be stopped. The result was that the monopoly Ryukyu had on Chinese goods was gradually lost to not only Chinese merchants, but also Japanese merchants who began an increasingly large private trade. It was these two factors, the European expansion into East Asia and the increase of private trade that would bring Ryukyu's Golden Age of Trade to a gradual close, and while international trade would continue in the Kingdom until its abolishment in the 19th Century, it never again reached the heights of this age. While Ryukyu's trade partners were threatened from the south, Ryukyu's own autonomy would be put in jeopardy from the north, with the invasion of the Satsuma samurai.

11

THE SATSUMA INVASION OF RYUKYU

The Satsuma Samurai and a Unified Japan
While the first Ryukyu Dynasty collapsed due to internal strife, the second was subjugated by external powers. In Southeast Asia many of the tributary states that Ryukyu ships visited faced foreign pressures. The Kingdom of Ayutthaya was defeated by an invading Burmese army from the east, while the Sultanate of Malacca was no match for the mercantilism and the cannons of the Portuguese.

What makes Ryukyu's subjugation by a foreign power different from its Southeast Asian partners is that even after a devastating military defeat, the kingdom was encouraged to maintain a façade of independence that would continue until the 19th century.

It was Japan's most southern samurai, the Shimazu clan of Satsuma domain in southern Kyushu which became the overlords with their 1609 offensive culminating in the King of Ryukyu's surrender.

After this invasion, the kingdom continued to function as it had before on the face of it, but it was ultimately the Japanese shogun, through the Satsuma, who was pulling the strings. For the Japanese samurai, the annexation of Ryukyu came with a particularly mouthwatering prize, access to the goods of the Middle Kingdom through the guise of a tributary state.

THE RYUKYUS

This coveted Japanese aspiration was only possible because of the country's recent unification into a centralized state under the Tokugawa Shogunate after centuries of infighting. This brought an end to Daimyō factionalism and brought stability to the country under a single regime. No longer having to wage skirmishes to expand one's own domain or protect it from others, the most southern of these samurai, the Satsuma, were free to expand their territory south.

In Japan, the warring states period (or Sengoku Period) began with the decline of the Ashikaga Shogunate (1336-1573) with feuding Daimyō fighting to expand their domains at the expense of their opponents. The Emperor, long reduced to a figurehead, held little real power and these ambitious samurai were quick to fill this vacuum.

By the mid-15th century, this period of warring states was bought to a close when the 'Three Unifiers of Japan', Oda Nobunaga (1534-1582) Toyotomi Hideyoshi (1537-1598) and Tokugawa Ieyasu succeeded in bringing most of what is now Japan under their direct rule.[cxl]

This centralization of power, first under Toyotomi Hideyoshi and then Tokugawa Ieyasu, allowed the Shimazu samurai of Satsuma domain in southern Kyushu to expand their own power into the Ryukyu Archipelago in the name of the Shogun.

Japanese trade in Ryukyu had long been a reality, there were both Japanese merchants in Ryukyu and Ryukyu sailors would visit Sakai and Hakata in Japan, but the potential of such a trade was limited, far less lucrative than the coming monopoly.

Until the early 15th Century, it was the Shogunate which issued official seals to any Japanese merchants who sought to trade in Ryukyu, and the Satsuma were bestowed a special role in policing this, and were ordered to confiscate any currency found aboard these unauthorized ships and bring it to Kyoto.

THE SATSUMA INVASION OF RYUKYU

By the early 15th Century, the Shogunate allowed the Satsuma to issue their own seal to ships going to the Ryukyu Kingdom, and following this, Satsuma Daimyō continually emphasized their right to control merchants from Japan who made their way to the Ryukyu Kingdom. These merchants were expected to obtain documents from the Satsuma before heading further south, and since the seal of the Shimazu was not free, it became a sources of revenue for the Satsuma.

However, while the Satsuma emphasized this right, there were plenty of Japanese merchants who were more than happy to ignore these requests, sailing on to Ryukyu without paying any dues to the Satsuma.

On numerous occasions, the Satsuma asked the Ryukyu Kingdom to apprehend any such Japanese merchants who appeared in the Kingdom's ports, and while Ryukyu agreed to seize these merchants in principle, little effort was made to enforce this. With the Ryukyu Kingdom paying little heed to the Satsuma's requests, these samurai attempted to force obligations onto Ryukyu.

In 1516, the lord of Tsurajima (in present day Okayama Prefecture) Miyake Kunihide was on his way to Ryukyu when he and his fleet of twelve ships were stopped at Bōnotsu on the Satsuma Peninsula in southern Kyushu.

Here, the Daimyō of Satsuma, Shimazu Tadataka (1497-1519) and his band of men killed those aboard the ships and set them alight in the harbor. The Satsuma's justification for this sudden massacre was that Kunihide had been going south not to trade, but to overthrow the King of Ryukyu.

In 1536, the Satsuma sent a letter to Ryukyu arguing that they had done the deed for Ryukyu's sake and since they had done the favor so altruistically, should not the kingdom be obliged to send away Japanese merchants who did not bare the Shimazu's seal? The historian Tanaka Takeo has concluded that this plot surrounding Kunihide was almost certainly a falsehold and, within the context of the Satsuma's numerous schemes towards Ryukyu, looks all the more suspect.[36]

Hideyoshi and Ieyasu

The Satsuma's scheme came during a time of war between the samurai, and before the Satsuma could press Ryukyu further they were caught up in local skirmishes in Kyushu. A miraculous blessing to the Ryukyu Kingdom which unlike Japan was enjoying a prosperous and stable era.

But the skirmishes could not be relied upon to keep the Satsuma at bay infinitely and by the 1570s the Satsuma had succeeded in extending their territory to nearby Hyūga and Ōsumi in Kyushu.[cxli]

With their newfound hegemony, the Satsuma once again sent a letter to the King of Ryukyu in 1572, in which they dispensed with formalities and ordered the kingdom to seize any merchants who were so brazen as to go south without the Shimazu seal.

If the Satsuma had succeeded in conquering Kyushu during this period, it is quite possible that they may have turned their attention to the Ryukyu Archipelago and launched an invasion. Once again, Ryuyku was saved by the internal affairs of Japan. The Shogun Toyotomi Hideyoshi, who had succeeded in solidifying his control over much of Honshu and Shikoku, sent an army of over 20,000 into Kyushu and subjugated the Satsuma in 1587.

However, any respite for the Ryukyu Kingdom was brief, and with stability Japanese pressure to Ryukyu once again returned. Under Hideyoshi, the Satsuma were called upon in 1591 to order

---

36 *Ryūkyū No Jidai*, 280.

THE SATSUMA INVASION OF RYUKYU

the Ryukyu Kingdom to send supplies to feed 7,000 troops for his planned invasion of the Korean Peninsula. This was the beginning of a vision that saw Hideyoshi conquering Korea, China and as far as India, a dream that died with the defeat of his army in the Korean Peninsula by joint Ming and Joseon forces.

The Ryukyu Kingdom first resisted such requests, just as it had ignored other Satsuma demands. Ryukyu was reluctant to aid in the invasion of a fellow tributary state, but fearing further retribution from the samurai, the kingdom eventually conceded to sending only a fraction of what Hideyoshi had requested.

During this period, Ryukyu's relationship with China was already under strain. The Ming themselves were facing harder times with the European encroachment into Asia and Ryukyu was increasingly stuck between China and Japan facing an uncertain future. This explains why the Ryukyu Kingdom did not completely ignore Hideyoshi's request, as perhaps even partial compliance could work towards keeping Japan out of Ryukyu affairs. This did not turn out to be the case, and not sending the full supplies would later be interpreted by the Japanese side as a lack of respect.

Tokugawa Ieyasu, the third of Japan's 'three unifiers' was quick to grab power after the death of Shogun Toyotomi Hideyoshi after his death in 1598. In 1600 the Battle of Sekigahara was fought between Hideyoshi loyalists and Tokugawa forces with the Tokugawa prevailing. In 1614, Ieyasu launched the siege of Osaka that culminated the following year in the death of the former Shogun's heir, Toyotomi Hideyori (1593–1615).

Once again, stability in Japan meant that there was an organized state in the north that could put further pressure on the small kingdom in the south, and under the Tokugawa Shogunate there were further attempts to forcibly open the Ryukyu Kingdom. In 1602, a Ryuyku ship washed ashore at

Sendai Domain in Tohoku. Under Ieyasu's orders, the 39 sailors were sent back to Ryukyu. For Ieyasu, the return of these sailors was a diplomatic bargaining chip and when he entrusted his retainer Honda Masazumi (1565–1637) to give the Ryukyu sailors to the Satsuma in Osaka, they were told there would be dire consequences if even a single one of them died.

By their return, the Shogun expected a formal delegation from Ryukyu to thank him and this delegation could be used to negotiate a formal relationship with the kingdom. Yet, the Ryukyu Kingdom failed to send a delegation to Japan, probably because Hideyoshi's invasion of Korea had put Ryukyu in an uncomfortable position.

The Shogunate was given another diplomatic opportunity when in 1604 another Ryukyu ship drifted ashore at Hirado (present day Nagasaki Prefecture). But before this could happen the Shogunate was furious to discover that the Ryukyu sailors had already returned home of their own accord, robbing the regime of any hopes of using the event as a diplomatic opening.

The samurai of Satsuma, who had initially fought against the Tokugawa at Sekigahara, were in a position of disgrace after 1600 but through their proximity to Ryukyu they were soon partially rehabilitated by the new regime. In 1606, Shimazu Tadatsune (1576–1638) changed his name to Shimazu Iehisa as an oath of loyalty to the Tokugawa clan and to Ieyasu in particular.

It is not clear when the Satsuma were given permission from the Tokugawa Shogunate to launch an attack on Ryukyu, but it was likely sometime after this display of new-found loyalty between 1606 and 1609. The justification for the invasion of Ryukyu was that the kingdom had not paid sufficient respect to the Shogunate and had failed to supply what was fully requested by Hideyoshi.

The reality was that this was a means for Japan to access

THE SATSUMA INVASION OF RYUKYU

the wealth of China and for the Satsuma to expand their own territory. While the Ryukyu Kingdom had been enjoying an age of peace and prosperity, trading with its partners in East and Southeast Asia, the samurai of Japan had spent almost two centuries fighting among each other and had become battle-hardened warriors. This coupled with an invasion of Korea and the subjugation of numerous rebellions within their own domains meant these were warriors who had honed their military skills, making them fully prepared to launch such an invasion. This was the opposite case for Ryukyu.

The Satsuma Offensive

The Satsuma entrusted Kabayama Hisataka (1560-1634), a man about whom little is known, to lead the armada of 100 ships. On these ships rode more than 3,000 samurai ready for battle.[cxlii]

Kabayama's fleet left the port of Yamagawa on March 4, 1609 and arrived at the small island of Kuchinoerabu in Northern Ryukyu, seventy nautical miles south of Satsuma Domain.[37] Here they were forced to wait for a day as bad weather and a torrid ocean prevented them from pressing further south.

By the 6th, Kabayama's armada once again set sail, arriving in Amami-Ōshima on the 7th. The Satsuma greeted the Ryukyu officials there with a volley from the ship and the officials quickly saw that their few numbers were no match for the thousands of samurai and capitulated.[cxliii]

The place the samurai saw combat was further south, on Tokunoshima where on the 16th the first blood of the Ryukyu Kingdom's soldiers was spilled. Due to this resistance, it took until the 22nd for the Satsuma to subjugate all of Tokunoshima, and due to a lack of wind it was not until the 24th that the armada

---

[37] Kenzen Uehara, *Shimazu-Shi No Ryūkyū Shinryaku: Mō Hitotsu No Keichō No Eki* (Yōju Shorin, 2009), 138.

could rendezvous at the island of Okinoerabu. From there, the armada was ready to launch an attack on northern Okinawa.

The Two Satsuma histories on the campaign differ in their accounts of what happened after leaving Okinoerabu. The *Nanpeikyō* records that the Satsuma went directly to Naha.[cxliv] While the *Ryukyu Tokai Hibi* says that the first attack on the kingdom proper was at Nakijin on the 27th.[38] It is the latter of these accounts which is generally referenced in contemporary histories of the Ryukyu Kingdom.[cxlv]

While the Satsuma bombarded Nakijin, the kingdom sent a member of the Council of Three, the highest political position in the country besides the king, to negotiate. But he was taken hostage and the soldiers stationed at Nakijin ultimately fled knowing they were outmatched. The Gusuku that had been the 'Conquer of the Aji' had fallen. Kabayama then divided the Satsuma army into two, one took the sea route along the west coast bound for Naha, the other overland headed for the royal capital of Shuri.

The ships taking the sea route set off in the dead of night on the 29th from Unten in northern Okinawa and after traveling south laid their anchors off the coast of Yomitan. With the failure of negotiations it dawned on King Shō Nei (1564-1620) that the kingdom had little choice but to resort to force.

On April 1st, Shō Nei ordered for 3,000 troops to protect both Naha and Shuri. At Naha gun batteries were lined up along both sides of the port and an iron chain was strung across the port to prevent the entry of any ships. Around noon of that very same day, the clash between Satsuma samurai and Ryukyu *hiki* began, with the Satsuma ships that had tried to make landfall at Naha being sunk, a minor victory for the kingdom.

---

38   *Shimazu-Shi No Ryūkyū Shinryaku*, 149.

THE SATSUMA INVASION OF RYUKYU

The Satsuma who had taken the overland route set fire to property and fields along their march south, inciting fear among the populace. Many cowered for their lives as they hid in the fields while the horde past.

Of particular significance was the Satsuma burning of Urasoe Gusuku, where Shō Nei had spent his younger years as a prince before his ascension to the throne. There is a song in the *Omorosaushi* composed by the Kikoeōkimi where she compels the god of the sun, who the king of Ryukyu is descended from, to crush the 'strange haired and impotent' Yamato and that the Japanese ships be 'run aground and sunk into the darkest depths of the ocean.'[39] Perhaps this was even written among the flames of war. On this occasion, the gods did not intervene to save the kingdom.

Kagoshima

Only a few days after the Satsuma had made landfall on Okinawa, on the 4th of April, Shō Nei surrendered.[40] The next day Satsuma samurai enter Shuri castle and began taking an inventory while loading rare goods onto their ships. In comparison to Tokunoshima, there was relatively little fighting in Okinawa.

Shō Nei must have decided that he had little choice but to surrender, facing overwhelming odds a decision to fight may have risked the total annihilation of the Ryukyu Kingdom. Apart from the sheer number and experience of the Satsuma samurai, there were other advantages the Japanese side had, such as the numerous Japanese merchants who were already familiar with the layout of Naha, the country's backdoor, giving the Satsuma inside information about the kingdom.

This is not to say that Ryukyu could not have prepared more.

---

39 Torigoe. *Ryūkyūkoku No metsubō to Hawai Imin*. 45-47.
40 *Ryūkyūkoku No metsubō To Hawai Imin*, 44.

THE RYUKYUS

The Ryukyu Kingdom had witnessed the fall of the Sultanate of Malacca to the Portuguese and knew that the Burmese had attacked Ayutthaya from the east. The kingdom had seen firsthand the dangers of a lack of military might. But rather than build up these forces within the kingdom the decision was instead made to shift to other trading partners in Southeast Asia.

> While the Satsuma samurai carried treasures from Shuri Castle back to their ships, the last king of an independent Ryukyu is moved north to Urasoe.[cxlvi] For days Shō Nei anxiously awaits what is to become of his kingdom, but he is kept in the dark. At last on the 16th of April samurai guards escort him further south to the port of Naha.[41] Here he is ushered through the stone arches of the temple of Sōgen-Ji and into the wooden hall of the temple proper.
>
> In the dim light, surrounded by timber walls there is the lingering scent of incense. Seated on the floor Shō Nei is consciousness that it is at this great temple where the kings of yore have been enshrined, the same temple where delegations from China would come to pay their respects. He wonders what they would think if they knew the kingdom had fallen to these Yamato barbarians.
>
> Two large figures enter the temple and sit in front of the king. There hair is tied up in the Chonmage style, their large bodies further accentuated by the by their shining lacquered armor. They are the generals who led the Satsuma offensive, Kabayama and his Vice General Hirata Masamune (1566-1610). The silence

---

41   *Shimazu-Shi No Ryūkyū Shinryaku*, 165.

THE SATSUMA INVASION OF RYUKYU

that hangs in the air is broken when Shō Nei is told that he has no choice but to go to Satsuma domain.

It is not until almost a month later, on the 15th May that the Shō Nei, his closet advisors from the Council of Three and about one hundred other officials board Satsuma ships to sail north to Kyushu.

The boats follow the coast of Okinawa, the next day stopping at Nakijin. From the deck of the ship Shō Nei looks out over the burnt remains of Nakijin Gusuku, the great northern castle that was the 'Conquer of Aji'. A painful reminder of the blow to the kingdom's power.

From Nakijin the fleet once again set sail on the 17th across the waves of the grey sea as storms clouds gathered in the sky. Amongst the rocking of the boat Shō Nei feels nauseous, while he is the king of a maritime empire he himself has never left the kingdom.

The voyage from Okinawa to Kyushu should have taken the fleet seven to eight days but the turbulent conditions cause the journey dragged on for ten days.[42]

The ship carrying Shō Nei eventually arrives in southern Kyushu and docks at the port of Yamagawa. Here the King of Ryukyu again waits in a temporary lodging until he is taken to a custom-built mansion in the Satsuma capital of Kagoshima on the 23rd of June.[cxlvii]

Kagoshima lies along the east side of the serpentine bay at the most southern tip of Kyushu. In the Meiji era, foreigner visitors to Kagoshima would call the

---

42 *Shimazu-Shi No Ryūkyū Shinryaku*, 166-174.

THE RYUKYUS

city the 'Naples of the East' due to the ever-present volcano Sakurajima, a Mount Vesuvius of the east. Kagoshima is the capital of Satsuma and one of the most prosperous cities on Kyushu, but the people here live in the constant shadow of this goliath. In some ways Sakurajima resembles Iōtorishima in his kingdom, both are volcanic islands but Iōtorishima is but a tiny speck compared to Sakurajima, and people do not live under its shadow. Everything here seems bigger than in Ryukyu.[cxlviii]

Shō Nei is treated well in Kagoshima, his arrival is met with a formal ceremony and during his adjourn there he is granted numerous meetings with officials from the Shogunate.

Despite the show of hospitality, Shō Nei and his inner circle are well aware that they had lost the battle in Okinawa and the Japanese had the fate of Ryukyu within their hands.

Time passes and he remains in Kagoshima, the spring blossoms fade into autumnal shade. The King remains far from his kingdom. In October, Shō Nei secretly writes a letter to the Ming, writing that the Satsuma had waged a war on the kingdom to increase their territory and that due to this tribute would be late. This was likely a discrete call for aid.

The letter is entrusted to Jana Rizan (1549-1611) a trusted member of the Council of Three.[cxlix] Jana takes the letter to the Chinese community in Kyushu who have a network that extends to Nagasaki and beyond to the Chinese mainland. The letter is discovered, and never makes it out of Kyushu.

THE SATSUMA INVASION OF RYUKYU

More time passes in Kagoshima. In winter temperatures drop to around four degrees, a frigid environment for a king used to lows of fourteen. Sakurajima occasionally erupts with clouds of ash that blankets the city in a sheet of silver. Winter passes through to spring again and then blooms into summer.

In August of 1610, the king is taken to Sunpu Castle to met the now retired, but very much in control Shogun, Tokugawa Ieyasu. The Japanese castle is unlike anything the Ryukyuans have seen back home. It is surrounded by a moat like a vast river coupled with steep walls, its dark colored tiles and white lacquered façade.

The castle also gives off an air of authority, its multi-layered castle tower is like a mountain that dwarfs the flatter Shuri. The top of the castle tower is crowned with *Shachihoko*, a fierce looking carp with the head of a tiger.

At Sunpu, the former Shogun meets with the King and compels Shō Nei to sign a vow of fealty expressing the kingdom's allegiance with the Satsuma. The Satsuma of course, will do as the Tokugawa command.

This show of protestation is too much for Janza Rizan, he serves the King of Ryukyu, has studied in the imperial power that was China and refuses to show allegiance to an army of invaders.

Ieyasu's retainers force Janza to his knees, his last chance to see the error of his ways. When he refuses, he is decapitated. Amongst the façade of diplomatic pomp and procession it is clear to all that there is no choice but to accept the conditions of the samurai.

THE RYUKYUS

In the same year, Shō Nei is also taken to Edo Castle to meet with Ieyasu's son and the Shogun of Japan, Tokugawa Hidetada (1581–1632). Edo castle, the center of the Shogunate, was far larger than Sunpu. While the castle tower of Edo, over 35 meters in height, looked over the city, it was at Sunpu, on paper at least, that the Ryukyu Kingdom's independence came to an end.

Shō Nei and his court remained in Kagoshima for another cycle of the seasons, and does not be returned to Okinawa until 1611.[43] During these long days the once proud king of Ryukyu wonders what is to become of his kingdom, as he waits under the cloud of the thundering Sakurajima.

---

43 *Ryūkyū No Jidai*, 284-285.

12

Puppet Kingdom

Japanese Reforms in Ryukyu

While King Shō Nei was exiled to Kagoshima, the Satsuma set about consolidating their hold over Northern Ryukyu. In 1610 a branch of the Satsuma government was created, becoming the Ōshima Magistrate in 1613, and this was followed by the Tokunoshima Magistrate in 1616 which oversaw the islands of Tokunoshima, Okinoerabu and Yoronto.[cl]

By 1611 the Satsuma had completed a survey of the entire archipelago to assess things such as the land, how much could be produced and the population.[cli] This survey included the most southern isles of Miyako and Yaeyama and must have been a fright for the islanders who had not experienced first-hand the battle with the Satsuma as had those in Amami and Okinawa.

In remote Yaeyama, the Satsuma found that there were no temples nor shrines, and advised Shō Nei to construct some. In 1614, the Tōrin-Ji Temple and Gongendō Shrine in present day Ishigaki City were built to meet this need.[clii] The building of shrines and temples was not just a pious act from the Satsuma but a means to assert Japan's presence in the most distant reaches of the Ryukyu Archipelago.[cliii]

When Shō Nei was eventually allowed to return to Ryukyu in September of 1611, the northern territory of Amami had been torn from the Kingdom, all trade with China had to be approved by the Satsuma, and no Japanese merchants were to be alowed to dock in Ryukyu's ports without the explicit permission of the Satsuma.

The loss of autonomy and the ever-expanding power of the Japanese state was not an experience unique to the Ryukyu Kingdom. Hideyoshi's failed invasion of Korea had shown that Japan, while not successful on that occasion, had the military prowess to take over neighboring peoples. A few years earlier than the Satsuma invasion of Ryukyu, the Shogunate had also authorized the Matsumae samurai to conduct a monopoly trade with the Ainu of Hokkaido, or Ezo as they were known to contemporaries.[cliv] The most tangible and painful of these changes for the Ryukyu Kingdom was the loss of the five islands of Amami-Ōshima, Kikaijima, Tokunoshima, Okinoerabu and Yoronto. The Ryukyu Kingdom was also now liable to pay a yearly tax to the Satsuma, which would further shape the policy pursued by the royal government within Ryukyu.[clv] The Satsuma called these five islands of Amami 'Michinoshima'.[clvi]

Yet despite these drastic changes, many things continued unchanged and many common people were none the wiser. The Satsuma could not have taken direct control of the entire archipelago as this would have stretched their resources, just as the Matsumae samurai of Hokkaido were not powerful enough to take over the entirety of that island which was also inhabited by what contemporaries considered as a foreign people, just like Ryukyu.

Even if the Satsuma could have taken direct control of Ryukyu, the possibility of insurrections from the local elite would have made governing such a large region burdensome, and such a blatant land grab could have prompted the Ming to send their navy.

Thus, the political structure of the Ryukyu Kingdom remained

PUPPET KINGDOM

largely intact, with the King and officials below him keeping their roles. Tribute continued to be paid to China, with Ryukyu reaffirming itself as a tributary state, although this fell to once every ten years under the Satsuma.

Without taking direct control of the Ryukyu Kingdom it was still possible for the Shogunate, through the Satsuma to extend its laws to Ryukyu. With the establishment of a Satsuma Magistrate, it was possible to keep a constant watch on the affairs of the kingdom. The Shogunate also warned the Dutch, who it had a commercial relations with, to stop any piracy towards Ryukyu ships, a tacit sign that Ryukyu was now under the protection of Japan.

Christianity had been a thorn in the Shogunate's side, the Shimbara Rebellion (1637-1638) was one such event with thousands of Catholic peasants rising up against the Shogunate. The response was a clampdown on all missionaries and converts, with Japan's ban on Christianity being applied all the way to Yonaguni, the most western of islands within the Ryukyu Archipelago.

While the King of Ryukyu still appeared to be in power, changes to royal rule were implemented under the Satsuma. In 1611, when Shō Nei returned from Kagoshima, a hostage system was begun in which an individual of high rank from the court would be sent as a captive to Kagoshima. This began with the Sashiki Prince in 1614 who spent ten years in Kagoshima. This prince would later become King Shō Hō (1590-1640). From 1626 this system was revised to a three-year period, and in 1630 it was loosened further, allowing for one member of the Council of Three to come to Kagoshima as collateral, with this system continuing until 1646.

From 1660 the formality began in which any heir to the throne would have to venture to Satsuma first before he could be crowned king.[clvii] In Satsuma, they would receive ceremonial garb, with kings from Ryukyu now being recognized by both Japan and China. Such formalities extended to the kingdom's bureaucrats, with a pledge of allegiance required every time a Satsuma Daimyō or Ryukyu King changed.

An Agricultural Kingdom
Under the Satsuma the Ryukyu Kingdom left behind its mercantile internationalism and became a very different sort of state as it entered the early modern era. With the kingdom no longer able to rely on trade as a stable form of income, the Ryukyu Kingdom began to shift towards an agricultural society in the mid to late 17th Century. This can be seen in reforms carried out under Haneji Chōshū (1617-1675), the compiler of *Chūzan Seikan*, one of the primary official histories of the kingdom, in his position as Prime Minister.[clviii] Haneji believed that peasants should put their efforts into farming and he ordered a blacksmith to be stationed at every Magiri so that farming implements could be readily produced.

Other political leaders such as Sai On (1682-1761) of the Council of Three saw that pines and Fukugi trees were planted along the coasts to protect the land and people from strong gales alongside tidal forests to prevent erosion. Other reforms ordered by Sai On included the reclamation of land for agriculture, the relocation and establishment of settlements, and the creation of forestry on islands lacking trees by bringing them from central and northern Okinawa. In 1682 an official role to inspect the level of cultivation was established, and under Sai On these officials spread across the entire countryside.[clix]

With this shift towards agriculture, the population boomed, and by the beginning of the 18th Century there were about 10,000 people in the Ryukyu Kingdom. By the mid-19th Century this number had risen to 30,000, and by the Kingdom's final year this was 35,000. The agricultural reforms begun in this era created the basis for an expanding Okinawan population, and by 1935 what had now become Okinawa Prefecture had a population of around 60,000.

These reforms were not always welcomed by the ordinary people of Ryukyu. In *Kyūyō* it is recorded that when islanders from Miyako were moved four kilometers off the coast to Ōgamijima to create a new village in 1725 they did not readily adapt to farming and continued fishing just as they had done on Miyako. It was not until the royal government moved a further two hundred villagers to Ōgamijima and stationed officials there to oversee them that they were forced to make the transition to agriculture.

Sugar and Sweet Potatoes

While the population may have been expanding, these reforms were still unable to protect the populace against natural disasters such as tsunamis or famine. In 1709 there was a particular severe famine caused by typhoons, a lack of rain and a scorching sun which resulted in the death of three thousand people, and a similar scale famine occured again in 1825. These are but two of many such natural disasters. It was during this same period that the sweet potato, which had made its way from the New World to the Old World, entered Ryukyu through China, said to have been bought by the tributary official Noguni Sōkan.[clx] This potato, which continues to be called the *Satsuma Imo* (potato) in Japan, has its name in these origins since many of these sweet potato entered Japan (Satsuma) through Ryukyu.

It is no exaggeration to say that the introduction of the sweet potato in the Ryukyu archipelago saved thousands of lives, and it became a staple food since rice, wheat, beans and millet were not grown in sufficient quantities throughout the archipelago. Following Noguni Sōkan's contribution, it was the noble Zama Shinjō (1557-1644) who researched methods of growing the crop which led to the sweet potato's proliferation throughout the archipelago.[clxi] The sweet potato alongside an increased number of sago palm's planted as an emergency food stock would serve to protect the people of Ryukyu from famine during many hard times. Although during the toughest crisis even these would not be enough.

Under the reign of King Shō Ho (1590 – 1640), the technology to process brown cane sugar, known as black sugar in Japanese, was bought to Ryukyu from China. The production of sugar in the Ryukyu Kingdom and the now Satsuma-held Amami bolstered the wealth of the Satsuma and it was this wealth that in part gave the Satsuma the power to overthrow the Tokugawa Shogunate in 1867.

Through the first century of the Ryukyu Kingdom under Satsuma dominion, the urban centers of Shuri and Naha boomed, agricultural activity flourished, and the class system of nobles (samurē) with a genealogy and common peasants lacking even a surname became increasingly fixed, with Ryukyu society increasingly divided into classes of bureaucrats and commoners.

Interactions between Ryukyuans and Japanese

Throughout this period there was an increasing amount of Japanese interactions with Ryukyuans and this was not limited to the august officials of the Ryukyu court. On the lower levels of society, Satsuma officials would meet Okinawan women who operated lodgings, by visits to brothels, and through trade. While the Satsuma forbade any Japanese from marrying Ryukyu women, Satsuma sailors were given the right to trade and many of their business partners were women. That is not to

PUPPET KINGDOM

say that relationships did not develop between the two peoples and while the Satsuma Magistrate in Ryukyu did try to limit any relationships between Ryukyu women and Satsuma men, issuing numerous ordinances against the matter, there were time when children were born between Ryukyu women and Satsuma men. In some cases these children were even given Samurē status and receiving stipends from royal government thanks to their Satsuma connection.

While both the Satsuma government and Ryukyu government attempted to ban any commingling between the two these attempts largely failed. Many of these Satsuma men would meet Ryukyu women in Okinawa's pleasure district, Tsuji (Chīji in Okinawan) and through the Satsuma sailors, these women gave letters, money and items from China, or Ryukyu products such as Awamori which would then be taken as far as Kyoto. Something we know as Awamori is recorded as an offering at Nishihonganji Temple, a major temple in Kyoto.

This increased Japanese presence extended as far south as Yaeyama. In the 1830s Japanese merchants began setting up temporary wooden shops along the south coast of Ishigaki. The people of Ishigaki called these wooden shops *Yamato Kuyā*. These merchants would have looked strange to the Yaeyamans, with their different clothes, language and Chonmage (top-knot) hairstyle. The Japanese merchants would begin setting up in October, returning to Kagoshima in early July or August of the following year.

As in Okinawa, these Satsuma merchants would father children with local women, and the success of these merchants led to those from Shuri and Naha setting up stock as far as Yonaguni off the coast of Taiwan in turn.

There was also an increased Ryukyuan presence within Japan. Whenever there was a change in Shogun or a new king in Ryukyu, the Ryukyu Kingdom would be required to send a delegation to the capital of Edo in congratulations. This practice was known as 'Edo Nobori' — going up to Edo. From 1644 to 1850 there were seventeen Edo Nobori delegations to Japan, and as with the journeys to Fujian, individuals could die of disease or exhaustion along the way.[44] The graves of these unfortunate Ryukyu individuals who fell during this endeavor can be found today in Shizuoka Prefecture.

The Ryukyu delegations to Japan were a chance for the Shogunate to show off its influence and power. Such great influence that it even extended to the foreign people of Ryukyu, who wore different clothes, spoke an unusual language and had come across the sea to pay their respects.

The Shogunate made ample use of these opportunities, with the Ryukyu delegations being paraded around the Toshōgū Shrines in Ueno and Nikko, shrines dedicated to the Tokugawa. Serving a more utilitarian purpose was the establishment of a Ryukyu Hall in 1654 below Kagoshima Castle, a dedicated base for tribute within Satsuma domain.[clxii]

Ryukyu and Sakoku

As in China, this Ryukyu Hall was erected to manage trade and this became all the more precious when in 1633 the Shogunate began implementing the Sakoku, or closed country policy.

The Sakoku policy limited Japanese from going overseas and foreigners from venturing to Japan. In reality, Sakoku limited movement rather than completely closing Japan off from the outside world, as is sometimes depicted. There remained four trade routes in and out of Japan throughout the entirety of this period. In the north there was Hokkaido, and the Ainu who

---

44 Kazuyuki Tomiyama, Ryūkyū, Okinawa Shi No Sekai, (Yoshikawa Kōbunkan, 2003) 57.

traded with mainland Asia, Sakhalin and the Kuril Islands, and then traded these goods to the Matsumae Samurai. There was Tsushima in between Korea and Japan, and Nagasaki where Dutch merchants were given the island of Dejima, and Chinese merchants were permitted. Then of course there was was the Satsuma's trade and taxation with the Ryukyu Kingdom. There are numerous accounts of Japanese ships carrying goods back from all over the Ryukyu Archipelago, and one item which was particularly coveted was sugar, which will be addressed in more detail in a later chapter.

While the Ryukyu Kingdom was a de-facto puppet state of the Satsuma, the Shogunate wanted the Ryukyu Kingdom to maintain its customs and traditions and to give off at least the façade of independence. This was so that the kingdom's relationship with China would not be damaged, which would have in turn cut off Japan's access from Chinese goods.

But after the events of 1609, the Chinese court was wary of the Ryukyu Kingdom. In 1612 and 1613, King Shō Nei sent a tributary mission to the Ming and there were suspicions regarding the copious amounts of Japanese tributary items included. The Ming were also still wary after Hideyoshi's invasion of Korea just over a decade before. It was because of these suspicions that the Ming changed Ryukyus allowance for tribute from once every two years to once every ten. Cautiousness towards Japan was never plainly stated to Ryukyu, and the kingdom was told that because of the Satsuma conquest of Amami, the kingdom required time to recover, and that the ten-year tribute system was chosen so as not to place a burden on Ryukyu.

But these measures were only short term, with the perception of the threat from Japan fading shortly after this. With this, the kingdom was allowed to make tribute once every five years from 1622, and by 1633 King Shō Ho had succeeded in convincing the

THE RYUKYUS

Chinese to allow Ryukyu to make tribute once every two years again. The historian Akamine Mamoru has written about how there were two types of Ryukyu during this period, a 'Ryukyu in Japan' and a 'Ryukyu in China' the kingdom continued to hold a unique place in both countries, acting as a buffer state while being a fully integrated part of neither.[45]

Reassessment of Ryukyu's Place in East Asia

Within the Ryukyu Kingdom itself, two schools of thought, not necessarily in opposition to each other, grew under this new state of order. One sought to reaffirm the history of the Ryukyu Kingdom, and this can be seen particularly in Omoro's (traditional epics) after the Satsuma invasion which continued to extol the greatness of the kingdom. There was also an amassing of historical documents to write the official histories of the kingdom, and the central texts of *Chūzan Seikan*, *Chūzan Seifu* and *Kyūyō*, the documents that help us understanding how the Ryukyu Kingdom came into being in earlier chapters, were written during this period.[clxiii]

In the *Chūzan Seikan* the institutionalization of the theory that the Ryuyku and Japanese people descended from common ancestors began to be seen for the first time.[clxiv] Some of the first proponents of this were the Confucian scholar, Nanpo Bunshi (1555–1610) in Japan and Haneji in the Ryukyu Kingdom. This theory implicitly justified the new relationship between Ryukyu and Satsuma, Haneji himself had studied in Satsuma, and his positive view on the Japanese influenced his editing of *Chūzan Seikan*, which argued that the Ryukyu Kingdom had been a vassal state of Satsuma almost two centuries before the Satsuma invasion and that King Shunten (1166-1237) of Chūzan descended

---

45   *Ryūkyū ōkoku: Higashiajia No kōnāsutōn*, prologue.

PUPPET KINGDOM

from the samurai Minamoto no Tametomo (1139–1170), himself a relation of the Japanese imperial family.[clxv]

The legend surrounding Minamoto is that he was an unruly child from a very young age. When only aged four, he flipped an ox carriage with nobles aboard. His father Minamoto no Tameyoshi (1096–1156), concerned about the mischief his son would get up to in the imperial capital, sent him south to Kyushu at the age of thirteen. Here Minamoto no Tametomo soon made a name for himself, conquering parts of Kyushu with his military prowess, and by age sixteen had conquered the government in Kyushu, Daizaifu. From his feats, he earned the nickname 'Chinzei Hachirō', Chinzei meaning 'conquer of the west'. [clxvi]

In 1156 a dispute erupted in the imperial court between the reigning emperor Go-Shirakawa (1127–1192) and the retired emperor Sutoku (1119–1164). The older Sutoku called upon warriors led by mostly Minamoto Tameyoshi (or Genji clan), while warriors led by Taira Kiyomori (or Heikei clan) came to the side of Go-Shirakawa, although Minamoto no Yoshitomo (1123–1160) another son of Minamoto no Tameyoshi did fight alongside the Taira.

What the emperors did not take into account is that within these two families were the seeds of the samurai class who would take power away from the imperial court. The Heikei side (who fought for Go-Shirakawa) were victorious and Minamoto No Tametomo was exiled to Izu Ōshima, an island off the coast of present day Shizuoka Prefecture.

The legend diverges here. In one account, Tametomo continued to misbehave on the island and was forced to commit ritual suicide by slicing open his stomach. However there is also a legend that he fled, going further south until he reached Okinawa. Here he married the daughter of an Anji from Ōzato in the south of the island and their son became the ancestor of the first ruler of Ryukyu, Shunten (1166–1237).

As the reader has already seen from the archaeological record discussed in previous chapters, there was no unified king of Ryukyu in this period, and as we have also seen, the 'kingdoms' of the Three Kingdoms Period were more likely collections of warlords rather than a kingdom in the sense of the centralized Ryukyu Kingdom. There are also other claims within the tale which raise eyebrows, such as a four-year-old overturning an ox driven cart, or a sixteen-year-old conquering Kyushu. Just as the official histories portray Shō Hashi as toppling corrupt and decadent rulers during the Three Kingdoms Period, such a story tells us more about how contemporaries wanted to portray themselves and their place within history—which in turn justified their present day position of power.

While this narrative in *Chūzan Seikan* was pro-Satsuma in nature, it did not call for the annexation of the kingdom, nor complete takeover by the Japanese state, as proponents of the same theory in the Meiji era would a few centuries later, but merely tried to contextualize the kingdom's new position in a way that saw it ever closer to Japan.[clxvii]

At the same time, this was was an era in which the Ryukyu Kingdom sought to emphasize its connections with China. After the Satsuma invasion, the kingdom began to increasingly emphasis the importance of Confucianism for nobles and by the 18th Century, Confucian schools had been built in Naha, Shuri and Tomari.

These Confucian teachings were also propagated among the common people of Ryukyu, with regional bureaucrats required to read the native text 'Articles of Instruction' to the peasants in the Magiri that they oversaw.[clxviii]

In 1671 the construction of a Confucian temple in Naha began with its completion in January of 1676, the Shisei-byō.[clxix] The dialectics between these two trains of thought, a Pro-Chinese and Pro-Japanese, would not be resolved until the creation of Okinawa Prefecture at the end of the 19th century.

13

AMAMI'S SUGAR SLAVES

The Tale of Kantimi
Nestled at the end of a long serpentine bay is the sleepy village of Yakeuchi. In the mid-18th century a beautiful girl called Kantimi is born to a once-proud Noro mother.[clxx] During her prime the villagers had come for advice to this mystic, a bridge between the spiritual and mortal realms. But like many in Amami this Noro and her family have fallen on hard times after the island was severed from the Ryukyu Kingdom. With profound regret the parents decide that the only way they can survive is to sell the now thirteen-year-old Kantimi as a Yanchu, an indentured servant.

Kantimi's new master is a cruel man driven only by his own desires, and he soon takes a fancy to Kantimi. This only evokes the ire of the master's jealous wife who takes every opportunity to scold the young Kantimi.

Kantimi spends her days toiling in the beating sun, the master's household offer no empathy, she is a piece of property, a slave in an island that is overseen by strange-looking samurai who do not speak her language.

Kantimi's drudgerous existence stretches on through the years, until one fateful day a scribe from a neighboring village crosses over the mountains to pay her master a visit. Kantimi learns he is called Iwakana and the two fall in love. They seize an opportunity to sneak away in the dead night from their villages. They meet in the forests of the mountains in between their villages. He plays the Sanshin and she sings along by an isolated mountain cabin far from the gaze of the master.

But these happy times in her life are not to last, news of their escapades eventually reach the ears of the master, and in a fit of rage he beats Kantimi, the master's wife takes her own revenge, forcing Kantimi into a cage, heating tongs by the fire and then prodding her like a feral beast.

Iwakana is unaware of what has befallen his love, and that night he heads to their secret meeting place, Sanshin in hand. He finds Kantimi there waiting for them, and together they sing beneath the moon light. Iwakana notices that there is something different about Kantimi tonight, not only the paler color of her skin but her strange demeanor. Iwakana prepares to part as they always do, he going down one side of the mountain and her the other. But this time Kantimi simply tells him 'we will meet again' before vanishing into thin air.

Unable to comprehend what he has seen, a shaken Iwakana gingerly pushes open the cabin door, there is a figure hanging from the ridgepole, limp and lifeless. As his eyes adjust to the dark, he is aghast to see that the figure hanging is none other than his Kantimi. She could no longer bare the confined life of a Yanchu, unable to be with Iwakana. She was only in her twenties.

The next day a grief-stricken Kantimi informs the master of his Yanchu's fate, he expresses little remorse. But misfortune soon befalls him, the following day he develops a mysterious fever and dies an agonizing death. Bad luck continues to haunt his household, one of his descendants is bit by a poisonous viper and perishes writhing in pain, another is crushed while erecting a house, despite not a hint of wind in the air. These series of misfortunes continue until the master's entire bloodline is wiped out.

If you visit the village of Uken in Amami today, you may stumble upon a monument erected in the forests to Kantimi, a slap of rock engraved with her name. Incense may be burning at its base, maybe there are even some offerings of food. hundreds of years later, someone still remembers Kantimi.[clxxi]

The above story is an Amami legend, based at least in part on real events. It is perhaps the most famous story about a Yanchu, the servant class that became all the more prominent with the Satsuma acquisition of the islands of Northern Ryukyu from the Ryukyu Kingdom. The legend of Kantimi is even sung about in an Amami folk song, and despite its blending of reality and fantasy offers a glimpse into the hardships of this subservient class that was increasingly tied to the cash crop that was sugar.[clxxii]

Amami

The islands that constitute the Amami archipelago are the most southern in Kagoshima Prefecture today. The 56 islands that make up this portion of Northern Ryukyu are mostly small islands floating around the mass of land that is the 712.39 square kilometer island of Amami-Ōshima, as if they are satellites caught in the gravitation of this mass of land. Studded with verdant mountain forests that become all the more clustered in the south, the majority of the population today, well over two-thirds, is concentrated in the island's capital of Amami City on the north of the island facing Japan.

Amami Ōshima is shaped somewhat like a squid, the narrower north begins to widen as one traces the island south, with the islands just off the coast the tendrils of this cephalopod.

Amami is now a prominent resort location, renowned for its beaches of white sand, unique textiles and its sugar. The latter of these is such a brand that it can be bought throughout the country, where it makes its way into lattes, castella cakes and a whole range of traditional desserts. Yet there is a darker history behind this sugar that remains relatively unknown even in Japan today, one that traces its origins to the Satsuma conquest of the Ryukyu Kingdom's most northern territory.

Black Sugar
While the Ryukyu Kingdom had become a puppet state of the Satsuma, on a superficial level it was allowed to maintain the façade of an independent nation, the king remained the head of state in name, his advisers carried out reforms and tribute with China continued. The same cannot be said for Amami, the first region of Ryukyu that was attacked by the Satsuma in 1609, and the only part of the kingdom that was annexed for direct control by the samurai. Unlike in the Ryukyu Kingdom, where any reform the Shogunate or Satsuma ordered was filtered through the royal government, in Amami this control was direct and immediate. Under the Satsuma, life in Amami increasingly revolved around one precious crop, sugarcane. Sugarcane was first bought to Amami by Sunao Kawachi (1596-1615) and planted in his hometown the village of Yamato in 1605. Sunao had been going to Okinawa but a typhoon set him off course to Fujian where he discovered the crop after spending a year and a half secretly learning about it in China.

For the Ming, the cultivation of sugar was a closely guarded secret, one they were not even willing to tell a tributary state such as Ryukyu.[clxxiii] This brown cane sugar, known as *Kuruzātā* in Okinawan (black sugar) would come to dominate the lives of the people of Amami.

The efficiency of extracting sugar from the crop were further enhanced in 1623, when Zama Shinjō, who played a central role

THE RYUKYUS

in the proliferation of the sweet potato, studied sugar processing techniques in China, and introducing wringers to Amami-Ōshima and neighboring Kikaijima.

Sugar soon became a despised crop in Amami as it was this 'black' gold that was the foundations for the early-modern Yanchu system, a system of debt peonage, which became structuralized when the Satsuma passed a law in 1745 which set a level of sugar for each islander throughout Amami to produce, and this was to be paid as a tax. One could become a Yanchu quite easily. If one was unlucky enough to have one's sugar crop fail because of a typhoon or just bad luck, one had little choice but to sell oneself in order to meet these obligations. Yanchu were indentured servants who were forced to produce sugar for bigger farmers other than themselves to meet this sugar tax.

By the final few years of the Tokugawa Shogunate and beginning of the Meiji Reformation in the late nineteenth century between 30 to 35% of Amami's population were Yanchu.[46] While the Amami native and reporter Nagoshi Mamoru estimates that by the early Meiji period, there were between 10,000 to 20,000 Yanchu out of a population of 100,000 in Amami.[47]

The Satsuma instigated a number of reforms to make Amami a monoculture. The use of currency was banned and all essential goods were to be traded to the Satsuma via excess sugar that was not required for tax. The Satsuma would then take this sugar, and sell it for up to ten times more in the markets of Osaka. However, when the Satsuma first took over Amami there was no sign that such a system would develop.

---

[46] Takara, Kurayoshi, Kenichi Tanigawa, and Ringorō Ōyama. *Okinawa Amami to Yamato.* Doseisha, 1986. 187.
[47] Nagoshi Mamoru, *Amami No Saimu Dorei Yanchu*, Nanpō Shinsha, 2006. 84.

AMAMI'S SUGAR SLAVES

The Origins of the Yanchu

The Yanchu system itself had its origins in Amami long before this period, although the system developed and changed into something new throughout a period that Nagoshi has described as 'Black Sugar Hell'. There is a record from Dazaifu, the regional government in Kyushu from the 8th to 12th centuries, that during the Heian Period (794-1185) people from Amami attacked Satsuma, Chikuzen and Chikugo in Kyushu taking 300 captives back with them who went on to become Yanchu.[clxxiv] What sort of lives these captives went to live in Amami is unknown as with this abduction they disappear from the historical records.

When the Satsuma first took over Amami in 1609, it appeared as if the Yanchu system of old would be confined to the past. In 1623, the Satsuma ordered that the Yanchu system was to be partially ended.[clxxv] The motivation was not necessarily benevolent; the aim was to encourage self-supporting agriculture in Amami that could then be taxed by the Satsuma, and was coupled with the banning of going overseas.

During the early days of Satsuma rule, the crop of interest was not sugar but rice, and it was during this time that the number of Yanchu throughout Amami began to decline. But this was not to last. The extortionate price of sugar was soon realized, and in 1695 a surveyor was sent to Amami-Ōshima to examine the prospects of turning Amami into a sugar colony.

Following this, the amount of sugar produced in Amami began to rapidly increase and by 1713 the Satsuma Domain through Amami was producing 678 tons of sugar a year. Further enhancing Amami's colonial status was the introduction of the sugar tax system in 1745, which changed payments of rice to sugar. This overproduction of a cash crop in place of food had disastrous results, such as in 1755 when 3,000 islanders died from malnutrition due to crop failure in Tokunoshima.[clxxvi] With sugarcane replacing essential foods such as sweet potatoes, crises forced the Yanchu to forage and even resort to the starch from within palm trees. During such hard times, islanders would scavenge for weeds in the mountains and seaweed in the sea, but such food would not sustain them for long, and many inevitably died.

Under this new system boys from the young age of fifteen, to age of sixty, and girls from thirteen to fifty were given allocations of land for the purpose of growing sugar called *Takawari*.[clxxvii] Punishments were also in place for those who produced poor quality sugar or refused to obey orders, such as having one's neck or feet shackled.

The production of sugar became even more focused in 1777 when a system was introduced which made the buying and selling of sugar illegal throughout Amami-Ōshima, Kikaijima and Tokunoshima.[clxxviii] This monopolization of sugar and goods in Amami bought about the early-modern Yanchu system, the beginning of Black Sugar Hell.

In 1830 an even more extreme version of 1777 began in the three islands, with local people being ordered to not use sugar themselves, and to abstain from habits such as chewing sugar while working.[clxxix] This focus was accompanied with an increase in the number of Satsuma officials and the introduction of the death penalty for anyone who was caught partaking in the smuggling of sugar. Under the sugar tax system, power throughout Amami became increasingly concentrated in the hands of a few wealthy families. As if one could not produce the stipulated amount of sugar one would have no choice but to sell oneself as a Yanchu.

The interest on these debts made it hard for many Yanchu to ever succeed in paying them off, and while some did manage this there were even cases of a master refusing to release a Yanchu who was eligible to be a Freemen. Through this process of debt peonage, the wealthier farmers became increasingly wealthy while the Yanchu became saddled with ever more debt.

Living Conditions of the Yanchu
The life of a Yanchu was tough. One of the biggest challenges was finding enough food to survive. One means Yanchu used was to secretly grow potatoes on flat land hidden in the mountains. As a last resort, people were forced to turn to the sago palm (*Cycas revoluta*) which while having a starch that could stave off hunger, also contained lethal cyanide. If processed properly the starch from these *Nari*, as it was called in Amami, could be eaten without harm, producing a food known as *Togaki*. But if not processed correctly it would be a slow and agonizing death.

The only time a Yanchu would be treated to eating something as luxurious as rice was during the Obon festivities, where they might be given a small serving, although this was dependent on the generosity of their masters.

The Yanchu themselves were well aware of how their efforts would only benefit their masters. One folk song includes the lyrics "Who are we working so hard for? No one but the Yamato (Satsuma) officials." [48]

The master's ownership of the Yanchu extended to the bodies, particularly of women. If a child was born between a Yanchu and a free man or a Yanchu women and a freeman the child would automatically inherit the parents' Yanchu status, despite having accumulated no debts of its own. These children born between Yanchu or from a Yanchu mother were known as *Hida*.

The places the Yanchu lived depended on the number of Yanchu owned by their master. In small households where there

---

48 *Amami No Saimu Dorei Yanchu*. 92.

was only one Yanchu, they were usually permitted to live with the household. But in some of the richer farmers who possessed hundreds of Yanchu, special lodgings were constructed for this purpose. The richer masters who owned large numbers of Yanchu offset any attempts at developing a class conscious by delegating Yanchu leaders who were entrusted to watch over other Yanchu while they worked.

A Yanchu's status as little more than property was evident in the tags that were assigned to them.[clxxx] These tags were the property of the master and they included the master's name. Some of the most influential masters owned hundreds of Yanchu, and in one of the biggest households of Amami-Ōshima in the mid-19th century a collection of over three hundred of these tags were discovered.

Escape

Due to the dire conditions and a potentially lifelong sentence, it is no surprise that some tried to escape life as a Yanchu. Women had the chance to become the local wives of Satsuma officials, called *Ango*. These wives would be permitted to have silver hairpins and would be granted special privileges such as being given rice, a luxury. While some women chose to become *Ango* to escape their life of debt servitude others were forced, sometimes even if they were already married. Parents could also give away their daughters, hoping to better their own lot in life through it.

Other Yanchu made attempts at desertion, although there were few places for them to go with the Satsuma indirectly controlled Ryukyu to the south and Satsuma domain to the north. Yet, how could the common people of Amami have known that the kingdom had been defeated by the Satsuma, and that no haven was to be found there? Some may even have hoped that a benevolent king in Ryukyu might free them from Satsuma oppression if only he but knew.

There is a record of three young men from the village of Isen on Tokunoshima, where three individuals Eibuji, Kishimasa and Nōetsu left for Shuri. Since it was forbidden for anyone in Amami to freely cross over to Okinawa, the trio left in the dead of an August night in 1736. But due to strong winds and choppy waves they were forced to stop over at the island of Okinoerabu, about half way between Amami-Ōshima and Okinawa, where officials found them and promptly returned them to Tokunoshima. After this, it is likely that they were exiled to outlying islands as punishment.

The Intabu Crusade

Fukushige looks out from his sugar fields to the ocean, he has seen much hardship over his seventy years on this earth.[clxxxi] There were times when insufficient rainfall caused the hard ground to crack, sub-tropical storms that would lay waste to the fields, and then there was the ever-present burden of the onerous taxes imposed on the islanders of Tokunoshima by their Satsuma overlords.

Fukushige had always managed somehow or other to make it through these crises, though in his seventh decade he now wonders if his luck had finally run out. The previous June, a devastating typhoon struck Amami. Like the other islanders, Fukushige was forced to take shelter listening to the howling gale and blankets of heavy rain, wondering if the sugar fields would make it through.

While Tokunoshima is a small island compared to Amami-Ōshima, it is the second largest island in the Amami archipelago. Like its northern sibling, Tokunoshima is a rugged mountain island blanketed in laurel rainforest, difficult land to raise crops in. Because of the island's topography Fukushige's sugar fields

THE RYUKYUS

were by the ocean an area of flatter more even land.

After the typhoon had passed, Fukushige goes to check his fields only to find that they had been covered in bracken water churned up from the sea during the gales. The typhoon had salted the sugar crop.

The elderly Fukushige is able to salvage about half the crop, but is well below his quota. With the deadline for the sugar tax approaching, there are even rumors that Fukushige had been brazenly profiteering selling sugar privately on the side, a crime punishable by execution. It is his niece's husband, the 38 year-old Tamemori who volunteers to go to the Satsuma officials and explain these circumstances, Tamemori believes once the situation has been explained there will be no need to torment the septuagenarian.[clxxxii]

But when Tamemori talks to the officials they do not believe him. He is thrust to the floor a stone mortar is place on his legs and he is beaten senseless as they demand to know where he has hidden their sugar. All Tamemori can do was scream that he had done no such thing. They do not believe him.

The Satsuma samurai had long viewed the people of Amami as inferior beings. They were peasants, and peasants under their yoke. This too was common knowledge to the islanders but something about this incident lit a spark. In March of 1864, more than 150 islanders gathered makeshift weapons and surrounded the place where Tamemori is being tortured.

The outnumbered Satsuma officials take flight to call reinforcements, leaving Tamemori pinned to the floor in their wake. Tamemori has been saved but sensing the fury of the samurai, the rebels create a makeshift stronghold in the interior forest. After a week of this stalemate, the Satsuma are finally able to convince the islanders to stand down. No blood is shed, but seven of the ring leaders are exiled to outlying islands as punishment. Tamemori makes a recovery and goes on to to live until 1908.

While this incident at Intabu on Tokunoshima in the spring of 1864 was a peasant uprising from the view of the Satsuma samurai, to the islanders it had a very different meaning.[clxxxiii] They dubbed it the 'Intabu Crusuade', a righteous war against feudal tyrants, a challenge to centuries of their subservient as sugar slaves.[clxxxiv] The incident continues to be remembered in Tokunoshima today, and in 1964 to mark the events centennial a stone monument with the characters 犬田布騒動記念碑 carved into stone was erected to commemorate the rebellion.

While the incident led to a degree of relaxation of the sugar taxes throughout Amami, it would not be until the Meiji restoration in 1868 that Amami would be released from the control of the Satsuma, becoming part of the newly formed Kagoshima Prefecture, in many ways the spiritual successor to Satsuma domain — something we will examine in a later chapter.

Sugar continues to play a central role in the economy of Amami to this day, although the dark history of the Yanchu is left largely untold.

14

POLL TAX IN MIYAKO AND YAEYAMA

The Legend of Mappe

Kuroshima is a small island between Ishigaki and Iriomote. It is a flat island with sandy beaches surrounded by coral reefs. In the distance, the more rugged Ishigaki can be seen during clear weather, crowned by the peak of Mount Omoto.

But Ishigaki is far across the sea and has little meaning to the daily life of the Kuroshima islanders.

On Kuroshima there are two children, a young boy and girl, he is called Kanimui, she Mappe. In a central road running down the island the two play together from dawn to dusk. Sometimes they even get into fights, but they always make up. The people of Kuroshima saw the young couple and knew that they would marry when they came of age.

Years later when Mappe and Kanimui are teenagers a group of Ryukyu officials comes to Kuroshima. They are wearing affluent black kimonos compared to the browns and greens of the islanders, they are also equipped with swords.

One of the officials, a man with a mustache, orders the islanders to gather, for there is a proclamation to be heard. Once all of the villagers have assembled he begins reading "under the orders of his majesty, the people are required to produce more rice and sugar, yet this land is not fruitful. It is necessary to open new lands for the production of rice and sugarcane."

There is a pause as the official looks at the expressionless faces of the islanders and then with a slight smirk he continues "In line with this, some of you will move to Ishigaki. See that central road running down the village, those of you on this side will be leaving for Ishigaki tomorrow morning." The surrounding officials cackle, losing control of their faces.

The silence that has descended on the villagers is broken when someone exclaims "We will not be moved!"

The mustached official hands move to the hilt of his blade. "Shut up! Silence with you! If I hear any more complaints from anyone, I will sever them in two."

Silence once again returns to the villagers who only stare at the officials. Suddenly, Kanimui steps out from the crowd, "I beseech you, I am to wed Mappe, please don't take her away."

The moustached official's hand does not move from the hilt of his sword, and he pays no heed to Kanimui's pleas.

That night as the villagers on one half of the village make their preparations, Mappe takes Kanmui's hand and says, "I'll still be here for you, look for the moon over Nosoko on a clear night, that will be me watching over you."[49]

At the break of dawn, Mappe and the other islanders are taken across the sea to begin building the village of Nosoko. In the dense jungle from dawn until dusk they move rocks, cut through the undergrowth and cultivate arable land.

Hemmed in between the ocean and the slopes of Mount Nosoko, after much toil, the villagers manage to successfully raise crops.

But the situation soon takes a turn for the worse, in the heat of summer some of the villagers begin to fall ill, they have been bitten by mosquitoes that are thriving in the stagnant water that

---

49 沖縄県立総合教育センター "野底マーペー."

has collected in Ishigaki's uneven terrain. Such a disease was never a problem in Kuroshima, and as many become bed-bound the villagers arrange for a festival in the hope that it will drive the affliction away and reinvigorate Nosoko.

But the infection continues and production declines. Mappe is also smitten and as she lies on a futon, sweating profusely, shivering, all she thinks about is Kanimui across the waves in Kuroshima.

Longing to see Kanimui on the day of the festival, Mappe leaves the village alone and climbs up the mountain.

She ascends until she arrives at the highest point on the island, Omoto Peak. On this moonless bitter night, she looks across the ocean longing to see Kuroshima but she cannot see it. Desperate to see her beloved Kanimui in the depths of despair she turns to stone, forever facing towards Kuroshima. Ever since the people of Ishigaki have called Mount Omoto, Nosoko Mappe.[clxxxv]

If you climb the mountain today, you may encounter a weathered sign detailing the story of Mappe.[clxxxvi] Ascending to the peak, there is a panorama of Yaeyama's islands and maybe if the conditions are right you will even see Kuroshima in the distance. Maybe you will even see the close-at-hand rock formation that is said to be Mappe herself.

While it is impossible to know if a girl named Mappe and a boy named Kanimui ever existed, the story itself is based in the suffering of the people of Yaeyama during the ear of poll tax.

Mappe's story takes place in the 1730s, an era in which the court at Shuri ordered numerous islanders from Hateruma, Kohama, Iriomote and Ishigaki to move and create more profitable villages for the Kingdom. This forced movement resulted in the deaths of islanders, many dying a slow death of malaria and ultimately many of these villages were abandoned.[clxxxvii]

POLL TAX IN MIYAKO AND YAEYAMA

Poll Tax in Sakishima

With the Satsuma dominance of Ryukyu, the Kingdom lost the foundations for much of its prosperity, the trade through China's tributary state network. In Northern Ryukyu an era of suffering was bought about under the direct rule of the Satsuma, while in the far south of the archipelago, the people would also experience an era of hardship under the Ryukyu Kingdom.

The Ryukyu Court envisioned a poll tax on Sakishima, the islands of Miyako and Yaeyama as a solution to fill this void and this system lasted for 266 years, from 1637 to 1903, a couple of decades beyond the life of the Ryukyu Kingdom itself.

The payments for the poll tax consisted of grains such as rice and millet alongside cloth, with men making the most payments of the former and women of the latter. In Miyako and Yaeyama this tax was levied on all men and women from the ages 15 to 50. Within these age groups, there was a further division of four ranks of payment, with the young and old have a smaller share of the burden.

From Ōgawa Village in Ishigaki as an example, men between the ages of 15 and 20 had to produce 21 liters of rice, for those aged 21 to 40, 53 liters, for those 41 to 45, 42.4 liters, and for those 46 to 50, 31.8 liters.[50] Men also had to produce a designated amount of cloth based on their age, but this was not as extravagant or as of high quality as was ordered for the women of Sakishima.

The Kuramoto, the royal government stations in Yaeyama and Miyako, came to play a central role as over watchers of the poll tax system, with the Hirata Kuramoto in Miyako overseeing as far as the island of Tamara, a small island far west of Miyako, while the Ishigaki Kuramoto in Yaeyama as far as Yonaguni.

The highest figures in these Kuramoto were Samurē from

---

50 Umi No Curosurōdo Yaima (Okinawa Prefectural Museum & Art Museum, 2010), 37.

Naha who would be stationed there for a period of three years. These bureaucrats from Okinawa were not enough on their own to man the Kuramoto, and local officials were also employed. With this, these local bureaucrats were recognized as nobles by Shuri, and were allowed to establish their own lineages. The officials working at the Kuramoto were often corrupt, but they were the highest authority in the land, and who was to stand against them?

The poll tax had unexpected results and the heavy tax burdens even prompted some to purge any who could not work from society, the youngest and oldest. One horrific example of this is a crevice in Kubaru on Yonaguni in which pregnant women were thrown down in order to force an abortion.

Kubaru Bari (Bari means chasm) is about 20 meters in length with a width of three to five meters in places, Kubaru Bari is above the cliffs of Yonaguni's west side, and the chasms drop is seven to eight meters. One can only imagine what these women felt as they stood above this crevice with the waves crashing against the cliffs a few meters away from them as they were forced to risk not just their own lives, but that of their unborn child. Today Kubaru Bari is marked by a sign providing information and a tiny Buddhist statue full of coins, green with patina from the salt sea breeze.

Forced Migration
At times these officials would extort the islanders on top of the already heavy burden of the poll tax. In the 1700s the royal government's policy shifted once again, and in a bid to increase productivity a plan was created to forcibly moved islanders in Yaeyama from the smaller outlying islands, to the larger islands of Ishigaki and Iriomote were they could create new villages.

Both Iriomote and Ishigaki were heavily forested, and had

sources of fresh water which were resources that had the potential to be exploited. However, the reason the islanders in Yaeyama mainly lived on smaller islands such as Kohama, Kuroshima and Taketomi was that these islands were free from malaria. Since these smaller coral islands lacked sources of fresh water, the denizens of these small islands would go across to Iriomote and Ishigaki to collect water, while the small settlements that already existed on these islands were on the coast, far from the mountains and forest where stagnant water would collect.

This forced migration under the Ryuyku Kingdom, brought many of these islanders little more than pain and suffering. Ōhama Nobumoto (1891-1976) jurist and former principal of Waseda University, himself an Ishigaki native, remarked that "the only freedom those who were made to build the new villages had was the freedom to die."[51]

When the poll tax system was first introduced the amount of payment that was required reflected the actual population of the villages throughout Sakishima, but seeking further revenue the royal government made the decision to levy a fixed poll tax regardless of the actual population of Yaeyama.

The result of this was that making the poll tax payments became an increasing burden on the people of Sakishima. In the past a decreasing population led to a decrease in the poll tax burden, thus reliving the common people to some degree.

The historian Tomiyama Kazuyuki has divided the almost three century long period of poll tax into three eras. The first lasted from the introduction of poll tax until the mid-18th Century. Over this period the population of Sakishima gradually increased to about 20,000 in Yaeyama and 35,000 in Miyako by 1770. It was under this era of population increase that additional

---

51 Ōhama Shinken, *Yaeyama No Nintōzei* (Sanichi Shobō, 1971), 9.

THE RYUKYUS

Samurē from Okinawa were sent to enforce the poll tax system, as well as supervise the forced moving of islanders to build new villages.

During Tomiyama's second era, Yaeyama entered a particularly dark phase of its history, when in 1771 the Meiwa Tsunami destroyed around half of the villages on Ishigaki, and killed over 9,000 people in Yaeyama and over a thousand in Miyako. In this tsunami alone one third of Yaeyama's population was killed with others dying after from the epidemic and famine that followed. The extent of the Meiwa Tsunami was so severe that the population of Yaeyama did not rise above 10,000 again until the late 19th Century.[clxxxviii]

Ōhama has called the period after the Meiwa Tsunami the 'Era of Suffering', partly caused by a policy of forced movement. Tomiyama's third era, which will be the focus of a later chapter, followed the birth of Okinawa Prefecture, in which despite the poll tax system continued up until 1903 when a movement centering in Miyako successfully petitioned the Japanese government to abolish it.[52]

Women and Cloth Production

Throughout the poll tax era, the labor of women was indispensable, although as with sugar in Amami, it was the product itself which value was attached to rather than the laborers who were forced to toil in order to produce it.

Under the Satsuma, the Ryukyu Kingdom was ordered to send cloth as a form of taxation, and it was luxurious cloth that was one of the items taken by Ryukyu delegations to the Shogun's capital of Edo. The dyeing techniques and styles differed in Yaeyama and Miyako, with Miyako becoming particularly famous for

---

52 Ryūkyū, Okinawa Shi No Sekai, 217.

POLL TAX IN MIYAKO AND YAEYAMA

its product of dark blue ramie fabrics. Many of the dyeing techniques throughout the Ryukyu Archipelago hark back to the Golden Age of Trade, and one only has to look at Okinawan Bingata, vibrant colors and depictions of flowers and wildlife to see how this differed from styles employed in mainland Japan.

The textiles produced by these women came under heavy scrutiny. Yaeyama villages were divided up with a few female leaders, called *Bunaji* who were responsible for supervising the village women that worked beneath them.[clxxxix] Cloth would then be taken to the Kuramoto by the *Bunaji* where it was inspected to make sure that its length, width texture and even pattern were precise. If this cloth passed satisfactory levels it would be stamped and placed in trunks wrapped in leather for water resistance, and shipped to Shuri, and then on to Kagoshima in Satsuma Domain.

The intensity of this production at the village level was high. There are records of women being shut into rooms and forced to weave throughout the night while their baby cried for milk in the neighboring room.

Raw materials for cloth, particularly Ramie and dyer's knotweed also came under the eyes of officials with orders from Shuri to plant these at every household in Yaeyama, to which Kuramoto officials would inspect. The production of cloth also led to changes in the dynamics of village life, since once the cloth had been stitched it was necessary to bleach or wash it, and this required water. There are numerous Yaeyaman folk songs about the process. For women who resided in villages that were far away from beaches or wells, it was easier to carry out the work close to the Kuramoto and continue working until the day of inspection, taking the women away from their homes and women could be away from their homes for extended periods of time.

THE RYUKYUS

Abandoned Villages and Dreams of Escape

The other feature of the poll tax system that drastically changed islanders' lives in Yaeyama was the forced building of new villages. The policy was proposed by Sai On, and began under the reign of King Shō Kei (reign 1713-1751). Unlike Sai On's many successful policies in Okinawa, his policy of relocation was a failure. Villagers were forcibly torn from their homes, sent to untamed land leaving a bloody trail of bodies in their wake.

The building of a new settlement was hard physical labor that was coerced, in uncultivated land that was near impossible to cultivate with the technology of the age. Examples of forced movement include; in 1713 when 300 Hateruma islanders were moved to Ishigaki to create the village of Shiraho, in 1732 when 400 Kuroshima islanders were moved to Ishigaki to create the village of Nosoko (the backdrop of the Mappe legend), in 1734 when 400 Hateruma islanders were moved to Iriomote to create the village of Haimi, and another 288 in 1755 to create the village of Sakiyama.[cxc] The islanders of the time also had little knowledge of sanitation practices, nor the causes of the malaria that led to one's friends and family dying before one's eyes. There are over eighty abandoned villages throughout Yaeyama from this period.[53]

Two of these cases of forced movements have had a particular legacy on the identity of Yaeyama that continues to this day. The first is Mappe's story and the other is the 1755 movement of Hateruma islanders to Iriomote to found the village of Sakiyama which is commemorated in the popular folk song *Sakiyama-Bushi*, which continues to be sung and recorded to this day.[cxci]

While the legend of Mappe is perhaps the most famous story from the era of poll tax, there are also plenty of other such stories

---

53   Ōhama Shinken. Yaeyama No Nintōzei (Sanichi Shobō, 1971), 9.

POLL TAX IN MIYAKO AND YAEYAMA

from across Yaeyama's islands. Under the poll tax system it was illegal for islanders to move freely; this kept them working and under the supervision of the Ryukyu officials. Nevertheless, many did dream of escaping to a better life.

In both Hateruma, Japan's most southern inhabited island, and Yonaguni, the most western inhabited island, there are legends of islanders escaping overseas to a southern paradise where they would no longer have to toil.

In Hateruma there is the story of Pai-Patirōma (Southern Hateruma), where islanders steal an official's ship in the dead of night and sail to a paradise south of Hateruma, and an almost identical story exists in Yonaguni of an arcadian Hai-Dunan (Southern Yonaguni).[cxcii]

The legacy of poll tax on Yaeyama and Miyako has been profound and is an important reminder of how even within the archipelago there are different histories and experiences as well as culture. The abolition of poll tax would not come until the Meiji era and this abolition was only after two centuries of suffering, as with Amami which is the focus of a later chapter.

Like Amami, Miyako and Yaeyama are today both renowned for their holiday resorts. Families across Japan head south to bathe in the sun on their sandy beaches. While the focus of the Satsuma era of Ryukyu tends to be on Okinawa itself, there is also a largely neglected history of pain at both ends of the Ryukyu Archipelago.

15

FOREIGNERS IN RYUKYU

The Execution of Ishigaki Eishō

The increasing number of foreigners arriving in the Ryukyu Archipelago was of great concern for the Shogunate, and following orders of the Tokugawa, it was up to the Satsuma to police Japan's southern backdoor. As early as 1636, the Satsuma had introduced regular checks between every six to nine years to check that no families had converted to Christianity.[cxciii] If such a discovery of hidden Christians were made, the Shogunate could be sure that a wily priest had managed to hide himself somewhere throughout the islands.

One of the most serious events to shake the Shogunate occurred in 1624, when a Spanish ship ran aground at Ishigaki. In the *Yaeyama Nenraiki*, a collection of documents from the 15th to 18th centuries, it is recorded that the official in charge of Miyara Magiri, Ishigaki Eishō furnished the Spaniards with cattle and even invited them to his home.[cxciv] On board was the missionary of the Dominican Order Juan de los Angeles Rueda, who succeeded in converting Ishigaki to Christianity, or if he had not, conversion was at least suspected by the Ryukyu Kingdom. Ishigaki was subsequently exiled to Tonakijima, a small island in between Kumejima, the Kerama Islands and Agunijima off the west coast of Okinawa.

Ishigaki's punishment did not end with exile. While Ishigaki was in Tonakijima, the Satsuma gave orders for his execution, burning him at the stake in 1634. Juan de los Angeles was none the luckier, exiled to Agunijima and subsequently killed there. Iriomote was also a particular flashpoint for the Satsuma. In 1640 a foreign ship kidnapped a woman from the island, and the following year Satsuma samurai were dispatched to the island to prevent further unwanted foreign incursions.

The Sakishima Beacons
Instability also came from China, when in 1644 the Ming dynasty fell to the Manchu Qing dynasty, which created concern about potential instability in the region. In response to these events, the Satsuma briefly moved their base in Yaeyama from Ishigaki to Iriomote.

The Satsuma army in Yaeyama was recalled in 1648 but the cultural legacy of this period continues to be seen in Yaeyama today, such as in the Shichi Festival in Iriomote.[cxcv] While the Satsuma army had moved out of Yaeyama, a new system to oversea these southern islands was built, the Sakishima Beacons.

These beacons were a series of stone platforms across Sakishima where officials could watch the seas for the approach of foreign ships. If such a ship was spotted the message would be relayed to Shuri, and then the Satsuma through a series of flares, horses and fast ships.

In Yaeyama all the beacons sent a series of relays to the Kuramoto in southern Ishigaki, and from here a ship was dispatched to Shuri. By the early 19th Century, foreign ships were appearing all the more throughout the Ryukyu Archipelago, even as far as Northern Ryukyu.

One such incident occurred in June of 1824 when a British whaling ship appeared off the Tokara Islands. Subsequently making landfall at Takarajima, north of Amami, with seven to eight British sailors alighting. Not knowing the language, at Takarajima they resorted to pointing and gestures, but failing to be understood by the officials on the island gave up and returned to their ship.

The following day they appeared again, and this time the officials give them vegetables and rice which they refused to take, for their real motivation was for the island's cattle, which they made no inroads in acquiring. Four hours later, the British sailors opened fire on some of the island's cows. The Satsuma official, Kichimura Kyūsuke returned fire killing one sailor, and causing the rest to flee to their ship and depart the island.[cxcvi] The incident at Takarajima, was one of the factors that prompted the Shogunate to issue an order to open fire at all foreign ships in February of 1825.[cxcvii]

Foreign ships

From the Western perspective, some of the earliest detailed accounts of foreigners' interactions with Ryukyu come from British captains. Basil Hall (1788–1844) first visited Okinawa as captain of the *Lyra*, alongside the ship the *Alceste* in 1826. Hall wrote how he expected ships had little motivation to visit Ryukyu, and he recorded that the locals had little interest in foreign goods and that nothing of much value was produced on the island.

Hall was mistaken about the interests of the island to foreign powers, and by the 19th Century even his own country Britain was considering a Ryukyu colony in the East China Sea. Locals' lack of interest in foreign goods, on the other hand, was a product of Japan's Sakoku policy, with the kingdom ordering common people to stay away from foreigners. While Hall was in Ryukyu, he was treated well, but always kept at a distance, not fully understanding the reasons behind the Kingdom's reluctance to interact too closely with foreigners.

In 1827 another British ship, *HMS Blossom* under Captain F.W. Beechey arrived in Ryukyu where it anchored in Naha for 20 days. Others followed, and in 1832, a British East India Company ship and an American ship, *The Morrison*, in 1837.[cxcviii] One sailor aboard *HMS Blossom*, once again ventured to the Ryukyu Archipelago, Edward Belcher (1799-1877) this time as the Captain of the *HMS Samarang* in the 1840s where he conducted the first survey of Sakishima.

Belcher became the captain of the *HMS Samarang* after a long career in the Napoleonic Wars (1803-1815) and the first Opium War (1839-1842) and he had conducted surveys of the northern coast of Africa and South America, being knighted in 1843. The *HMS Samarang* left for its survey of Asia in 1843. In Southeast Asia, the Samarang conducted a survey of northern Borneo before arriving in Hong Kong, a newly acquired British colony, on September 14, 1843.

Belcher had originally been instructed to survey the coast of China, but the foreign office decided it would be wiser to avoid causing any tensions and redirected him to Taiwan and the uncharted islands past which British ships regularly passed through. Belcher recorded his experience of Yaeyama and Miyako in, *Narrative of the Voyage of H.M.S. Samarang, During the Years 1843–46*, published in 1848. Belcher like all Western writers of the period made mistakes when recording the names of the islands and places within them, this was often caused by a mispronunciation of Chinese, Japanese or Okinawan words.[cxcix]

The *Samarang* first arrived on the south-west coast of Ishigaki on November 30, 1843, Belcher recorded that four officials gave the crew of the *Samarang* permission to survey the island provided this survey was kept to the coast and that his crew were strictly forbidden from entering any village. Belcher believed that the islands were essentially independent of each other writing:

> "The people of these Islands are not only independent of each other, but either pretend to be, in great measure, ignorant of the other's affairs; and it was not without some pressing that I persuaded the chief of [Yaeyama] to communicate to the authorities of [Miyako] the nature of my visit, and our peaceable observance of their habits and custom."[54]

As the reader will know, this was not the case, but over his 21-day expedition Belcher and his crew succeeded in providing the first Western descriptions of Sakishima as well as maps of Ishigaki, Yonaguni, and Miyako. It was not just Belcher who was recording his surroundings, the Satsuma stationed in Yaeyama noted that a ship with white flags anchored at Miyara and that from it alighted nine British and one Chinese individual. Having set their feet on land, the party used telescopes to observe their surroundings and three of them stayed in a tent on the island. Belcher's description was an introduction to those in Europe and the Americas of the island's subtropical climate:

> "The variety and beauty of the vegetation clothing the sides of mountains of [Ishigaki], and its neighbor [Iriomote] is very striking. The light glaueous foliage of a species of *Spondias*, mingled with the leaves of the [screw palm] Pandanus and broad fronds of Palmyra Palm, varied with masses of dark green Cyeas, and here and there the feathery sprays of elegant Acaeias, with large-flowered [Hibiscus] , [Morning Glory]

---

54 Edward Belcher, *Narrative of the Voyage of H.M.S. Samarang during the Years 1843-46* (Reeve, Benham and Reeve, 1848), 77.

FOREIGNERS IN RYUKYU

climbing plants and Creepers interspersed with broad patches of ...Pines, rising from the beds of tall grass and gigantic reeds, formed together a scene of singular botanical interest."[55]

Belcher also provided one of the first descriptions of houses in Sakishima:

"Throughout the Islands, the construction of their villages appeared to be nearly similar, the houses being arranged with squares on parallelograms, intersected by narrow lanes or streets, bounded by stone walls. Each house appears to stand separate with a neat and picturesque garden of shrubs and shady trees; they are constructed of massive wooden framework, and slightly raised above the earth, having a very sharp-pitched thatched roof. The sides, as well as internal divisions, are of moveable sliding panels, which can be opened at pleasure; and the floors are covered with neat mats, of prescribed dimensions, formed of rice straw, generally of three inches in depth, each mat being intended to serve as a bed."[56]

Of particular interest to Belcher, and later arrivals such as Commodore Matthew Perry, were the burial practices of the archipelago, which were far removed from the graves of Europe:

"They sometimes bury their dead in caverns hewn out of the sides of the rocks, in natural caves or holes near the sea, the apertures being carefully closed, in wooden coffins; and, not unfrequently in simple cerements only. The better classes erect

---

[55] *Narrative of the Voyage of H.M.S. Samarang during the Years 1843-46*, 95.
[56] *Narrative of the Voyage of H.M.S. Samarang during the Years 1843-46*, 80-81.

THE RYUKYUS

stone tombs, surmounted by piles of loose stones, and, in one instance...we noticed a very extensive plastered mausoleum."[57]

Belcher, like Perry after him, was correct in his suspicions that the languages spoken throughout the archipelago were related to that of Japan. But Belcher was mistaken in his assumption that Yaeyama and Miyako were penal colonies. Having completed his survey of Ishigaki, on January 18, 1844 Belcher left for Miyako. The Satsuma preferred that no Western ships anchor in the Ryukyu archipelago at all, but if they could not be stopped the individuals who embarked from them came under heavy scrutiny, as did Belcher and his crew on Miyako:

> "There was an old man, a native of [Ishigaki]...with a quick and piercing restless grey eye, a venerable beard depending to his breast, and mustachios to match, a man evidently of high authority...who was especially jealous of our movements; if we strayed from the party it was he who spurred on his little wiry horse in pursuit. He very soon earned for himself the appropriate soubriquet of 'The Spy'; and yet the old fellow was fond of a joke, and would sing as he journeyed on his way, and excite you to race across the sands. I have seen the old man, however, frequently assume a stern look and fierce demeanor, when the lower orders showed themselves refractory or insolent; then his ire would get the better of his dignity, and, seizing a stick, he would belabour them unmercifully."[58]

Belcher left Miyako on February 4, 1844 and from there attempted to dock in Yonaguni but was prevented due to choppy

---

57 *Narrative of the Voyage of H.M.S. Samarang during the Years 1843-46*, 82.
58 *Narrative of the Voyage of H.M.S. Samarang during the Years 1843-46*, 88.

waves and heavy rain. By May 7, 1844 Belcher entered Saint Domingo Harbor at the island of Batanes in the Philippines, and later returned to Yonaguni before going on to Naha and finally Nagasaki.

The Robert Bowne Incident

Not all Westerners who visited these islands respected local officials and made records of what they had witnessed. More violent incidents, akin to the British sailors in Takarajima were also prevalent.

One of the most infamous of these was the Robert Bowne Incident of 1852. The *Robert Bowne* was an American ship that partook in the coolie trade. The abolishment of slavery in the mid-19th Century prompted those who wanted cheap and exploitable labor to shift to contracted labors from India and China.

Many of these contracts were spurious and coolies were often told they were bound for one destination only to be taken as far as the opposite hemisphere. British colonies, such as the British West Indies were particularly desperate for labor, as their economies depended on plantation labor.

The British through their orientalist world view, saw the Chinese as industrious and well-suited to the Caribbean climate and free of the restraints of a caste system such as that in India, although this did not stop the British from transporting India coolies around the world either. Chinese coolies also had the advantages of their connections with overseas Chinese communities which made it easier to access markets for coffee, indigo, rice, sesame and cotton.

These coolies were also sent beyond British colonies in the Barracoons, the name given to the coolie camps by Europeans, they would be branded with letters on their chests, 'C' for

California and 'P' for Peru. Under Chinese law, citizens of the country were not freely able to leave, but this was also a time in China in which the population was rapidly growing, and those who believed they could have a better life for themselves overseas paid for this passage, others who were in a weaker situation had to rely on treacherous middle men.

In Xiamen, one of the centers of the Coolie trade, these Chinese were gathered in such Barracoons. The *Robert Bowne* was one of many coolie ships which left Xiamen in 1852 bound for California.

But the journey soon ran into trouble. Off the coast of Taiwan on March 30, fears over the spread of disease among the coolies led to the captain, Lesley Bryson, ordering some of the Chinese to be thrown into the ocean. The 400 or so coolies on the ship revolted, killed seven members of the crew, including the captain and his first mate. The coolies ordered the 11 remaining members of the crew to redirect the ship to Taiwan. But having lost the ability to navigate, the crew directed the ship to two islands unknown to them, until about three to four days later they hit a reef in the process and the ship ran aground at Ishigaki on April 4, off the island's southwestern coast.

The place the ship stopped happened to be in front of a Kuramoto, and the majority of Chinese alighted here and a temporary place to stay was erected for them.

The *Robert Bowne* then returned to Xiamen, sending an urgent report to the American vice-consul calling for the coolie's recapture. This urgent request was relayed to the British vice-consul in Xiamen also, and together they dispatched three ships, two British and one American.

It was the American ship, the *Saratoga* that found the coolies, shooting many to death before capturing the rest, and the British did likewise. In contrast to the behavior of the Americans and

British, the people of Ishigaki secretly gave the Chinese food as they did in the forest and mountains and even made graves of piled stones when coolies died. Other coolies died from starvation or committed suicide. Today the 128 Chinese who died are enshrined in a monument at the place they alighted at Ishigaki.[cc] About a year after the revenge of the British and Americans, the royal government at Shuri sent two ships to Fujian to carry those who had not been captured or killed back, although this unfortunately was attacked by pirates with only 125 surviving.

Commodore Matthew Perry
The Westerner who made the most inroads with Ryukyu, often by force was Commodore Matthew Perry of the US Navy. Perry made numerous stops in the Ryukyu Kingdom on his way to and from Japan—where he succeeded in forcing the Shogunate to open select ports to US ships. Perry first arrived in Naha aboard the *USS Susquehanna*, accompanied by the *Mississippi*, the *Supply* and the *Saratoga* on May 17, 1853. Perry and his crew's account of the Ryukyu Kingdom is recorded in *Narrative of the Expedition of an American Squadron to the China Seas and Japan* (1856).[cci] Bayard Taylor (1825-1878), who joined the *Susquehanna* while Perry's fleet had stopped in China, offered the first description of Okinawa, as the ship approached the islands shores:

> "The shores of the island were green and beautiful from the water, diversified with groves and fields of the freshest verdure. The rain had brightened the colors of the landscape, which recalled to my mind the richest English scenery. The swelling hills, which rose immediately from the water's edge, increased in height towards the center of the island, and were

picturesquely broken up by abrupt rocks and crags, which, rising here and there, gave evidence of volcanic action... the hills were dotted in various places with white specks, which I at first took to be dwellings, but which were tombs of limestone rock."[59]

One of the most notable features of the Ryukyu Archipelago's landscape was the tombs, and Taylor remarked that, "Upon the first approach of the squadron, their size, color, and position on the hill-sides caused them, at a distance, to be mistaken for dwellings."

One of the first individuals the Perry expedition met after anchoring was the British missionary Bernard Jean Bettelheim (1811–1870) whose lodgings were completed with a hoisted Union Jack flying out front. Bettelheim was a Jew from Hungary and had converted to Protestantism while in England. At the time of Perry's arrival, Bettelheim had been in Ryukyu for about five years.

Bettelheim had ignored the ban on missionaries and succeeded in pushing himself onto the kingdom, which reluctantly provided him with lodgings.[ccii] By the time Bettelheim arrived in the Ryukyu Kingdom, the Shogunate was struggling to prevent the increasing frequency of 'black ships' that were appearing off not only the coast of the Ryukyu Archipelago but mainland Japan itself.

Much of the Perry expedition's thoughts on the Ryukyu Archipelago can be gleamed from an exploration party led by the Chaplain, Mr. Jones and again narrated by Bayard Taylor. While the expedition traversed through Ryukyu, accompanied

---

[59] Matthew Calbraith Perry and Francis L. Hawks, *Narrative of the Expedition of an American Squadron to the China Seas and Japan: Performed in the Years 1852, 1853, and 1854, under the Command of Commodore M.C. Perry, United States Navy, by Order of the Government of the United States* (Beverly Tucker, 1856), 152.

FOREIGNERS IN RYUKYU

by royal officials, they found that while local people bowed as they passed, women and children ran away,

"We strolled into a temple, from the walls of which several persons, probably females, had been watching us. They disappeared with great rapidity as we entered the door."[60] Prior to Berry, Basil Hall had also noted that he was never permitted to see the women of Ryukyu up close. The Ryukyu Kingdom explicitly ordered women to stay as far away from any European as possible, although it was impossible to hide them completely. The French missionary Le Turdu, who was in Ryukyu between 1846 and 1848 wrote that:

> "Their most beautiful decoration is the tattoos on their hand. From the viewpoint of a foreigner they may be ugly, but within this country they are valued very highly, because of this this custom is even necessary for the noble women and even the Queen herself."[61]

Although by Perry's fourth visit to Ryukyu, it was noted that women working in the markets, who had previously run away, would instead approach them to sell their wares.

The Americans themselves were an object of fascination for the Okinawans. During the exploratory expedition, the party discovers a jagged rock jutting out of a pine forest up to eight feet in height. Due to its notable height, the tallest thing they had discovered in Okinawa, they christened it 'Banner Rock' and unfurl an American flag on top of it while the local people looked on in wonder, probably musing at what exactly the Americans were doing.

From Banner Rock the party stumbled across Naka Gusuku,

---

60 *Narrative of the Expedition of an American Squadron to the China Seas and Japan*, 158.
61 *Okinawa Ken Shi Kakuhen Ron 8 Joseishi*, 28-29.

the very same that was given to Gosamaru in 1430. The description of the now over four centuries old Gusuku is as follows:

> "We were surprised by the discovery of an ancient fortress, occupying a commanding position upon the summit of one of the spurs of the central ridge. Its outline was irregular...while some parts of it were in perfect preservation, other portions were overgrown with vines and shrubbery, and hardly to be distinguished from the natural rock upon which it was based... the material was limestone, and the masonry of admirable construction. The stones, some of which were cubes of four feet square, were so carefully hewn and jointed that the absence of any mortar or cement did not seem to impair the durability of the work."[62]

As per long held orders from the Satsuma, the kingdom's officials attempted to prevent Perry from forcing his way as far as the royal capital of Shuri. At first, officials beseeched Perry to visit Naha instead. In the hopes of convincing him, a banquet was prepared, which Perry and his crew deliberately snubbed. Realizing this, the official brought the banquet aboard the ships, although "the Commodore...from considerations of policy, thought it best to be invisible."

Still reluctant to give Perry any reason to visit Shuri, he was then told that the Queen Dowager had been sick with shock, after a British naval officer insisted on entering Shuri with a letter from Lord Palmerston the previous year, and that if the Americans made any such attempt, it could potentially kill her. The Americans saw this as little more than an attempt to halt them.

---

62   *Narrative of the Expedition of an American Squadron to the China Seas and Japan*, 169.

FOREIGNERS IN RYUKYU

"The Commodore, who did not believe one word of the queen dowager's illness, and who was quite convinced also that this maneuvering and trickery was designed merely to satisfy the spies kept about the [Ryukyus] by the Japanese government."[63]

Perry himself was belligerent, saying that if a British official had been allowed to go anywhere, he too must be granted the same privilege. The Ryukyu officials had little choice to but accede to the Americans, and the ships were allowed to move to Tomari.

At Tomari, there were already hundreds of Okinawans gathered, and Perry treated them to the spectacle of the marines and the rest of the crew marching to Shuri:

> "Very soon the procession emerged from the village, and came out upon the undulating country of [Shuri]. The picture here was perfect. The fields of upland rice were gracefully bending like waves before the wind; the groves and hill sides were dark with deep-green foliage, so suggestive of cool shady retreats, while, in the distance, the roof-tops of [Shuri], glittering in the sun, revealed, here and there, a spot of dazzling brightness amid the thick leafy covering of the trees in which the city was embosomed."[64]

At Shuri Castle, Perry met with the regent, since King Shō Tai (1843-1901) who would be the last king of Ryukyu, and was still only a child. Following, this a feast was held at the regent's mansion in which Perry toasts "Prosperity to the [Ryukyuans] and may they and the Americans always be friends."[65]

---

63 *Narrative of the Expedition of an American Squadron to the China Seas and Japan*, 188.
64 *Narrative of the Expedition of an American Squadron to the China Seas and Japan*, 189.
65 *Narrative of the Expedition of an American Squadron to the China Seas and Japan*, 192.

THE RYUKYUS

It is impossible to know whether Perry realized that the consequences of his actions played a major role in the destruction of the Ryukyu Kingdom, as it was fears that Westerners powers such as America could make the archipelago a colony which in part prompted the creation of Okinawa Prefecture by the Japanese state, something we will look at in more depth in following chapters.

Around the time of Perry's arrival, the Satsuma in Amami extended the sugar purchasing system to the island Okinoerabu in 1853, and planted sugarcane in Yorontō in 1857, as sugar was one of the Satsuma's main sources of finance that they could use to protect themselves against foreign ships if need be.

After Perry's first successes in Ryukyu, he took the *Susquehanna* and *Saratoga* to survey the Ogasawara Islands, returning on the evening of June 23, 1853 where the other ships, the *Mississippi*, the *Plymouth* and the *Supply* were anchored at Naha. During this return to Okinawa, more thoughts were offered about the role of women. They, like others before them had already noted women's role as merchants in the markets, and this time further add that:

> "(the women) "half naked, delving with the hoe or the spade, in the adjacent gardens, under a scorching sun...When the poor females are not thus employed in the cultivation of the earth, there is still found work enough for them of some other kind, for their destiny is labor. In every house may be seen the loom for weaving grass cloth...What has been said here must be understood as applying to the men who are not of the very lowest class."[66]

---

66 *Narrative of the Expedition of an American Squadron to the China Seas and Japan*, 219.

FOREIGNERS IN RYUKYU

While Perry and his crew had little evidence, they also suspected Japanese control over the islands:

> "The Japanese are to be found in numbers in [Ryukyu], and stroll about as uninterruptedly as the natives; they marry with the [Ryukyuans], cultivate lands, build houses in [Naha], and in short, seem to be perfectly at home" and that, "Japan sends annually thirty or forty junks to [Ryukyu], of about four hundred and fifty tons each; only one [Ryukyu] junk goes to China, and every alternate year one more, said to carry tribute, but not a single Chinese junk is ever allowed to enter [Naha]."[67]

But Perry had higher orders than to just stop in Ryukyu, and from here the ships departed for Uraga at Edo Bay to open Japan via gunboat diplomacy. Perry would again appear in Ryukyu, arriving in Naha from Hong Kong on January 20, 1854 on his way back to Japan after giving the Shogunate an ultimatum the previous year. Perry once again met with the regent, although a different one from the first occasion, and attempted but failed to get a Ryukyu coin, which would in theory prove whether or not the kingdom was independent.

This stop in the Ryukyu Kingdom also provides us with a detailed description of the Ryukyu Kingdom during its final years. Of particular note is the mention of Banyan (Gajumaru) trees that are so prevalent throughout the archipelago even today:

> "The trees that are most abundant, are the pine and the banyan, [Ficus microcarpa]..these are found

---

67 *Narrative of the Expedition of an American Squadron to the China Seas and Japan*, 222.

growing in regular lines along the highways, forming beautiful avenues, leading to the tombs and villages, it is reasonable to suppose they have been planted. The banyan is particularly abundant and is much used for hedges, being planted on the tops of the coral walls which surround the houses, and pruned and cut into symmetrical forms."[68]

In contrast to the earlier description of Shuri, the scene of a farmer's house is also described:

"The cottages in the country are generally thatched with rice straw, and surrounded by either stone walls or bamboo picket fences, within which there is not only the house, but the usual farmer's concomitants of stable, pig pen, and poultry hutch. The furniture is of the simplest kind, consisting of thick mats spread upon the plank floor, upon which the natives sit crossed legged."[69]

Finally, there is also an account of beards as a status symbol for noble men:

"The men in [Ryukyu] in youth have almost invariably a rich jet black beard, which in age becomes as white as snow. The higher classes allow their beards to grow of great length, and cultivate them with great care and pride, while the inferior people are obliged by law to cut theirs."[70]

---

[68] *Narrative of the Expedition of an American Squadron to the China Seas and Japan*, 312.
[69] *Narrative of the Expedition of an American Squadron to the China Seas and Japan*, 318.
[70] *Narrative of the Expedition of an American Squadron to the China Seas and Japan*, 315.

FOREIGNERS IN RYUKYU

Again leaving for Japan, Perry signed the Treaty of Kanagawa in March of 1854 in Yokohama, the country's first treaty with a Western nation, and the beginning of the end of the Shogunate's Sakoku policy. After his return from a survey of Hakodate in Hokkaido, Perry arrived in the Ryukyu Kingdom for the last time on July 1, 1854. During Perry's absence a major incident had happened, concerning the arrival of Lieutenant Glasson aboard the *Lexington* in May.

The incident had involved the death of a sailor named Board, who had been hit on the head with a blunt object and had fallen into the water. Glasson had demanded an explanation, but the Kingdom had done little in response. With Perry's arrival the order was complied with, and six judges on the Ryukyu side concluded that three sailors, including Board, were intoxicated in Naha, and Board had climbed over a wall to find a woman and her niece. Board had pulled out a knife and attempted to rape the women. Her cries brought the crime to the attention of other men, who chased him out, hurling stones until he met his death at the waters edge.

The Ryukyu side convicted the six men who had thrown the stones, but Perry said he only wished to see Ryukyu law carried out. The two America's were court-martialed, with those on the Okinawan side exiled to outlying islands.[cciii]

Despite this incident, Perry's final journey to the Ryukyu Kingdom is mostly remembered for the July 11, 1854 Treaty of Amity between the United States of America and the Ryukyu Kingdom. Like its Japanese predecessor, the treaty agreed that the treatment of US citizens while in the Ryukyu Kingdom would be with "great courtesy and friendship", that any item they requested would be made available to purchase, that ships wrecked in the archipelago would be aided by the kingdom, and that those on US ships be able to "ramble where they please, without hindrance, or having officials sent to follow them".[71] This final comment about the hindrance of officials following them was a particular remark to the Perry expeditions own experiences in the Ryukyu Kingdom.

The treaty also recognized the couth behavior of Americans in Ryukyu, and while the Board incident is the most notable, it was not the only such incident. The treaty states that if Americans "trifle with women, or force people to sell them thing", they are to be arrested by the kingdom and sent to the captains of their ships, where they would be punished.[72]

The US treaty with the Ryukyu Kingdom prompted other Western Powers to pursue their own treaties with the kingdom. In 1855 a treaty with France was concluded, when three battleships arrived in Naha commanded by Nicolas Francois Guerin. From the ships alighted over 200 soldiers, with the kingdom having little choice but to agree, and another treaty was signed with Holland in 1859. Over the next few decades the Ryukyu Kingdom as it had existed for four centuries was brought to an end, first being reclassified as a Japanese 'domain', and then in 1879 a prefecture of Japan.

In the final years of the kingdom, or 'domain', Westerners in the Ryuyku Archipelago were treated well, such as when on May 1, 1877, 109 men and women from the Spanish Philippines ran ashore at a reef of Hateruma. The officials saw that they were housed in huts, and Shuri prepared for a boat to take them back to the Philippines.

After the arrival of Perry and through the following tumultuous decades, the former Ryukyu Kingdom was formally integrated into Japan, with the foundations for what we know as Okinawa Prefecture being slowly and at times laboriously laid.

---

71 "Loochoo (Ryukyu) Commerce and Navigation"
72 "Loochoo (Ryukyu) Commerce and Navigation"

16

Contested Archipelago

The Meiji Restoration

The Meiji Restoration of 1868 came about precisely because of the Shogunate's inability to prevent foreign powers forcing 'unequal treaties' upon Japan. During this era of crisis, disgruntled samurai rallied around the phrase "Revere the Emperor, Expel the Barbarians".[cciv]

It was thought that by restoring the Emperor to his rightful place as the head of the Japanese state, the country could be justly governed, with the barbaric foreigners expelled. While there were lone wolf samurai who took it into their hands to assassinate shogunate officials and foreigners in Japan, it was the Satsuma-Chōshū Alliance in 1866 that led an organized movement. What followed was the Boshin War (1868–1869) to overthrow the Shogunate and reinstate the Meiji Emperor.[ccv]

While under the new Meiji government the decision was not taken to "Expel the Barbarians", it was clear to the Meiji oligarchs that the country had to be reformed to survive in an era of Western imperial power and colonization.

The end of the era of the Samurai came a few years after the Meiji restoration itself, when on August 29, 1871 the new government announced the abolition of feudal domains and the establishment of prefectures.[ccvi] The justification behind this sweeping reform was that the Daimyō had only taken land from the Emperor, who it had rightfully belonged to, and that it was only being returned to its rightful owner.

What to do with Ryukyu?
But what was to be of the Satsuma colony of Amami, or the indirectly controlled, once independent Ryukyu Kingdom which had never 'taken' land from the Emperor? The case of Amami was relatively simple, due to its colonial status. It was informally governed by the new Kagoshima Prefecture before being formally integrated in 1879. But the Ryukyu Kingdom technically still had a king, even if he was a puppet, and was not directly governed by Japan, nor necessarily loyal to it.

There was also the problem of the Ryukyu Kingdom's position suspended between Meiji Japan and Qing China with both sides claiming that they held the historical precedent justifying their possession of Ryukyu. Within the Meiji government, there was general consensus that Ryukyu should be at least partially integrated into Japan, and this led to the abolishment of the Ryukyu Kingdom and its reclassification as a feudal domain in 1872.

Under this mostly cosmetic change, King Shō Tai became a Daimyō and a residency was constructed for him in Tokyo's Iidamachi, as all Daimyō had estates in the Shogun's capital of Edo under the Tokugawa Shogunate.

The irony, that a Ryukyu King would be recognised as a samurai lord only in the heyday of the feudal system only serves to underline the subjugated status of Ryukyu within Japan by the time Shō Tai was recognized as a Daimyō, the shogun's capital of Edo had for some years been renamed the more modern Tokyo. This change occurred on September 3, 1868 with Tokyo 'the eastern capital' in contrast to the historic capital where the emperor resided that was Kyoto.[ccvii]

CONTESTED ARCHIPELAGO

A year before this, in 1871 the domain system was abolished and replaced with prefectures, leaving Ryukyu as both the newest and only 'feudal domain' of Japan. This reclassification of Ryukyu is characteristic of the uncertainty about what was to become of the archipelago in the early years of the Meiji regime.

By 1872, control of Ryukyu had shifted from Kagoshima Prefecture to the Ministry of Foreign Affairs with a government office replacing the Satsuma Magistrate. There were voices of protests in Kagoshima Prefecture, as losing the former kingdom was a loss of revenue for what had recently been Satsuma Domain.

In November of the same year, those stationed in Kagoshima's Ryukyu Hall were sent back to Ryukyu Domain, and to further emphasize the point that these islands were part of Japan the government ordered for the Hinomaru flag to be flown at Miyako, Ishigaki, Iriomote and Yonaguni.

Despite abolishing feudal domains in the mainland, it was important for the Meiji government to make the Ryukyu Kingdom appear to be as close as possible to Japan. This involved bestowing Ryukyu Domain an official seal, with the kingdom, now holding both the seal of Ryukyu Domain from Japan as well as a seal provided by the Qing Dynasty.

Changes also came to those of all classes in the kingdom, most notably the adoption of surnames in December 17, 1872. The Meiji government introduced surnames for all people in Japan via a family register in that year. Prior to this, surnames had been a privilege of nobles in Japan and the same had been true for Ryukyu. Under the era of the Ryukyu Kingdom, surnames were held by the Samurē and since these names were often tied to a given territory, it was not rare for these names to change from father to son, or brother to brother. The 1872 reform made surnames for all fixed.[ccviii]

THE RYUKYUS

With the rebranding of the Ryukyu Kingdom as Ryukyu Domain, the Japanese government did not necessarily want to annex Ryukyu, but rather emphasise Japanese influence while maintain the buffer state status between Japan and China. Additionally, within the Meiji government a debate about whether the Ryukyu Kingdom should be a fully integrated part of Japan continued all the way until 1879.

The Ryukyu Kingdom, now Ryukyu Domain, also wished to maintain its status as a semi-independent state in East Asia. In 1873, the member of the Council of Three Yonabaru Ryōku (1718-1797) visited the foreign minister Soejima Tanetomi (1828-1905) at his private residence in Tokyo, and was reassured that, "The polity of Ryukyu Domain shall remain forever unchanged."[73]

Yet, only two years later on July 1, 1875, Matsuda Michiyuki (1839—1882) the Meiji official who was later put in charge of bringing the kingdom to an end, was dispatched to Shuri to give orders.

From the heart of the kingdom, Matsuda read a proclamation to Prince Shō Hitsu, in which the prince was told that the kingdom was to halt all tributary delegations to China, forbid any Chinese ships from coming to Ryukyu, abolish the Fujian Ryukyu Hall, adopt the Meiji calender system and allow for the creation of a garrison. These were unmistakable signs that the Ryukyu Kingdom was under the direct control of Japan.

Some of those who harked back to what they saw as a golden age made frequent trips to China, requesting that the Qing intervene by military force if necessary to restore the former kingdom to its former status.

Yet the Qing court did not have much leverage, and its other tributary states were then under pressure from imperialist

---

[73] Kazuyuki Tomiyama. *Ryūkyū, Okinawa Shi No Sekai*. Yoshikawa Kōbunkan, 2003, 235.

powers. When France acquired Tonkin in Vietnam in 1884, the Qing sent troops, leading to the outbreak of the Sino-French War.

This war at least gave hope to some who longed for a return to the recent past and wanted to see an intervention by the Qing in the Ryukyu Archipelago also. Such hopes were soon dashed, with the French destroying the Qing fleet at the Battle of Fuzhou. It was soon evident that the Qing had enough problems defending even its nearest tributary states. A battle with Japan for Ryukyu's sake seemed increasingly unlikely.

The Mudan Incident
Despite the changes since the creation of Ryukyu Domain, the Japanese government had yet to settle the question with Qing China as to which Ryukyu belonged to. Such an opportunity presented itself when on October 18, 1871 a ship from Miyako that had made annual tax payments in Naha was caught in a typhoon on its journey back.[ccix]

On November 6, the ship foundered off Taiwan's southeast coast. Out of the 69 members of the crew, three drowned and 66 scrambling onto the shore. But the majority of the survivors, 54 of them, were murdered by the local Paiwan aboriginals. The twelves survivors of the Mudan Incident, as it came to be known, where saved by Qing officials and sent to the Ryukyu Hall in Fujian.[74]

Around seven months later, on June 7, 1872 they were at last returned to Naha. It was the Meiji bureaucrat Ijichi Sadaka (1826–1887) who compiled a report that same year in Naha, submitting it to the governor of Kagoshima, Ōyama Tsunayosi (1825–1877) who urged that these events justified a Japanese invasion of Taiwan.

---

74 *Ryūkyū, Okinawa Shi No Sekai*, 236.

THE RYUKYUS

Following this, Ijichi was dispatched to Tokyo where me met with the foreign minister Soejima on the matter. For those within the Meiji government who wanted to integrate not just Ryukyu, but Taiwan as well into the Japanese Empire, this was an ideal scenario. The following year, 1873, offered further justification and cries for compensation, when a ship from Okayama ran adrift at Taiwan and was subsequently pillaged.

As far as the Qing government was concerned, the actions of the 'uncultured' Taiwanese natives were not their responsibility and they also maintained that Ryukyuans were not Japanese. What's more, the Qing argued, the Ryukyu Kingdom was under their suzerainty, and that there was no need for Japan to be getting involved in matters that did not concern it.

While the Qing emphasized Ryukyu's historical and tributary relationship. For the Japanese side, any Chinese relationship with Ryukyu had been little more than ceremonial since the 1609 Satsuma invasion, and this coupled with Ryukyu being a Japanese 'domain' as well as the theory that King Shunten of Chūzan was descendant of the samurai Minamoto no Tametomo was more than enough justification for them to stress that what happened to Ryukyuans was in fact a matter of Japanese concern.

The Meiji government had been considering the possibilities of making Taiwan a colony from roughly the same time the Ryukyu Kingdom became Ryukyu Domain.

Soejima talked to the US diplomat Charles Egbert Delong (1832–1876) about the Taiwan matter, with Delong pointing out that the Qing had failed to establish law across the island, making it a no-man's land under international law. The advisor to the Ministry of Foreign Affairs, and former American consul in Xiamen, Guillaum Joseph Émile Le Gendreals (1830–1899) also mentioned to Soejima that it would be quite possible to make Taiwan into a colony.

CONTESTED ARCHIPELAGO

During this period there was also a faction that was in favor for an invasion of Korea, led by Saigō Takamori (1828–1877) one of the central leaders in the Meiji Restoration. But while the invasion of Korea was off-putting to many within the Meiji government as they rightly expected it could lead to international condemnation, an annexation of 'no-man's land' Taiwan was unlikely to result in any such criticism.

In January of 1874 the Meiji oligarch, and later Prime Minister of Japan, Ōkuma Shinobu (1838–1922) launched an investigation into the potential for a Japanese takeover of Taiwan, with the proposal submitted to the Diet on February 6th.[ccx] Sending soldiers to Taiwan was agreed on, with the expedition serving two purposes. One was to show China that Ryukyu was a Japanese territory, the other was to expand the empire. Although due to later negotiations, Taiwan would not become a Japanese colony until almost twenty-years later, in 1895.

Since the expedition to Taiwan was also about justifying Japanese control of Ryukyu, two months before soldiers were sent in May 1874, the jurisdiction of Ryukyu moved from the Ministry of Foreign Affairs to the Ministry of Home Affairs. Ryukyu, thus went from being an official foreign matter to a domestic one.

The General entrusted with Taiwan was Saigō Jūdō (1843-1902) the younger brother of Saigō Takamori. The 3,000 man Japanese army arrived in Taiwan on May 22, having left Nagasaki. While few died from combat, by as early as July over 500 had died from malaria.[75]

Upon the Japanese army's arrival in Taiwan they erected a stone monument to commemorate those from Ryukyu who had died in Taiwan which read "Resting Place of the 54 Citizens of

---

75 *Ryūkyū, Okinawa Shi No Sekai*, 240.

THE RYUKYUS

Ryukyu Domain of the Empire of Japan".[ccxi]

The conflict itself did not last long, with British arbitration wrapping it up by November of 1874. With this, Japanese troops agreed to withdraw from the island by December. Through this arbitration, the Qing Government also agreed to compensate the Japanese side with a payment of over eighteen tons of silver, a sign in itself that the Qing had fallen far from their heights of power.

While the Taiwan Expedition had failed to solve the Ryukyu question, the Empire of Japan had succeeded in showing modern military prowess to the Qing. But for those in Ryukyu Domain the question of suzerainty remained unanswered. Ryukyu contact with the Qing continued with Shō Tai sending a tributary delegation to China. In June of 1875, Japan once again ordered Shō Tai to halt such tributary missions, but this did not deter him and he sent one again in 1887. Since China was dealing with Russian incursions to its west, there was not an immediate nor constant response to the Ryukyu matter from China.

Ulysses S. Grant and the Proposed Division of Ryukyu
In October of 1878, the Qing formally protested the Disposition of Ryukyu, and in the following year of 1879 the former US President, Ulysses S. Grant (1822-1885) helped broker an agreement that envisioned the Ryukyu Archipelago split, with Miyako and Yaeyama becoming Chinese territory and the majority of the archipelago Japanese territory.

The Chinese petition to Grant began in May of 1879 when politician Li Hongzhang (1823-1901) and Prince Gong (Yixin 1833-1898) requested he intervene in the dispute, while he was visiting China. It was as a private citizen on a trip to Nikko that a conference was held with Itō Hirobumi (1841-1909), the first Prime Minister of Japan.

During the conference, Itō stressed that Ryukyu had long

been protected by Japan, and that China's territorial claims were quite frankly baseless. The Japanese side presented Grant with documents that proved to them that Ryukyu had been part of Japan since ancient times, stressing a shared history, language, religion and ethnicity. Of particular note was the legend of the samurai Minamoto no Tametomo (1139-1170), a samurai with imperial blood who had fought in the Hōgen Disturbance (1156), a dispute regarding imperial succession.[ccxii]

Minamoto no Tametomo had supposedly come to Ryukyu after being exiled to Izu-Ōshima. In Okinawa, Minamoto no Tametomo fathered a child with the daughter of King Shūnten of Chūzan, and this legend allowed the Ryukyu court to claim it had links to the Japanese emperor. On the Ryukyu side this can be seen written in *Chūzan Seikan*, as well as allowing the Japanese side during the early Meiji period to make bold claims that the Ryukyu royal family was a scion of the Japan's imperial lineage.[ccxiii]

The Japanese side also offered Grant more tangible reasons why Ryukyu was an indisputable Japanese territory. These included that the Shogun Ashikaga Yoshinori (1391-1441) had given the islands to Shimazu Tadakuni (1403-1470) and the pledges that Shō Nei had made under the Tokugawa Shogunate. The argument was also made that the Ryukyu language(s) were a Japanese dialect, and therefore part of Japan.[ccxiv]

During the Nikko conference, Grant made the following suggestion:

> "I have heard it suggested, but I have no authority to speak on the subject, that a boundary running between the Ryukyu Islands so as to give China a wide channel to the Pacific would be accepted."[76]

---

76 Richard T. Chang, "General Grant's 1879 Visit to Japan," *Monumenta Nipponica* 24, no. 4 (1969), 380.

THE RYUKYUS

The Japanese side followed Grant's advice, and the decision was made to cut off the Sakishima islands, giving Miyako and Yaeyama to China, while the rest of the Ryukyu Archipelago would remain under Japanese control. The Qing initially agreed to this proposal, but protests from Ryukyu elites who had fled the kingdom after it had become Ryukyu Domain led to the Qing eventually rejecting this scenario.

The matter was left unsettled until the Japanese victory in the first Sino-Japanese War (1894-1895). With the Treaty of Shimonoseki, which concluded the war, Japan was able to force the Qing to agree that Korea was independent and that it would forfeit all claims to Taiwan. With the Qing now subjugated and having lost Taiwan, China was in no position to claim the even more distant Ryukyu Archipelago.

17

THE DISPOSITION OF RYUKYU

What to do with Ryukyu?

Before the Japanese victory over the Qing in 1895, there were two ways of thinking about whether Ryukyu should remain in semi-colonial status: should the islanders remain indirectly tied to Japan? As had been the Ryukyu Kingdom and Ryukyu Domain or fully integrated into Japan as a prefecture.

Those against the creation of a new prefecture mainly cited financial, as well as racial reasons. A legislative body of the early Meiji era, the Chamber of the Left (1871-1875)[ccxv] was opposed to the Ryukyu King becoming a Japanese noble as "the people of Ryukyu are not the same ethnicity as the mainlanders and they should not be mixed."[77]

Other statesmen also voiced their sentiments that the people of Ryukyu were not Japanese, such as the Meiji oligarchs, Ōkuma Shigenobu and Kibo Takayoshi (1833-1877).

A degree of public opinion was also against the integration of Ryukyu and Ezo (Hokkaido) with an 1875 editorial in the Hōchi News proclaiming that "Ryukyu should be let go and Ezo should be sold".[78] Such an opinion was based on the high costs that would be required to turn a kingdom in the south and a

---

77 Oguma Eiji. *"Nihonjin" No kyōkai Okinawa, Ainu, Taiwan, Chōsen: Shokuminchi Shihai Kara Fukki undō Made* . Shinyōsha, 1998, 20-21.
78 *"Nihonjin" No kyōkai Okinawa, Ainu, Taiwan*, 20.

THE RYUKYUS

vast undeveloped island in the north into central parts of the Japanese state.

The same year as this editorial, the Ministry of Home Affairs dispatched Kawarada Moriharu (1842–1914) to provide an assessment of Ryukyu Domain. Kawarada returned arguing that it would be astronomically expensive to simultaneously modernize Japan proper in addition to a foreign kingdom.

While the arguments against a formal integration of the Ryukyu Kingdom in Japan were largely economic or racist, those in favor argued from the point of national defense.

This held particular sway in an era in which European and American colonial powers were carving up the world. By extending the boundaries of Japan as far as possible, it became in turn easier to protect the Japanese mainland at the expense of these borderland regions.

Numerous Westerners had come to Japan via Ryukyu, most notably Commodore Matthew Perry of the US Navy, and the Shogunate had centuries of contention with the Russians regarding Hokkaido and, further north, Sakhalin and the Kuril Islands, which were also considered territories of Japan.

In May of 1872, the Finance Minister, Inue Kaoru (1836-1915) proposed that Ryukyu become part of Japan to solidify the countries southern border saying that "Ryukyu is a strategic position for Japan's defense".[79] Other Meiji oligarchs where in agreement, the Japanese Field Marshall and twice Prime Minister of Japan, Yamagata Aritomo, proposed that while the islands of Ryukyu themselves were small they spanned a great distance between Japan, Taiwan and the Chinese mainland and could not be overlooked in terms of maritime transportation.

Of particular alarm was the interest of foreign powers in

---

79   "*Nihonjin*" *No kyōkai Okinawa, Ainu, Taiwan*, 21.

THE DISPOSITION OF RYUKYU

the Ryukyu Archipelago. In 1877, the Meiji oligarch Iwakura Tomomi (1825-1883) submitted a report that showed the British emphasizing the region's military value. It was clear that if Japan did not take Ryukyu, Britain or some other colonial power would attempt to. Ultimately these arguments of national defense trumped the economic and racial arguments against.

The Disposition of Ryukyu

In March 1879, Matsuda Michiyuki led an army of over 500 police, soldiers and bureaucrats to Shuri Castle, to declare the end of the Ryukyu Kingdom/Domain. On March 31, Shō Tai, his family and forty women and children were made to vacate the seat of the Ryukyu Kingdom.

Shō Tai first attempted to resist attempts to be moved to Tokyo, stating that he was ill, but was finally forced to move by May 27. As a king exiled from his own kingdom, Shō Tai was given a mansion in Kōjimachi, in what is today Tokyo's Chiyoda Ward and granted a stipend of 200,000 yen a year from the treasury.[ccxvi] With the king exiled to Tokyo, an era of over four-hundred-years came to a close. The Ryukyu Kingdom was no more. From its ashes Okinawa Prefecture was born on April 4, 1879.

While the Meiji Restoration was in 1868, it was not until the end of the 19th Century that both Okinawa and Hokkaido began to reach the same standards as the rest of Japan and both can be understood as 'internal colonies' during the Meiji period.

At a superficial glance, Okinawa and Hokkaido appear quite different, one is sub-tropical the other boreal. Okinawa is a chain of relatively small islands while Hokkaido is the 21st largest island in the world, bigger than Hispaniola but smaller than Ireland. Okinawa is closer to China and Southeast Asia, while Hokkaido is closer to the Russian far east.

But if one thinks about them from the viewpoint of Meiji era

THE RYUKYUS

Japan, they share a number of similarities. Both have indigenous people who spoke different languages, both were only partially integrated into Japan in the era of the samurai, and both were now border regions of the fledgling Japanese nation state.

In Hokkaido, the process of integration began with Enomoto Takeaki (1836–1908), who fought a final battle to preserve the Shogunate in Hakodate, when he was defeated Ezo was bought under the Meiji government, which rechristened the island as 'Hokkaido'. Hokkaido went through numerous forms of government, until in 1886 the centralized Hokkaido Government was formed to govern this vast island.

Unlike Hokkaido, which is not technically classed as a prefecture, Okinawa was on face value a prefecture just as any other from its inception, just like Kagoshima Prefecture to the north.[ccxvii] Yet the level of reforms required in an attempt to bring Okinawa to the same standards as a mainland prefecture were considerable and while classified as a 'prefecture', Okinawa was never treated the same as prefectures in mainland Japan.

Unlike in Hokkaido, where large numbers of immigrants from the mainland were encouraged, displacing the indigenous people, in Okinawa rule by mainland Japanese over a majority Okinawan population became the norm. The first governor of Okinawa, Nabeshima Naoyoshi (1844–1915) arrived on May 18, 1879 and within the prefecture government building a department of general affairs, education department, tax department and sanitation department were founded as the first bid to bring Okinawa in line with mainland prefectures.

The lack of trust in Okinawans to rule themselves can also be seen in the right to vote, which in Japan was granted to men aged over 25 (albeit with a high tax requirement) as early as 1889, amounting to only 1.1% of the population.[80] Such a right was not given to Okinawans until 1912, and it was not until 1920 that this was extended to Miyako and Yaeyama. It seemed that the further one was from the center of Japan the less trust the central government had in you.

To prevent any resistance against the new order, in May the Major General of the army, Masumitsu Kunisuke (1849–1899) collected all the weapons of the Ryukyu Kingdom and stored them in Shuri Castle. In July a police station was founded with branches throughout Okinawa including Shuri, Naha and Kumejima as well as in Miyako and Yaeyama.

'Preserving the Old'
Under Nabeshima some reforms that would have been unthinkable to the nobles of the former kingdom were carried out, such as the abolition of the religious system tied to the now defunct Ryukyu court. This began with the abolishment of the highest ranking priest, the Kikoeōkimi in 1884, followed by other courtly Kaminchu ranks. Although it was not until 1910 that the national treasury stopped paying Noro their stipends.[ccxviii]

Despite the abolishment of the Ryukyu court religion, the Ryukyu religion itself continued on the local level albeit without the centralization that had begun under King Shō En. One form of this is the presence of Yuta, who are women who are said to have supernatural powers that allows them to communicate with the spirits and the gods.[ccxix] The act of visiting Yuta for advice is called *Yutakōyā* and some people in Okinawa continue to visit Yuta today for all sorts of reasons including, health and prosperity for their family, for their ancestors, or to consult about an unfortunate event.

---

80   Milton Walter Meyer, Japan a Concise History (Rowman & Littlefield, 1992), 144.

THE RYUKYUS

In 1881 Nabeshima was recalled to Tokyo, and the time period for the governors that followed was limited to only a few years, no longer than five and sometimes as short as a single year. This changed with the former Kagoshima samurai Narahara Shigeru (1834-1918) who would assume the post for close to sixteen years (1892-1908). Like Nabeshima, Narahara's focus was on building a stable Okinawa that could be integrated into the larger Japanese state. Narahara's tenure in Okinawa was so long that he was sometimes referred to as the 'King of Ryukyu', and his reign of fifteen years and ten months was indeed longer than many of the Ryukyu Kings of yore.

In contrast to women of high rank under the former Ryukyu Kingdom, Narahara continued a policy called 'preserving the old' for men of high rank, under fears that too much change too fast could lead to open revolt. Such fears were not unfounded, given the Satsuma Rebellion (or Seinan War) in 1877, in which disgruntled samurai led by Saigō Takamori rose up against the new regime.

With Japan's abolishment of the feudal class system, even once honorable samurai lost their stipend from the state, and further military reforms left many of these low-ranking samurai in particular at a loss in this new world, in which they had become a living relic.

Saigō had established an academy for such down-and-out samurai in 1876, and the Meiji government which was already concerned after numerous rebellions in Kyushu, moved warships to Kagoshima as a precautionary measure. This resulted in an open rebellion.

If such a response could come from samurai within Japan, and no less from the former Satsuma who had helped lead the Meiji Restoration, the potential for resentment to bubble up into rebellion in Okinawa was certainly worrying. With the

THE DISPOSITION OF RYUKYU

Disposition of Ryukyu there were Samurē who resisted, with attempts to boycott the new government springing up across the prefecture, but the new regime quickly took to arrests and if necessary used torture to dissuade any such resistance.

Under the policy of 'Preserving the Old', officials in the Magiri districts created by the Ryukyu Kingdom continued their role as before, and the five to six percent of the population who had received stipends under the Ryukyu Kingdom continued to do so under the Meiji government, and this system lasted until 1903.

While this was a short-term relief for a degree of the former kingdom's nobles, it was the opposite for the former kingdom's agricultural peasant class who had to continue paying taxes. This included the deadly poll tax in Miyako and Yaeyama.

The frustration spilled over in a number of cases, such as in 1888 when villagers of Nakijin Magiri who were sick of paying a heavy tax burden stormed the guard house and Magiri, and in the following year a similar event happened at Chinen Magiri. There were hopes that the new regime could create a more equal society, and in Miyako a plea was submitted to the Diet in Tokyo, because as out of the island's population of around 35,000 there were 340 local officials, almost one for every 100 people.[81] However, even the Samurē who continued to receive stipends were only a portion of the total nobles there had been in the Ryukyu Kingdom, with about 2,000 completely losing their stipend.[82]

To remedy this, the Meiji government created the Development Association which encouraged former Shuri and Naha nobles to develop the land through agriculture.[ccxx] Other means involved the creation of a weaving factory, but neither this nor the Development Association managed to solve the new

---
81 *Ryūkyūkoku No Metsubō to Hawai Imi*, 77-78.
82 Ryūkyū, *Okinawa Shi No Sekai*, 255.

THE RYUKYUS

sense of poverty for the nobles who had lost their stipends.

The aim behind the early policy of the Meiji regime was the stability of Okinawa, rather than the plight of the common people. The government encouraged sugar production which meant that the Yanchu system in Amami was not immediately abolished either. In 1891, 25 noble households from Shuri moved to Shiinahara in Yaeyama in an attempt to further expand sugar production throughout the prefecture, but due to outbreaks of malaria this project was a failure.[ccxxi]

The resentment some of the Samurē held towards the new regime can be seen in Iha Fuyū's (1876-1947) reflections on his grandfather and father who were nobles from Naha under the days of the Ryukyu Kingdom. Iha's family despised the Japanese to such an extent that they refused to let out any rooms to them: "Even though we had room in the family house, we would not rent out any space to *Naichijin* (mainlanders). Also, if I wasn't listening properly someone in the family would threaten me saying "there's a *Yamatonchu*".[83]

Naha nobles such as Iha's father had made their fortune because of Naha's role as the kingdom's center of trade. But with the birth of Okinawa Prefecture merchants from Osaka and Kagoshima began to dominate this market. Iha's father was so distraught with matters that he tried to drowning his frustration with alcohol. Iha's grandfather took particular pride in his contribution to the Ryukyu Kingdom, reminiscing about his role on the tributary ships:

"When my grandfather was seventeen, he looked at his family tree only to be overcome with grief that not a single one of his ancestors had succeeded in life. With great energy he

---

83 "私の子供時分"

became involved in the China trade and went over to Fuzhou six or seven times."[84]

The end of the Ryukyu Kingdom for Samurē such as these was devastating:

> "In 1879 I was four years old. That was an unforgettable year for us...of course at the time I didn't know what all the fuss was about. My grandfather who had succeeded in creating a name for himself lost all hope for the future with the change in governance. Both his mind and body were suddenly weakened."[85]

The End of the Yanchu and Poll Tax

This era also marked significant movements that attempted to free the people of Amami and Sakishima. In Yaeyama and Miyako one of the pioneers in ending the poll tax system was Nakamura Jissaku (1867-1943). Nakamura had come to Miyako in 1892 to conduct a survey about the possibility of pearl cultivation around the islands.

It was in Okinawa that he met Gusukuma Seian (1860-1944) an official from a noble family in Naha who had been sent to Miyako in 1884 to oversee sugar production, after passing the prefecture's agricultural exam.

Both Nakamura and Gusukuma were horrified at how the people of Yaeyama and Miyako suffered under the burden of the poll tax. Nakamura and Gusukuma sent numerous appeals to the newly appointed prefectural governor, Narahara, calling for the reduction in the number of officials overseeing Sakishima and an abolishment of the poll tax system. But with resistance from the local officials themselves and the policy of 'Preserving

---

[84] "私の子供時分"
[85] "私の子供時分"

the Old', the two made little headway in Okinawa Prefecture.

After countless rejections the pair went to the Imperial Diet in Tokyo to directly appeal for an abolition of the poll tax. They were eventually able to submit an appeal directly to the Home Minister, with poll tax being finally being abolished in Sakishima in 1903.

In Amami, the Yanchu system technically came to an end with an order to release the Yanchu in 1871, followed by a law banning the buying and selling of people in 1872.[ccxxii] Yet, these laws alone did not bring an end to the practice.

In 1875, Ijichi Seizaemon a former samurai of Satsuma domain who had formerly been exiled at Amami-Ōshima came to the island and organized the islanders to not pay the sugar tax.[ccxxiii] This of course led to a great deal of tension from the masters of these Yanchu, and Ijichi was thrown in jail. But thanks to his efforts the movement against the Yanchu system gathered momentum, and it became increasingly difficult for masters to hold onto Yanchu.

The gradual end of the Yanchu system did not change the sugar monoculture in Amami in the short term. In 1873 the Meiji government moved the buying and selling of sugar to a free trade system. The governor of Kagoshima Prefecture was quick to adjust and the Ōshima General Trade Company was created to continue the now over two century long monopoly of sugar.

The company's monopoly was broken after only five years by Maruta Nanri (1851-1886). Maruta had illegally gone to the United Kingdom before the Meiji Restoration with the help of the Nagasaki based Scottish merchant Thomas Blake Glover (1836-1911). Maruta had studied how to construct a sugar factory during his time in the United Kingdom, and when he returned to his native Naze, he was appalled to see the monopoly of Kagoshima merchants.

THE DISPOSITION OF RYUKYU

Led by Naze, a movement consisting of the people of Amami, including Yanchu began against Kagoshima domination and called for a breakup of the company.[ccxxiv] While Maruta was imprisoned numerous times during the process, in 1878 the movement succeeded with the abolishment of the Ōshima General Trade Company.

Education

The most central of all reforms was education, as it was only the younger generation, with no direct experience of having lived in the Ryukyu Kingdom that could be fully molded into loyal citizens of Japan.

Under the Ryukyu Kingdom, education had followed a Chinese model. Officials studied such subjects as arithmetic, Confucianism and writing. The highest center of education within the kingdom was the Meirin-Dō in Kuninda. Meirin-Dō was built by a member of the Council of Three, Tei Jūnsoku (1663-1735), on the request of the Royal Government.[ccxxv] Tei had made numerous trips to China and was well versed in the Chinese classics.

Construction for the school finished in 1714 and those who attended learned what was needed to be a high-ranking official who would make the tributary voyage to China, such as diplomacy and Chinese.

With the advent of Okinawa Prefecture, Meirin-Dō and all the schools below it were temporarily shut down. But with their closure there was no means of education in Okinawa Prefecture at all, thus in June 1879 Governor Nabeshima allowed for their reopening.

In the same year, Okinawa's first Middle School opened, and in February of 1880 the training of elementary school teachers to speak 'standard Japanese', the dialect of Tokyo, began. Many

THE RYUKYUS

of these early teachers hailed from the Ryukyu Kingdom's educational system.

By the middle of 1880, fourteen elementary schools had been established across Okinawa, three in Shuri, ten in Shimajiri and one in Kunigami.[86] Of great concern was the difference between the Ryukyu languages and standard Japanese. In December of 1879, Governor Nabeshima wrote in a letter to the Minister of Finance that the most pressing issue in the development of the prefecture was to bring the language to the same level as that of Honshu.

This standardization of language was not an issue not limited to Okinawa Prefecture. In schools around the country, students were encouraged to drop their regional accents and speak the new standard Japanese, the dialect of Tokyo. This often meant that students would use this way of speaking while in class, but revert back to their regional accent when talking to friends. But in Okinawa, as with the Ainu in Hokkaido, there was a higher barrier to overcome as there was a greater linguistic chasm to cross than the regional accents of mainland Japan.[ccxxvi] These children would be not just learning a different dialect but a new language.

When Nabeshima assumed the role of Governor his first order was the creation of a Conversation School in 1880 and this marked the beginning of the new education system.[ccxxvii]

The first attendees of this school to study the "words of Tokyo" were elite boys of Okinawa. Following this, four years later, an Instructor School was created, replacing the Conversation School.[ccxxviii] Within three years of this, 51 schools had been created throughout Okinawa Prefecture.[87] While the initial focus was on boys, by 1886 education for girl's had also

---

86   Ryūkyū, Okinawa Shi No Sekai, 257.
87   "Nihonjin" No kyōkai Okinawa, Ainu, Taiwan, 49.

begun in earnest.

Education was particularly important from a perspective of defense, as Yamagata Aritomo said in 1886, "Okinawa is our Southern Gate" and one did not want a populace who would welcome the enemy.[88] The historical precedents of the tension between the Qing over the Korean Peninsula, and the British government offering to pay Japan to establish military bases in Okinawa were particularly shocking. In February 1887, the Minister of Education Mori Arinori (1847-1889) and Prime Minister Itō Hirobumi paid a visit to the prefecture, with both emphasizing the island's military value.

In March 1887, *Goshinei*, which are portraits of the Meiji Emperor, went up in the Instructor Schools, and not only the rest of Okinawa but the entire country soon followed a few years later.[ccxxix] A magazine of the period '*Kyoiku Jiron*' featured an article that extolled destroying the dual identity of Hokkaido, Okinawa, Tsushima, the Ogasawara Islands and the Oki Islands. Like Mori and others, the article stressed the strategic location of these borderland areas, extolled feelings of "Honor for the Emperor and Love for the Country", a common language and a reform of customs.[89]

The education of boys alone was not enough to create this loyalty, and Mori also gave a speech about the importance of educating women, who would raise the next generation of Okinawans. This education followed the Meiji period phrase "Good Wife and Wise Mother".[ccxxx] The first schools for girls focused on their practical skills and the contributions that they could make to Japanese industry, this had its foundations in an 1893 regulation which aimed to increase the production of key

---

88 "*Nihonjin*" *No kyōkai Okinawa, Ainu, Taiwan*, 36.
89 "*Nihonjin*" *No kyōkai Okinawa, Ainu, Taiwan*, 38.

industries through a practical education.[ccxxxi]

The first time this was seen in Okinawa was when the Shuri Elementary School added a course for girls. In 1899, education for all girls was expanded with the teaching of sewing, household chores and looking after children.[ccxxxii] The following year, in 1900, the Shuri Girl's Vocational School for Supplementary Education opened its doors.[ccxxxiii] The focus of Okinawa's girls was textile-making, with girls learning how to weave and dye. However, due to the policy of Preserving the Old, these schools were not accessible for most of Okinawa's common women.

At the school, customs of the Ryukyu Kingdom were frowned upon and seen as unfitting for a modern Japan. This included the Hajichi tattoos on women's hands, which had been outlawed in October of 1889, as well as seeking advice from Yuta and the practice of *Mōashibi* which, while not illegal, were frowned upon.[ccxxxiv]

It would not be until a decade later, in 1899 that the education of girls was made closer to that of boys, with an increased emphasis on the literacy and general education of girls.[ccxxxv]

The Pro-Qing Faction
When the new education system began in Okinawa it was also met with resistance and in some cases disinterest. When the first Instructor School began recruiting, it struggled to find enough applicants. To encourage Okinawans to become teachers it began waiving fees, offering financial assistance and providing free lunches.

From the perspective of the Meiji government, large expenditure in Okinawa was worth the price, as these islands were of vital strategic importance. Yet, despite these efforts, by the latter half of the 1880s the elementary education uptake in Okinawa was only 3%, well behind the 40% of the Japanese

THE DISPOSITION OF RYUKYU

mainland that had already been achieved in the first half of the 1880s.[90]

The discrepancy in enrollment rates between boys and girls was particular large in Okinawa; in 1887 in mainland Japan this rate was 60% for boys and 28% for girls, while in Okinawa the number was just over 11% for boys and only 1.6% for girls.[91]

While there was unfamiliarity and suspicion of the new education system, the main reason for the low rates is that the many poorer households in Okinawa required their children to work, and a lack of education for these parents under the Ryukyu Kingdom also meant that many doubted the value of education.

Many Okinawans of the era called the new schools '*Yamato-ya*' where children would be sent to learn the foreign 'Yamato education'. The more sensational of rumors surrounding the *Yamato-ya* was that Okinawan children who were sent to these schools were kidnapped and taken to the mainland, never seeing their families again. There was also resistance from some former nobles, particularly those of the pro-Qing faction who were hostile to all things Japanese.

Okinawan society would remain divided about reforms under Japan right up until the 1895 Japanese victory in the first Sino-Japanese war. By the 1880s, some former officials of the Ryukyu Kingdom, including members of the Council of Three, Tomikawa Seikei (1832–1890) and politician Kōchi Chōjō (1843–1891) while first attempting to work with the new government of Okinawa Prefecture both escaped to Qing China where they submitted numerous petitions. Both passed away their campaign unsuccessful.

While the Qing may have been sympathetic to Tomikawa and Kōchi's pleas, they were made during an era in which not only

---
90 "*Nihonjin*" *No kyōkai Okinawa, Ainu, Taiwan*, 38.
91 *Okinawa Ken Shi Kakuhen Ron 8 Joseishi*, 116.

THE RYUKYUS

China's tributary states but the Qing empire itself was under the threat of becoming carved up into colonies. The Qing had already lost Myanmar (Burma), which became a British colony in 1886, and the French annexed Vietnam (French Indo-China) by 1887.

While the elders of the Restore Ryukyu movement had fond memories of the kingdom, there was also a younger generation of Okinawans who had been educated in the new schools, and who bought into the idea of the emperor. There was also an elite who had even studied in Tokyo and increasingly saw themselves as Japanese.

During the build up to the Sino-Japanese war, this new elite began to increasingly criticize those who still supported the former Ryukyu Kingdom. The *Ryukyu Shimpō*, a newspaper founded on September 15, 1893, was one such mouthpiece that derided those who longed for the days of yore. The *Ryukyu Shimpō* lambasted the Restore Ryukyu Movement as an "anachronism".

The Sino-Japanese War began as both China and Japan claimed influence over Korea. The war was a particular shock to the Restore Ryukyu movement. Korea had been the final tributary state to hold out as a suzerain state of China, and this war also determined the future of Okinawa Prefecture. Those who supported the Qing during the Sino-Japanese war took to wearing traditional clothes, and on the first and fifteenth day of every month they would visit sites that were central to the Ryukyu Kingdom, such as Enkaku-Ji, Benzaiten-Dō, and Sonohyan-Utaki, praying for the health of Shō Tai, Ryukyu's last king now exiled in Tokyo.

The *Ryukyu Shimpō* looked on these processions with scorn, labeling those who participated as "the stubborn party".[92] The

---

92   *Ryūkyū, Okinawa Shi No Seka*, 264.

THE DISPOSITION OF RYUKYU

paper's attacks on the pro-Qing faction within Ryukyu reflected a wider anxiety that Okinawa Prefecture would again be cast into the unknown, if Japan did happen to lose a battle with the Qing. Such anxiety was also felt in Japan, reflect in rumors such as that a Qing ship had captured Okinawa, and was now in a position to attack Kyushu.

Such a rumor, while false was even reported in some mainland papers. The pro-Japanese faction within Okinawa also took the possibility of a Qing invasion seriously. The Principal of Jinjō Middle School, Kodama Kihachi, proposed the creation of a volunteer army of middle school student and teachers, and during this period they practiced with live ammunition at the Kumamoto Garrison Outpost.[ccxxxvi]

Volunteer armies were also formed by civilians to repulse a Qing offensive. Fumoto Jungi established a volunteer army of Japanese merchants in Okinawa who would gather every day to practice in Naha's Nanyokan, the first western building of its kind in Okinawa. Regardless of whether one was pro-Japanese or pro-China, the Japanese defeated the Qing and the 1895 Treaty of Shimonoseki meant that there was no chance that the Ryukyu Kingdom would ever be revived, as the Qing was compelled to even recognize the separate 'sovereignty' of Taiwan and Korea. Out of this, the *Ryukyu Shimpō* emerged as the prominent newspaper of Okinawa, and just as they had decried the pro-Qing faction during the war, the editors of the paper soon took to voicing their support for the modernization, and further Japanazation of Okinawa Prefecture.

18

BECOMING JAPANESE

The Turn towards Japanese Nationalism

In 1900 the editor-in-chief of the *Ryukyu Shimpō* newspaper, and later Mayor of Shuri, Ōta Chōfu (1865-1938) said in a speech that:

> "If we talk about the most pressing matter in Okinawa today, the (issue) is making this prefecture similar to the other [mainland] prefectures. If you'd allow me to give an extreme example, this should extend to Okinawans even sneezing the same as those in the other prefectures."[93]

Other targets of the Ryukyu Shimbun's editors scorned the practice of *Mōashibi* and traditional music in rural areas of Okinawa, which were described as "the height of barbarity".[94]

The defeat of the Qing was a fatal blow to the Restore Ryukyu movement, and it was now evident that the Qing were in no place to exert force on Japan and that Japan was now the hegemonic power in the region.

With this affirmation, the Meiji government finally ended the policy of Preserving the Old and instigated a wave of sweeping reforms across Okinawa Prefecture. The first of these was the end

---

93 *"Nihonjin" No kyōkai Okinawa, Ainu, Taiwan*, 281.
94 *"Nihonjin" No kyōkai Okinawa, Ainu, Taiwan*, 286.

BECOMING JAPANESE

of the land system that had existed under the Ryukyu Kingdom on March 5, 1896 with Okinawa Prefecture now rearranged into the five districts of Shuri, Naha, Shimajiri, Kunigami and Miyako and Yaeyama.

The next year, in March 29, 1897, the majority of the former kingdom's bureaucratic ranks were abolished, and the bureaucrats holding them in turn lost their government stipends. Following this, in 1898 conscription was introduced in Okinawa, and in 1902 for Sakishima. By 1889, private land had been recognized and national tax collection had been instigated, and from this point on any laws that were applied in Japan were also introduced to Okinawa, marking the prefectures move from a colony to a central part of Japan, at least in terms of legislation.

The Japanese victory over the Qing was also significant for increasing education attendance across the prefecture, which were the foundations for the Meiji government to build a modern Japanese state, as well as the modern Japanese citizen. Such a citizen would ideally have a shared language, culture and world view — those that had been decided by the Meiji Oligarchs. With the defeat of the Qing, even the nobles who had formed the pro-Qing faction were forced to concede, and the education rate in Okinawa shot up in this era, although it still remained the lowest in the country.

With Japan's victory, children could be seen playing soldiers and singing war songs. For boys the education rate went up by 54% following the war, for girls 17%, and by 1907 the general rate of education in Okinawa Prefecture had shot up to 93%.[95] In schools, children were taught their own history that bought all things together with their relationship to the Japanese state.

This went far back to the origins of the Ryukyu people, and stressed that since Okinawans were ethnically and historically

---

95 *"Nihonjin"* No kyōkai Okinawa, Ainu, Taiwan, 39.

THE RYUKYUS

Japanese, it was a natural course for the creation of Okinawa Prefecture. In contrast, the Ryukyu Kingdom's long history with China was treated as a variation from this norm, with the Ryukyu Disposition realigning the Ryukyu Archipelago into its rightful world place.

Before this, the Ministry of education had already published special elementary school text books for Okinawa and Hokkaido to reinforce such narratives, but 1897 saw the creation of a national elementary school textbook which meant that all Japanese children learnt the same history. The textbook stressed the same points that had been told to Ulysses S. Grant, that the Ryukyu Kingdom could trace its origins back to Minamoto no Tametomo, that the language had the same roots and that ethnically they were the same as mainland Japanese.

Although the Qing had been subjugated, this did not change Okinawa's place as the 'southern gate' of Japan, and the militaristic ethos alongside national ideas were drilled into the young of Okinawa. In April 23, 1886 a naval and military law divided Japan as a nation into five naval divisions, one of these was the Sasebo Naval District in Okinawa.[ccxxxvii]

Before even the establishment of such military posts, the militarization of Okinawa's young citizens was already well underway. In schools there were military drills which were carried out alongside school sports days.

Songs of the era also reinforced this mindset extolling the borderland areas of Japan, such as the 1885 song 'The Light of the Firefly'.[ccxxxviii] The song contains the lyrics,

> "From the Chishima Islands (Kuril Islands) to Okinawa,
> All is under the rule of Japan"[96]

---

96 *Ryūkyū, Okinawa Shi No Sekai*, 258.

emphasizing the regions that had only decades ago been formally integrated into the Japanese nation state, while also extolling Japan's young men to extend the land under Japan's rule even further still, displaying Japan's imperial ambitions which accompanied its modernization.

The lyrics of the song were ready to be changed, whenever the borders of Japan were extended further still, and after the first Sino-Japanese war and the Russo-Japanese war 'Taiwan' and 'Karafuto' (Sakhalin) were also added to the lyrics of the song.

Alongside militarization, ethnic ideas of a unified race were also important to create a new identity as loyal citizens of Japan. While the idea that the Okinawan and Japanese people were related began after the Satsuma invasion of the Ryukyu Kingdom in 1609, these ideas were originally not taken to mean that the kingdom should be absorbed into the larger Japanese state. But under the Empire of Japan, these ideas were used to justify the Disposition of Ryukyu and the development of Okinawa Prefecture.

The Okinawa Private Education Association was one such reflection of this.[ccxxxix] The organization was half government controlled and was made up of teachers who subscribed to the official line on Okinawa's future. The organization published one-hundred-and-sixteen issues of the magazine '*Ryukyu Education*' between 1895 and 1906 in which these views can be seen.[ccxl]

The writers consisted of both Okinawan and Japanese teachers, with most of the Okinawans agreeing that the indigenous language should be banned in schools, although some teachers continued to use it. In 1895, a teacher at the Okinawan Jinjōshihan School for the training of teachers wrote an article for the magazine in which he pointed out that the name 'Okinawa' had its origins in the Okinawan word for the island,

'Uchinā'. Following this logic, Okinawa had always been closer to Japan, with the islands true name Okinawa. Ryukyu was a name derived from Chinese.

The same author wrote that "The Japanese ethnicity, Japanese race, Japanese fellow countrymen and same ancestors are clearly [the same as Okinawa]."[97]

Articles in *Ryukyu Education* also referred to the Japanese language as the 'normal' or 'national' language, and articles were not just directed at the students of Okinawa, but the teachers themselves, with one article criticizing the bad pronunciation of many teachers. The same terminology applied to other things Japanese, with traditional clothes being referred to not as being Japanese but as being 'normal'.

Moves to become more Japanese were also proactively taken up by some Okinawans in school. This can be seen in the 'Dialect Tag', a thick piece of paper or wood that students had to wear if they accidentally used Okinawan instead of Japanese while at school.[ccxli] The wearing of the tag was a way of shaming the individual, and they could only exchange it once another student had accidentally uttered something that was not the standard dialect of Tokyo. There were ways of making an unsuspecting student speak quickly, which usually meant hitting them on the back of the head to make the shout out *"Aga"* ("that hurts" in Okinawan), to which they could give the tag to them.

The social anthropologist Higa Masao even recalls how the practice continued even as late as his time in middle school in the postwar era. In many cases, even this failed to remove the use of the native language. When Higa Masao was in elementary school in 1943, he used to talk Okinawan to his family, neighbors and friends on the way to school, only switching to standard

---

97 *"Nihonjin" No kyôkai Okinawa, Ainu, Taiwan*, 49.

Japanese upon entering the classroom.[ccxlii]

The Role of Women in Language Reform

The language reform movement in Okinawa was not just a top-down measure imposed by the state. As has already been seen, many Okinawan teachers themselves proactively took up the state line. This enthusiasm extended to wider Japanese society with women's organizations, parents and the students themselves taking up this role. There was ample reason for this. Japan was seen as the country of development and strength for the future, while there were also hopes that if Okinawans could become more Japanese, they could escape discrimination and stand on equal footing with their mainland counterparts.

Examples of slogans used by the women's organizations that drove this message home were "women who use dialect are coarse" and "if the [children's] words are bad, it is the fault of the mother".[98]

Kuba Tsuru the prefecture's first women teacher of Okinawan descendent first wore traditional Ryukyu clothing when she began work at an elementary school in Shuri.[ccxliii] However, by her second term in 1899, she had begun to wear Japanese clothing. This drew the ire of some local people, with comments such as "Kuba Tsuru has become a Yamato, soon she will become Dutch (a foreigner)".[99]

Kuba, who was one of the many women who led reforms in Okinawa aimed at making the populace more Japanese, was in an archetypical role. As a teacher she was in a natural position to influence the minds of the younger generation and likely saw the Japanazation of Okinawa going hand in hand with the

---

98 Chikashi Furukawa et al, *Taiwan Kankoku Okinawa De Nihongo Wa Nani o Shitanoka: Gengo Shihai No Motarasu Mono.* Sangensha, 2007, 143.
99 *Taiwan Kankoku Okinawa De Nihongo Wa Nani o Shitanoka*, 292.

prefecture's modernization.

There were also other movements that enthusiastically attempted to banish the traditional clothes of Ryukyu to the dustbin of history. Numerous women's groups encouraged the Japanese-style kimono over traditional Ryukyu clothes, and in 1942 the Ministry of Health and Welfare recommended that women wear 'standard' clothing.

Despite these calls traditional Ryukyu or Okinawan clothing remain popular in the prefecture today, and such movements failed to lead to an abandonment of Okinawan customs across the archipelago.[ccxliv]

Nevertheless this movement still gained momentum, and by the Taishō Period (1912-1926) 'patriotic' women's organizations began to spring up across Okinawa, marking an even closer alignment with the goals of the state. Traditional Okinawan names for girls also began to fall out of favor, with Okinawan names such as Nabe, Kamado and Ushi being replaced with such Japanese names as Hanako, Naeko and Setsuko.

Colonial Subjects

Yet no matter how hard individuals within Okinawa endeavored to reform the customs of their brothers and sisters, Okinawans themselves were usually held at arm's length by mainland Japanese.

This colonial aspect sometimes came to the fore. Of particular alarm to those within the prefecture who supported this Japanazation was the 1903 Fifth National Industrial Exhibition held in Osaka, which showcased not only the industrial developments of the age but also Japan's new colonial endeavors. What infuriated some Okinawan commentators was the living anthropological exhibition which featured different peoples from inside and outside Japan's territories, including Taiwanese aboriginal peoples, Ainu and as far as Zanzibar.

The Ryukyu Shimpō bemoaned how the people of Okinawa were mixed in with such people, when they after all were the same as the mainlanders, and there was no one from Tokyo on display. Of particular resentment was the association of Okinawans with Ainu and aboriginals of Taiwan. Both were, like Okinawa, recent colonies, and as in Okinawa these indigenous people were ruled over by the Japanese and such a comparison hit too close to home for many.

What followed was a prefecture-wide protest movement, leading to the eventual removal of Okinawans from the exhibition. Such an incident provided all the more impetus for those who believed in the cause to throw away the customs of old.

Iha Fuyu's Education Experience

While a section of the population was pro-Japanese, such reforms were not always welcomed, and this can particularly be seen in the school experience of Iha Fūyu. While Iha's grandfather and father resented the new regime, his mother understood that such an education was necessary for the young Iha to make his way in this new world, and thanks to her he managed to be enrolled in an elementary school attached to a teacher's school in Naha. Iha reflects that:

> "My mother realized that if she left me as I was it wouldn't be good for my future and decided to send me to school. My father didn't really agree but my mother made the decision."[100]

---

100 "私の子供時分"

By March 29, 1896 Iha had been enrolled. Iha's family were lucky to find a place, and it was thanks to his mother who seized the following opportunity:

> "Fortunately, around that time, the superintendent Togawa of the elementary school came to us to rent a room, my mother grabbed him and made a deal with him, that would allow me to be admitted to the school if he was allowed to rent the room. Togawa soon accepted the application and two or three days later came over to move. I was at last going to elementary school at the age of eleven."[101]

Those living in the early years of Okinawa Prefecture had more to overcome than just the gap between the archipelago and the Japanese mainland. There were significant cultural differences within the prefecture itself. These differences were not just the result of isolated islands separated by miles of ocean, such as Okinawa and Miyako, but also within Okinawa itself.

Both Shuri and Naha spoke different dialects, making it obvious from where each one hailed, despite being parts of the same city of Naha today. This difference was soon to become apparent to the young Iha, and in his memoirs about his childhood, he recalls how "the way the students spoke and customs differed to Naha", and how "the distance between [Naha and Shuri] was a mere [two and a half miles] but to people of the time it was thought of as if one had been sent to Tokyo".[102]

Iha spent only one to two months at the school in Naha, before the decision was made that the instructor school was to be moved to Shuri. The elementary school in Naha was divided up.

---

101 "私の子供時分"
102 "私の子供時分"

BECOMING JAPANESE

Students of the Naha school were sent to other schools throughout Okinawa, with Superintendent Togawa recommending Iha for Shuri.

It was in Shuri that Iha first noticed the differences between those from Naha and Shuri:

> "At that time, the old hierarchical system still remained, and the children of nobles looked down on those of commoners. I couldn't stand entering such a place as an outsider. They were always making fun of me calling me a Nāfā-Jin (person from Naha)."[103]

However, Iha soon adapted. He realized that one Naha student who had been at the school for a year longer than him was already talking with the Shuri accent, and that it was practically impossible to tell him apart. Iha soon followed suit. Iha also reflected that while the Ryukyu Kingdom may have been abolished, even the divisions from the time of the Three Kingdoms remained in the hearts of Okinawans.

For being different, Iha was bullied when he first moved to Shuri and longed to return to Naha. When he was able to go back to Naha for the weekends he recalls how "...my friends would come to visit me and I rejoiced in telling them about my life in Shuri. But sometimes they would hear a strange rhythm in my way of speaking and they would laugh."[104]

At the school in Shuri, Iha's teacher was from mainland Japan and he spoke to the students of things that he believed were necessary reforms in Okinawan society, the hairstyles, the tattoos of women, early marriage of girls, the education of women, and the language.

---

103 "私の子供時分"
104 "私の子供時分"

THE RYUKYUS

After finishing five years of elementary school, in April 1891 Iha moved on to middle school where, "I was able to make friends with students from Naha. I recall that the students who were in their second year and above mostly had their haircut short."[105] Iha's observation was that many of the middle school students had their hair cut short, a common trend in Meiji Japan in which many western fashions became the norm.

A small incident in Iha's life captures the battle within Okinawa between ideas of preserving the glorious past of the Ryukyu Kingdom, and the modernization and westernization under the modern nation state.

"One day after first period had finished the teachers suddenly stood in the doorway. I sensed something unsettling, and the head teacher barged in, stepped onto the podium and began lecturing. While I can't remember what he said, I remember being shown the photographs of American Indians students who all had short hair and western clothes. The gist of the speech was that regrettably in the Empire of Japan's schools there were still students with slovenly hair and that those students should get a haircut or better they drop out of school."[106]

But the grumblings of the headmaster were met with a very different response from the children, many of whom were, like Iha, from formally noble backgrounds.

> "All the students went pale, one or two stubborn students kowtowed and managed to leave saying they would consult their guardians. After a short while a number of hairdressers appeared. In a moment, the teachers and older students intruded into the classroom and went around cutting off *Chonmage*

---

105 "私の子供時分"
106 "私の子供時分"

(top-knot) wherever they could find them.[ccxlv] During this confusion there were some students who jumped out the window and ran away. One student who had come from Miyako refused. One teacher tried to cut off his *Chonmage* by force, but he took out his *Kanzashi* hairpin and using it as a weapon resisted. I could hear crying children all around me. After about one or two hours, not one *Chonmage* could be seen throughout the school."[107]

Iha himself would take part in challenging the top-down orders coming from the prefectural office during his middle school years. The cause of this disturbance was in the summer of 1895, when the Okinawan Prefectural Jinjō Middle School the decision was made to drop English from the curriculum.

This event happened during the start of the first Sino-Japanese war, during a time in which Iha and other middle school students were made to partake in shooting practice while at school, alongside the general militarization of Okinawa during this period. The removal of English from the curriculum led to a backlash by the students, with Iha emerging as one of the leaders of the movement, in which the students submitted an appeal to resign, and then going on strike from November of 1895.

The principal of the school was Kodama Kihachi. This Kagoshima native was also the head of Education at the Okinawan Prefectural Office, and he could not allow for these young Okinawan upstarts to question such decisions. Kodama had been considering the removal of the English language from the curriculum before this, commenting the previous year that "You all can't even speak the standard language yet, to make you

---

107 "私の子供時分"

learn English would be an unfortunate situation."[108]

The strike itself went on for about six months, with Kodama eventually being transferred to Taiwan due to the incident in 1896. Iha and the other leaders of the strike were subsequently dismissed from the school. The strike had at least helped the students get over regional identities within Okinawa, and brought them to work together to campaign as one people.

The success led Iha to briefly consider becoming a politician, before deciding he did not have the stomach for it. In 1897, Iha went on to study at a high school in Tokyo, and then onto Tokyo Imperial University. During this time in Tokyo, Iha alongside other Okinawans laid the foundations for Okinawan Studies.

Going into the 20th Century, there were increasing movements led by both Okinawans and Japanese that sought to place an increased value in the indigenous culture of the Ryukyu Archipelago. Such movements occurred in tandem with those who viewed the best course for the people of these islands to become as Japanese as possible. But there is was also a parallel history alongside this, of the tens of thousands of Okinawans who emigrated abroad, beginning in the Meiji period and continuing up to the 1940s.

---

108 "Nihonjin" No kyôkai Okinawa, Ainu, Taiwan, 289.

19

ACROSS THE WAVES—OKINAWAN IMMIGRANTS

Okinawans Around the World

Every few years there is a grand parade down Kokusai Dōri, the main street of Naha with over 5,000 people of Okinawan descent from twenty countries marching down the streets. If you happen to attend, you can see flags from South America, Asia, and to a lesser extent North America and Europe. People hold signs in Spanish, Portuguese, French, Japanese and English to name a few, and chatter to each other in all these languages. While they may come from all corners of the world, these people are united by their Okinawan heritage and their signs proudly proclaim so.

It was Okinawa's unsteady position after the Disposition of Ryukyu that was one of the main push factors that prompted many Okinawans to seek a better life for themselves overseas. Some had the intention of starting a whole new life abroad, while others had plans to return richer to Okinawa. Most of this emigration (72,134 people) took place between 1899 and 1938, the very same years the newly born Okinawa Prefecture was going through tumultuous change while a further 17,726 went abroad to South America between 1953 and 1993.[109] Much of the latter emigration was encouraged by the US authorities who sought to

---

109 沖縄県, "沖縄と移民の歴史"

address a shortage of land caused by the proliferation of military bases after the Battle of Okinawa.

Okinawan Emigrants between 1899 and 1938[110]

Country	Migrant Numbers
Hawaii	19,507
US Mainland	803
Canada	403
Mexico	764
Cuba	131
Peru	11,311
Brazil	14,829
Argentina	2,754
Bolivia	37
The Philippines	16,426
Other	5,187
Total	**72,134**

This final section will examine how and why Okinawans migrated to all corners of the world, far from their island home. Both these chapters are quite statistically heavy, a necessity to understand the extent of this migration. This might at times be a bit dry, but in later chapters we will look at the more personal experience of what it was like to live in what would have been completely different worlds for these Okinawan pioneers.

Following the creation of Okinawa Prefecture, migration

---

110   沖縄県,"沖縄と移民の歴史"

overseas reached such an extent that by 1940, 9.9% of Okinawan Prefecture's population had gone overseas, one in ten Okinawans.[111] Compared to other Japanese prefectures that had high levels of immigration over this same period, the immigration level of Okinawa was well above second place Kumamoto Prefecture (4.78%) and Hiroshima Prefecture (3.88%).[112] As of 2016, Okinawa Prefecture has estimated that there are around 415,361 people of Okinawan descent around the world, an increase of near double from around 270,000 in 1990.[113]

While this parallel history takes us away from the islands themselves, it is a direct result of the situation within Okinawa. Emigration began only a few decades after the Disposition of Ryukyu and within just a few decades of the establishment of Okinawa Prefecture. Within this small space of time, Okinawans migrated all around the world to other parts of Asia, Oceania, and North and South America. More than half of all these migrants had gone to Hawaii and the Philippines in particular as of 1938.

Okinawan migrants followed patterns of emigration that were already established by mainland Japanese, and in most cases Okinawans emigrating abroad followed their mainland contemporaries. In Hawaii, immigration opened to Okinawans in 1899, and by this time there were already over 10,000 mainland Japanese in Hawaii.[114] By 1924, 16,536 Okinawans and their descendants were recorded as living there by the Japanese consulate in Honolulu. By the mid-1920s Okinawans constituted about 13% of the total Japanese population in Hawaii.[115] By the outbreak of the Pacific War these Japanese citizens, both from the

---

111 Takeshi Miki. *Kuhaku No Iminshi: Nyūkaredonia to Okinawa*. Shinema Okinawa, 2017, 117.
112 *Kūhaku No Iminshi: Nyūkaredonia*, 177.
113 "海外の沖縄県系人、約41万5千人 県が5年ぶり推計:5年に一度の祭典「世界のウチナーンチュ大会」特集."
114 Munehiro Machida et, *Yakudō Suru Okinawakei Imin: Burajiru Hawai o Chūshin Ni*. Sairyūsha, 2013, 256.
115 *Okinawa Ken Shi Kakuhen Ron 8 Joseishi*, 218.

mainland and Okinawa and their descendants constituted 44% of the islands' population.[116]

Emigration to the Philippines began in 1904, and the number of Okinawans choosing to move there dramatically increased following the success of the early pioneers, alongside the 1920s closure of Hawaii with the passing of the Immigration Act of 1924, which banned migration from Asia to the United States.

In the same year that migration to the Philippines began, the first Okinawan migrants left for Mexico, although the numbers were comparatively low.[ccxlvi] A year after this, in 1905, some Okinawans left for the French Territory of New Caledonia. In New Caledonia today there are about 8,000 people of Japanese descent, of whom more than half came before the Pacific War, and of this 20% are of Okinawan descent.[117]

The early 20th Century also saw large numbers of Okinawan migrants to South America, beginning in 1906 for Peru, 1908 for Brazil and 1913 for Argentina. In Brazil the numbers were particularly large, with 4,342 Okinawan immigrants coming to Brazil in 1917 and 1918 alone.[118]

The expanding Japanese Empire also provided a new frontier closer to home, with Japan became a possibility after the creation of Okinawa Prefecture, and Taiwan in 1896.[ccxlvii] With the Japanese acquisition of the former German territories in the Pacific in 1919, large-scale immigration offered opportunities in what was now the South Seas Mandate, consisting of Palau, the Northern Marina Islands, the Marshall Islands and Micronesia.

By 1939, out of 77,000 Japanese citizens in the South Seas Mandate, about 46,000 were Okinawan, with the prefecture making up 60% of all immigrants to the South Seas Mandate.[119]

---

116 *Yakudō Suru Okinawakei Imin*, 255.
117 "The New Caledonia Weekly, 22-29 August 2008."
118 *Yakudō Suru Okinawakei Imin*, 266.
119 *Okinawa Ken Shi Kakuhen Ron 8 Joseishi*, 240.

ACROSS THE WAVES—OKINAWAN IMMIGRANTS

The communities of Okinawan immigrants scattered throughout the globe became a large source of finance for Okinawa, with immigrants at times contributing as much as 60% of the prefecture's revenues.[120] The descendants of many of these Okinawan migrants continue to live in these countries today, and the preservation, continuation and maintenance of these links creates a vast network that has its origins in these relatively small islands.

Why did so many Okinawans move abroad? One of the main drivers was financial, and many moved with dreams of escaping poverty and carving out a better life for themselves and their families.

The Geographer Ishikawa Tomonori has also provided a romantic notion alongside this more practical aspect, saying that since Okinawans already had a legacy of seafaring going back to the days of the Ryukyu Kingdom, going abroad was an extension of their maritime past. Torigoe Hiroyuki has also highlighted the unease that accompanied the fall of the Ryukyu Kingdom, coupled with a freedom from the restraints that had burdened the common people of Okinawa under the kingdom's rigid class system.

Of course, on an individual level each had their own personal reasons for leaving. Ishikawa further elaborates:

> "It can certainly be said that there were economic motives for the many overseas immigrants overseas that came from Okinawa Prefecture. However, other than these economic factors there were numerous social motivators, the abolition of the [old] land system and shift to the new...the presence of

---

120 "土地と移民."

middlemen and leaders of immigration, avoiding the draft etc., there were also more than a few cases where people had personal motivations for going abroad."[121]

This shift from the old land system under the Ryukyu Kingdom occurred between 1899 and 1903. Under the kingdom, it was only the noble class that was permitted to own land, while the common people would be permitted to work on the land, the yields of their labor also going towards paying taxes.

With the ending of 'Preserving the Old' system followed by the Meiji government up to 1903, this system was at last brought to a close. In its place, private ownership of land was permitted, and while this at face value appeared to better the lot of Okinawan's common people, the numerous new taxes made it unfeasible for many to keep land, with some selling what land they had to be able to pay for their passage overseas.

Why Hawaii?
Today Hawaii has the highest percentage of people of Okinawan descent outside the prefecture and it was the particular historical circumstances of these islands that led to Hawaii becoming such a gateway for immigrants from Japan. The Kingdom of Hawaii (1795–1893) came into being after Captain James Cook (1728–1779) and his crew visited the islands in 1778. It was thanks to weapons that the British brought that Kamehameha (1782–1819), the first Hawaiian king, was able to unify the islands in 1795.

This European contact proved to be devastating for the indigenous people and by 1840 infectious diseases had wiped out 84% of the population.[122] This decline presented opportunities to

---

121 *Kuhaku No Iminshi*, 117.
122 "ハワイ王国最後の「悲劇の女王」、リリウオカラニの物語."

missionaries and capitalists in the United States who increasingly bought up cheap land. With this, a plantation boom began that used cheap labor from East Asia to raise tons of sugar for export, and by 1874 the sugar exported annually to the US from Hawaiian plantations reached 10,000 tons.[123]

The US also coveted Hawaii due to its strategic position in the middle of the Pacific, and to put pressure on the island kingdom, heavy tariffs were imposed which had a devastating effect on the economy.

In 1874 Kalākaua (1836—1891) who would be the last king of Hawaii, ascended the throne and the following year, he signed a treaty with the US that seceded Pearl Harbor on Oahu and a small island now known as Ford Island, in return for the kingdom being once more allowed to freely export sugar to the US.

Kalākaua also opened up the kingdom to Japanese immigrants after a world tour in 1881 during which he discussed with the Meiji Emperor in Japan about opening the country to Japanese immigration.

Hawaii then was one of the first places migration became possible for Japanese citizens in the Meiji era, but it would not be until almost twenty years later, at the dawn of the 20th century that Okinawans began to venture to these shores. This was thanks to efforts by the 'Father of Okinawan Emigration' Tōyama Kyūzo (1868-1910) who first championed migration to Hawaii. It was under his leadership that the first Okinawan migrants left for Hawaii in December 3, 1899.

These first 26 people, like many of those who would emigrate after, were contracted migrants who had agreed to undertake stipulated work for a number of years.[124] The first generation of Okinawans in Hawaii were almost all laborers on the sugar

---

123 "ハワイ王国最後の「悲劇の女王」、リリウオカラニの物語."
124 *Ryūkyūkoku No metsubō to Hawai Imin*, 92.

plantations of Oahu. From Naha, they arrived in Yokohama where they boarded another ship, arriving at Honolulu in January 8, 1900 at the dawn of a new century. While Tōyama pioneered the first Okinawan passage to Hawaii, this was part of a wider People's Rights Movement led by his friend Jahana Noboru (1865—1908).

Jahana had small circular glasses and short hair, and was one of the few Okinawans working in the Okinawan Prefectural Government; most of his colleagues are from Kagoshima. While education in Okinawa was mostly for the sons of former nobles, with his diligence and hard work Jahana successfully graduated from Tokyo Imperial University with a degree in Agriculture. This had not been an obvious path for a rustic boy such as he, and Jahana's father warned his son that "peasants have no need for scholarship". But this did not deter a young Jahana as he snuck away to listen to the teachers from outside the classroom.

His mother took pity on him and eventually succeed in persuading the father to allow Jahana to go to school.

At the age of 17 he moved on to the Okinawa Instructor School, where his classmates were mostly the sons of nobles. These boys were irritated that a peasant could even make it into the school and frequently chided him as a "country bumpkin". In 1882 Jahana's brilliance was realized and he was chosen as one of the few students who would go on to study in the imperial capital of Tokyo.

Such a chance was only possible because of reforms under Governor Uesugi Mochinori (1884-1919) who had changed the education system so that those who were not from a noble background, commoners such as Jahana could attend high education in Okinawa. Jahan completed his studies at Tokyo Imperial University and became the first graduate from Okinawa Prefecture.

Jahana was a role model for what Okinawans could become if they endeavored to modernize and adapt Japanese ways.

Yet when Jahana began working in the Prefectural Office it became evident that he was not content to only follow orders. Jahana derided many of Governor Narahara's policies which he believed were making the life of Okinawa's poorest only more difficult.

Of particular alarm was Narahara's decision to open the former *Soma-Yama* of the Ryukyu Kingdom. The *Soma-Yama* were forested areas that had been set aside to protect the land from rampant deforestation.[ccxlviii] Under the Ryukyu Kingdom only designated lumberjacks were permitted to chop down trees in the *Soma-Yama* thus preserving the ecology and resources of the kingdom. However, towards the end of the Ryukyu Kingdom the *Soma-Yama* were increasingly the target of illegal logging and Narahara saw the *Soma-Yama* as resources ripe for development by former nobles who had lost their stipends from the kingdom.

On one occasion, Jahana visited one of these *Soma-Yama* that had been given to nobles in Motobu during his official duties. He is aghast to see that the nobles who had been given the land were already receiving payments from the government, this land was not helping most of the former noble class, let alone the people of Okinawa who also depended on this land.

Narahara was not entirely malicious, he had sympathized with the poll tax imposed on the people of Sakishima and had moved to abolish this, but to Jahana he was out of touch with the masses of Okinawa and this set him on a path for collision with the most powerful man in the prefecture.

Despite his misgivings, Jahana continues to work within the Kagoshima-dominated government. In 1897, Narahara made plans to sell government land to private buyers, a precedent that had already been set in Japan.

While the government had owned this land, the common people had been able to make use of water, materials for building and fuel there. With the sale of this land these privileges were removed, sparking a backlash that could be seen across Japan, even in Kagoshima Prefecture, where Narahara hailed from.

In Okinawa this privatization destroyed agriculture for many, forcing them to move to wage-labor. Trees sold to Taiwan to build a railway meant that fields became all the more vulnerable from typhoons and with wooden building materials in short supply the only choice left was to buy them. The common people of Okinawa did not have large reserves of cash, making building all the more difficult. Many agricultural villages went bankrupt during these reforms, and when Jahana refused to carry out orders, he was sacked from his role in the Prefectural Office.

Despite overcoming the challenges of his common background and being an Okinawan, Jahana accepted his fate and in 1898 left for Tokyo.

It was in Tokyo that Jahana met other like-minded Okinawans, such as Tōyama and together they founded the Okinawa Club.[ccxlix] The Okinawa Club aimed to increase the betterment of Okinawans, political inclusion, the financing of agriculture and reforms to the political system, a Freedom and People's Rights Movement for Okinawa to bring equality to the people.

One solution for the betterment of the people was stumbled upon almost by chance by Tōyama. One day he enters an old bookshop, and as he leafed through the volumes of all sorts of colors and sizes, he discovered a work on Japanese migration to Hawaii.

The first Japanese to leave for Hawaii had left four months before the Meiji restoration, 149 individuals who went on three-year contracts. The Meiji government continued this, making an agreement with the government of Hawaii in 1885 (not yet part of the United States) for regular migration. Some of these pioneers stayed in Hawaii, others crossed over to the mainland US, and others still returned to Japan. In the first ten years of this system, about half of all Japanese laborers in Hawaii eventually returned to Japan on the completion of their contracts.[125]

Both Jahan and Tōyama attempted to put the ideas of the Okinawa Club into practice, securing a better life for the poor masses. But the movement met with resistance from Governor Narahara, and Jahana became increasingly frustrated. By 1901, Jahana secured a job in the government of Yamaguchi Prefecture, but while on the train he was overcome with a sudden nausea. He stumbled out at Kobe station, and took refuge in a friend's house. Jahana's spirit had been crushed and his attempts to better the people of Okinawa had failed. He quietly returned to Okinawa and spent the next seven years there until he passed away in 1911 at the age of only forty-four. In the same year Jahana died, the governor he had worked so hard to remove from office concluded his term, an ironic coincidence of fate.

A year before Jahana's passing, Tōyama was making progress with his dreams of freeing the people of their poverty through migration. Like Jahana, he was captivated with the stories of the abundant resources that could be found in America and Hawaii. Tōyama had even taken the bold move of talking to the Kumamoto Immigration Company about the prospect of Okinawan migration to Hawaii.[ccl] However, there remained a problem: permission from the governor was necessary and Narahara flatly turned down the proposition. Unlike Japan, Okinawa was not ready for emigration. But pressure from the Okinawan Civil Rights Movement eventually led to Narahara changing his mind, and in 1900 the first Okinawan migrants left

---

125 *Yakudō Suru Okinawakei Imin*, 255.

THE RYUKYUS

for Hawaii under the lead of Tōyama.

Both Jahana and Tōyama were titans of a movement that championed a better life for the people of Okinawa. In the town of Yaese there stands a bronze statue of Jahana on a limestone podium. He has one hand in the pockets of his long suit jacket, a bow tie and his characteristic oval glasses as he looks out over the people of Okinawa.[ccli]

Likewise, in Kin stands a statue of Tōyama. He stands with his arm outstretched pointing across the waves to the prospect of a more prosperous life.

The First Immigrants to Hawaii

In terms of sheer numbers, Okinawa Prefecture by no means stood out in terms of immigrants to Hawaii. That distinction goes to Hiroshima with around 72,000 by 1940, while Okinawa had around 57,000, in third place after Kumamoto Prefecture.[126] However, taken as a percentage of population, Okinawa was by far the highest with 9.97% of the population migrating overseas in those years, about one in ten Okinawans. Hiroshima on the other hand was only 3.88%.[127]

Thanks to Tōyama, the first twenty-six Okinawans took up work on Hawaii's sugar plantations. Most of these immigrants were men who found themselves among a large number of Portuguese, Chinese, Philippine, Korean and Japanese immigrants.

Since the Okinawans did not understand the language, they were dubbed as '*Pake*' the Hawaiian word for Chinese person, and often they were referred to as '*Japan Pake*'. The second wave of migrants came in 1903, with 41 Okinawans moving to Hawaii. The second wave of migrants had the advantage of being able

---
126 *Ryūkyūkoku No metsubō to Hawai Imin*, 15.
127 *Ryūkyūkoku No metsubō to Hawai Imin*, 15.

ACROSS THE WAVES—OKINAWAN IMMIGRANTS

to gain the assistance of relatives who had already migrated to Hawaii, and these immigrants became known as *'Yobiyose Imin'*, or 'called-over immigrants'.

Such immigration was possible until 1924, the year the US decided to ban Japanese immigration. Anti-Asian sentiment in the US had been building since the arrival of Chinese to work on the railroads and in mines in the mid-19th Century, and Japan's victory of Russia in the Russo-Japanese war only accelerated delusions that the 'yellow' race would take over what was seen as a 'homogeneous' white America. Valentine S. McClatchy in a Sacramento newspaper claimed that the Japanese were 'unassimilable' and 'dangerous as residents', while the *American Defender* decried them:

> "Whenever the Japanese have settled, their nests pollute the communities like he running sores of leprosy. They exist like the yellow, smoldering discarded butts in an over-full ash tray vilifying the air with their loathsome smells, filling all who have misfortune to look upon them with a wholesome disgust and a desire to wash."[128]

Despite such bans, this did not mean the end of Okinawans in Hawaii. There would still be a new generation, a second generation born to Okinawan parents in Hawaii.

Higa Seitoku (born 1891), who was seventeen at the time, was one of the first migrants to Hawaii. Higa had been born in Nakagusuku and knew of people from his village who had already gone over to Hawaii. He left with a group arranged by Tōyama, although he never directly talked to him. Like those

---
128 Paul R. Spickard, Japanese Americans: the Formation and Transformations of an Ethnic Group (Rutgers University Press, 2009), 63.

before, Higa first boarded a ship to Naha to Yokohama. In this bustling port city, there was a medical inspection before the boat departed across the Pacific for Oahu in Honolulu.

In Honolulu, Higa stayed at the Komeda Hotel, one of the Japanese-run establishments where guests normally slept ten a room on mats. In those days, the boat entered Honolulu Harbor and docked not far from River Street near an immigration bureau in today Hawaii's Chinatown. Higa began his life in Hawaii toiling in the sugar fields where he works for twenty years. For the Okinawan immigrants, plantation work in Hawaii was similar to Okinawa where the main crops were also sugar cane and potatos.

For the Okinawans who decided to make Hawaii their home, many became prosperous over the years. By 1915 some immigrants could afford to buy a Ford automobile for about $4,000.[129] A shift away from plantations to other jobs, such as owning restaurants, hotels or pig farming also occurred over time. In 1921, only 125 Okinawans were recorded as residents of the big city, Honolulu, with the majority working in plantations in the countryside. However, by 1929 the number in Honolulu had risen to 989, and by 1944 to around 3,000.[130]

Taiwan and Japan 'internal immigration'

Immigration throughout Asia was also prominent at the end of the nineteenth century. With Taiwan becoming a Japanese territory following the 1869 Treaty of Shimonoseki, the door opened for Okinawans to migrate further south.

Unlike the Americas, Taiwan being a part of the Japanese Empire made it feel like a more permanent place to migrate to,

---

129 *Ryūkyūkoku No metsubō to Hawai Imin*, 124.
130 'Documents Concerning Psychological Warfare in the Battle of Okinawas' cited in 『沖縄県史 資料編2 THE OKINAWANS OF THE LOO CHOO ISLANDS, etc.』沖縄県立図書館史料編集室 1996, 91.

rather than just making money abroad and returning home, as was the intention of many who went to Hawaii.

Taiwan was also seen as more cosmopolitan. This was particular true for Okinawans from Sakishima, who despite being part of Okinawa Prefecture were closer to Taipei than Naha. Taiwan had numerous middle schools, high schools to which one could send one's children, and double the number of schools by the 1930s.[131] There was even a university from 1928, an institution that would not appear in Okinawa until after the Battle of Okinawa.

Japan, in particular the Kansai region, was also a prominent place for Okinawans to work. In 1883, the Osaka Bōseki a spinning company was established with the first steam powered loom introduced to the country.[cclii] A mere three years after this, an electric version was introduced and numerous spinning companies soon followed, to such an extent that 40% of such companies could be found in Osaka, the 'Manchester of the Orient.'[132]

Osaka's booming industry led to people from the surrounding countryside moving to the big city, and in the 1920s Okinawan immigration to Kansai took off at times as high as 20,000 per year.[133] Okinawan communities sprung up throughout Osaka such as in Taishō Ward. As of 2011, out of the ward's 70,000, residents one in four was of Okinawan descent.[134] If one takes a walk there today, you will see Okinawan food shops, Karate Dōjōs and training halls for Ryukyu dance. There is even the Kansai Okinawa Library with more than 8,000 books on Okinawa.[ccliii]

Taishō Ward was not the only area with a high number

---

131 *Okinawa Ken Shi Kakuhen Ron 8 Joseishi*, 247.
132 *Okinawa Ken Shi Kakuhen Ron 8 Joseishi*, 105.
133 Mitsuaki Ono, *Okinawa Toso No Jidai 1960/70: Bundan o Norikoeru Shiso to Jissen* (Jimbunshoin, 2014), 105.
134 "大阪にリトル沖縄、誕生の理由住民4分の1が出身者."

of Okinawan immigrants, there was also Minato Ward and Nishinari Ward. And Okinawan immigration was not limited to Osaka or Kobe in Kansai. In the vast industrial metropolis stretching from Tokyo's Ota Ward, through Kawasaki and into northern Yokohama, tens of thousands of Okinawans moved to work in Japan's industrial core. As with Osaka, these numbers took off during the 1920s.[ccliv]

While a better of standard of living was a pull factor, the economic situation back in Okinawa left many with little choice but to migrate. By the late 1880s, Okinawa's economy had become increasingly tied to sugar with many farmers turning towards the cash crop.

The value of sugar was heavily tied to international markets, to the point that it was more profitable to grow sugar and used the proceeds to buy rice than to grow such crops domestically. In the short term, this was beneficial to Okinawa, but if global markets suddenly had less need for sugar, then the people of Okinawa would quickly fall into poverty.

Such an event occurred after the First World War, when an oversupply of sugar in the market caused prices to collapse, pushing many Okinawans into starvation. The problems this caused were evident to those even in the mainland. One reporter visiting Okinawa for a Tokyo newspaper wrote about how he saw barefoot villagers, derelict houses on the brink of collapse, people drinking rainwater, and rampant prostitution.

With a lack of food, people resorted to eating starch from palm trees. This could be dangerous as, if not processed correctly, it would lead to an agonizing death due to naturally occurring cyanide. With Okinawa's suffering frequently reported in the mainland press, it was not long before the phrase 'Palm Tree Hell' began to symbolize the difficulties the people were facing.

Immigration to Japan's industrializing cores was one way

to escape Palm Tree Hell, and there was a boom of Okinawan migrants to the mainland. In 1910 a regular ship between Naha and Osaka left only ten times a month, but by 1920 the frequency had almost doubled to eighteen times as more and more people left.[135]

The Philippines

Further than Taiwan and mainland Japan but closer than Hawaii, the Philippines also became one of the destinations for Okinawans seeking a higher quality of life. In 1898 the US defeated the Spanish, ending the Spanish-American war and bringing the Philippines under American influence. The Philippines first became a US territory following the December 10, 1898 Treaty of Paris which saw Spain secede the territory.

However, due to local resistance, it was not until July of 1901 that this collection of islands was placed under the Philippines Commission, US military government rule.

An opportunity for Okinawans to come to the Philippines opened in 1903 with the beginning of the Benguet Road (now Kennon Road). This project was to be a sign of modernization of the Philippines with the construction of a serpentine road that would cut through the mountains and forests from the lowland town of Baguio to Rosario in La Union, and the American road chief recruited 4,000 men from 46 nationalities for the project.[136]

The pioneer of Okinawan immigration to the Philippines was Ōshiro Kōzō (1881–1935), a student of Tōyama's when he was a teacher at the elementary school in Kin, who was captivated in his teens by Tōyama's ideals of solving Okinawa's poverty through migration. On 20 February, 1904 Ōshiro left on a boat

---

135 *Okinawa Ken Shi Kakuhen Ron 8 Joseishi*, 260.
136 Rebecca Tinio McKenna, *American Imperial Pastoral: the Architecture of US Colonialism in the Philippines* (The University of Chicago Press, 2017), 50.

from Kobe for Manila as Okinawa's first Immigration Supervisor to the Philippines. At the time he was only twenty-three and still only part way through his studies as an agriculturalist at Tokyo Imperial University.

He was followed in April of the same year by a further 111 Okinawans.[137] After grueling days of work building the Benguet Road, the majority of the Okinawans moved to Davao on the island of Mindanao, the most southern of the Philippines large islands. In Davao, Ōshiro together with Ōta Kyōsaburō from Hyogo Prefecture founded Ōta Industries which oversaw the development of Abacá (a species of banana) plantations which could be spun into Manila hemp.[cclv] While working as the vice-president of the company, Ōshiro continued to call Okinawans over for a better life in the Philippines, and his contributions to developing the city of Davao have led to his name still being featured on the map with part of the east of the city called 'Bago Oshiro' after the him.

Ōshiro was not just a central figure for Okinawans in the Philippines but for all Japanese. In 1916, he founded the Okinawa Davao Association, then broadening this to found the Davao Japanese Association in 1918.[cclvi] Like his mentor Tōyama, he is commemorated in Okinawa today with a statue in his home town of Kin 'the Father of Philippine immigration.

It was in the capital that Okinawans really began to find a place for themselves in Philippine society. Manila was seen a modern city, miles ahead of Naha back home. Immigrants to Manila could find flushing toilets and refrigerators, there were cinemas showing the latest Japanese films only a few months after their release back home and department stores with names such as 'Osaka Bazaar' and 'Kobe Bazaar' which sold products

---

[137] "移民人物伝 2." 琉球文化アーカイブ

ACROSS THE WAVES—OKINAWAN IMMIGRANTS

from Japan. To many Okinawans, the Philippines felt like a blend of the modern parts of both America and Japan. In comparison, contemporary Okinawa seemed backwards. Outside of Naha, the common diet was potatoes rather than rice, and for water, one had to share a well as a common source and most toilets were outdoors next to pigsties. Many of the Okinawans who left for the Philippines did so to make a better life for themselves, and by 1904 there were 19,288 Japanese in the country, with 9,899 of these from Okinawa, making them close to half of all migrants from Japan.[138] Those bound for the Philippines would first go to Kagoshima, and stop over in Nagasaki before spending twenty days on the crossing to the Philippines.

Okinawans also migrated further still, past Hawaii all the way to the Americas. The majority of this migration was to Latin America, with some going to Mexico, but far more headed further south to Peru, Argentina and Brazil. These Okinawan pioneers boarded boats to this vast continent of extremes. While the Ryukyu Archipelago is a treasure trove of biodiversity, it is geographically tiny. In South America, these immigrants would be on the continent of the world's largest river, the Amazon, and also featuring vast deserts such as the world's driest, the Atacama Desert, and the world's longest mountain range, the Andes.

The legacy of this Okinawa in Latin America can still be felt today. The Okinawan historian Yamazatu Junichi was able to confirm multiple *Ishigantō* in São Paulo all erected by first generation immigrants that still stand in the city today.

This Okinawan presence in Latin America is not confined to the past, and is very much alive today. In Okinawan societies

---

138 Okuno Shūji, Natsuko: Okinawa Mitsubōeki no Joō (Bungei Shunjū, 2007), 115.

in Brazil, the Okinawan language continues to be spoken, there are language classes for the younger generation and the musical traditions of the Sanshin and Eisa dance continue to be popular. Many of those of Okinawan descent continue to eat *Iricha*, a fried pork dish, and some continue to leave offerings in their homes for the Okinawan god of fire, Hinukan, together with pictures of the Virgin Mary.

Okinawans also moved across the Pacific throughout the islands of both Micronesia (Marshall Islands, Guam and Saipan) and Melanesia (New Caledonia and Fiji). However, most Okinawans throughout Micronesia and Melanesia were forcibly returned to Japan at the end of WWII.

In New Caledonia, the Okinawan men tended to marry local French or indigenous Kanak wives, while in Australia they were forced into internment camps during the war. Many were forcibly repatriated back to Okinawa afterwards, but those who stayed and their descendants continue to be proud of their Okinawan heritage. In 2011 the Okinawan community in New Caledonia opened the Maison de Okinawa, featuring an exhibition hall about the Okinawan migrants to New Caledonia and their descendants. During the opening ceremony, a traditional Kanak dance was performed, a sign of the links with the indigenous people of New Caledonia.

South America
South America was one of the focal points of Okinawan migration. This first began with Peru in 1906, followed by Brazil in at least 1908 and Argentina in 1913.

It was on August 29, 1906 that the Ryukyu Shimpō newspaper first placed an advert calling for 'urgent applications' for immigration to Peru. Like many of the places Okinawan's immigrated to, the early conditions were for contract laborers but by 1923 Peru had scrapped this system allowing for free immigration. Like Hawaii, common work for Okinawans in Peru was on sugar plantations.

For South America's largest nation, Brazil, there is less certainty about when the first Okinawans immigrated to South America's largest nation. However, it is known that on March 10, 1908 an article appeared in the Ryukyu Shimpō which contained a dialogue with an agent of the Imperial Colony Company talking about immigration to Brazil.[cclvii]

In the piece, the agent talked about how as many families as possible were welcome to board a ship to begin their new life in Brazil. While families were seen as the ideal unit to work in Brazil, the Company was more than happy to form its own 'families' of single people who could then go on to work in Brazil, as the more people it sent, the more money it made. The Imperial Colony Company was in such a frenzy to recruit migrants to work on coffee plantations in São Paulo that it was still pitching the idea to Okinawans right up until the departure of the *Kasato-Maru*.

Ōgusuku Kame from the village of Tomigusuku was just a girl of seventeen at the time when she was put into one of these created families of ten people. She married the patriarch of the family, a twenty-nine year-old man a mere two months before they left for Brazil.[cclviii]

The *Kasato-Maru* left for Brazil on 28 April, 1908 and immigration continued on and off until the 1920s, the peak being between 1917 and 1918 when conditions in Okinawa remained poor.[139] After this, both the Brazilian and Japanese governments agreed to ban migrants from Okinawa under the justification that they were prone to run away from plantation life and that the rampant creation of "fake families" was an abuse of the

---

139 *Okinawa Ken Shi Kakuhen Ron 8 Joseishi*, 233

migration agreements.

Since migration to Brazil placed special emphasis on families, there was a considerable number of women compared to other countries where contracted labor tended to attract men. Of the 47 Okinawan families consisting of 325 people, 49 of these were women.[140]

From Japan the *Kasato-Maru* took fifty-two days to reach Brazil, arriving at the port of Santos on June 18. The following day both the Okinawans and Japanese alighted from the ship and boarded a steam train to São Paulo where they were sent to an immigration camp to have their documents surveyed.

Of particular suspicion to some of these Brazilian inspectors is how, despite many of these people being husband and wife in name, they chose not to eat or spend time together. When asked about this, some even gave excuses such as their wife becoming ill and her sister coming in her place. Once the processing was complete, the migrants were sent to plantations across Brazil.

While it was only a small number, two Okinawans who had arrived aboard the *Kasato-Maru* were unsatisfied with the conditions there, as we will examine later, and the same year moved to Argentina, marking the first Okinawan presence there, although large scale immigration would not begin in earnest until a few years later.

The Okinawan immigration presence to Brazil and Argentina was to such an extent that as of 2008 there were at least 170,000 of Okinawan descent in Brazil and 25,000 in Argentina.[141]

Micronesia and Melanesia

During World War I (1914–1918) Japan was allied with the Triple Entente (France, Russia and the UK) and used this opportunity

---

140 *Okinawa Ken Shi Kakuhen Ron 8 Joseishi*, 229
141 "沖縄県人ブラジル・アルゼンチン移民100周年と世界に広がる沖縄ネットワーク."

to take over Germany's colonies in Micronesia as early as the first year of the war.

During the 1919 Treaty of Versailles, the victors made the decision to give Japan these territories, what is now the Federated States of Micronesia, the Northern Mariana Islands, Palau and the Marshall Islands all became Japanese territories.

Even a few years before this, in 1915, Okinawan fisherman had already been going to these islands but with the creation of the South Seas Mandate, formal immigration could now begin.

The professor of History and International Relations at Clark University, George Hubbard Blakeslee (1871–1954) described the mandate in 1922 thus:

> "The Japanese Mandate, including all of the former German islands north of the Equator, compromises many hundreds of islands, some of them rocky peaks of volcanic origin, but the greater number low-lying tiny coral islets. The total land area is less than that of the state of Rhode Island. The population is small, 52,222 according to the Japanese census of 1920. The natives vary greatly, from the barbarians of the Western Carolines to the civilized and Christianized inhabitants of the Marshalls. The economic value of the islands is not great...scarcely one-ninth of that of such a small and backward country as Salvador."[142]

But the islands were of great interest to Japan. From 1922 the Japanese population rose from under 4,000 to just under 20,000 by 1930, and then to more than 62,000 by 1937. In some places, the Japanese population could be considerably extensive. In Palau,

---

142 George H. Blakeslee, "The Mandates of the Pacific," Foreign Affairs 1, no. 1 (September 15, 1922): pp. 98-115, 101.

the Japanese outnumbered the indigenous people two to one, in the Marianas ten to one and throughout Micronesia as a whole the Japanese population was larger than that of the indigenous people by 20%.[143] Japan's vision for the islands and the Japanese citizens living there was clearly for the long term. Schools, hospitals and restaurants were built and even a Japanese shrine complete with Torri gates and stone lanterns, Nanyō Shrine was built in Koror on Palau in 1940.

In Melanesia, it would be New Caledonia's island of Grande Terre that would see immigrants from Okinawa, although this was heavily skewed towards men compared to the South Seas Mandate's more gender balanced migration. New Caledonia would have been viewed by these men as a place to work and then return richer to Okinawa rather than somewhere to settle down.

Grand Terre is a long island of about 400 kilometers in length about 1,300 kilometers east of Australia. Across the island, a mountain chain runs 1,500 meters dividing the east and west of the island. Like Okinawa it is a sub-tropical climate, though the difference here is that since this is in the southern hemisphere, the seasons are reversed.

Some of the Okinawans who emigrated to New Caledonia eventually found their way to the capital city of Nouméa. New Caledonia and it's indigenous people (Kanak) first became known to the outsider world when Captain Cook visited in 1774. Cook christened the island New Caledonia, the Latin name for Scotland, since the island's mountains reminded him of Scotland.

The 2019 census of New Caledonia showed that 111,860 people said they belonged to the Kanak community, 41.2% of

---

[143] Peattie, Mark (1988). Nan'Yo: The Rise and Fall of the Japanese in Micronesia, 1885-1945. Pacific Islands Monograph Series. Volume 4. University of Hawaii Press. ISBN 0-8248-1480-0. P. 115

the island's population. The Europeans makes up 24% of the population, while 30,800 people declared that they were mixed race.[144] The majority of the European population is concentrated in Nouméa. Then there are people without a clear background, including Wallisian and Futunian, Vietnamese, Japanese, Italian and of course Okinawan.

When Miki Takeshi the head of Okinawa-New Caledonia Friendship Association described New Caledonia in his 2018 work on the Okinawan legacy there he remarked that the French tricolor reminded him of the US stars and stripes during the post-war occupation of Okinawa.

New Caledonia first became a French colony in 1853 and by 1864 the island was being used as a penal colony. In total about 22,000 criminals and political prisoners were sent to the island.[145] This included 5,000 rebels who were part of the Paris Commune of 1871 and it would not be until 1896 that this penal colony status was abolished.[146]

But a French penal colony held no attraction for Okinawan immigrants. In that year the engineer Jacque Jules Garnier (1839–1904) discovered nickel on the island in the north of Grand Terre and the economic potential was unlocked. Since New Caledonia's population was too small to capitalize on these ore deposits, in part due to the diseases the Europeans had bought with them decimating the indigenous population, the French government began a campaign to introduce workers from Asia.

In 1890, France petitioned the Japanese diplomat Aoki Shūzō (1844–1914), urging him to consider allowing migration on a five-year contract system. Yet Aoki had reservations since due

---

144 "Communautés - Une Mosaïque Pluriethnique."
145 Robert Aldrich and John Connell, *France's Overseas Frontier: Départements Et Territoires D'outre-Mer* (Cambridge University Press, 2006), 46
146 Takeshi, Miki. *Kūhaku No Iminshi: Nyūkaredonia to Okinawa*. Shinema Okinawa, 2017, 110

THE RYUKYUS

to the island's primary use as a penal colony. His successor, Enomoto, was more proactive and agreed for Japanese migrants to move there on a contract system provided that they would not be working alongside convicts. Enomoto reached agreement with France around the same time he finalised plans for Japanese migrants to go to Mexico, and to facilitate this process, the Japanese government set up the Japan Yoshisa Emigration Company where foreign companies could post contracts.[cclix]

With this, 600 Japanese men from Kumamoto Prefecture between the ages of 25 and 30 scheduled to work as miners on five-year contracts on January 6, 1892 left Nagasaki aboard the freight ship *Hiroshima Maru*, and ten days later they crossed the equator and on January 25 arrived off New Caledonia's coast having completed a 7,000 kilometer journey in twenty days.[147] But it would be almost two decades later before Okinawans first came as contract laborers to the island. This began in 1905 with a total of 821 Okinawans moving to New Caledonia.[148]

Immigrants to New Caledonia also found conditions to be different from what they had expected. While New Caledonia's penal colony status had been revoked before the arrival of the first immigrants, the penal colony mentality was very much alive. Fetters which had been used in this recent past were put to use against the first Japanese miners from Kumamoto who did not follow orders to the letter, and the conditions were so bad that out of the initial 600, only 97 saw out their contracts through the end, with a mere eight choosing to remain in New Caledonia.[149]

Conditions had slightly improved by 1905, but even then the Okinawan immigrants were sold a lie. An October 19 advert

---

147 Kūhaku No Iminshi, 113
148 Kūhaku No Iminshi, 1
149 *Kūhaku No Iminshi: Nyūkaredonia to Okinawa*, 114

ACROSS THE WAVES—OKINAWAN IMMIGRANTS

by the Oriental Immigration Company in the Ryukyu Shimpō declared that "the work is not harsh, and ore can be dug out of hillsides, there's really little difference to tilling a field."[150]

The reality was of course different. A great deal of physical strength was required to hack the nickel out, and contrary to the advert was also highly concentrated at the upper reaches of the mountain.

Alongside such brutal conditions, the immigration companies also held on to a portion of the miners wages, a stick to prevent them from bailing halfway through their contract. Yet even this was not a deterrent. At a mine at Thio on the island's east coast the miners would have to climb to the top of the mountain to even begin work. Here they were given low quality food with no vegetables or meat, and were forced to labor in the sub-tropical sun. Some even died from a lack of malnutrition and exhaustion.[cclx]

In such grueling conditions even the company's holding back salaries was not enough to prevent desertions. Some of the miners were so convinced they would die that they erected fake graves for themselves, and then ran away and survive before their contract ended.

As we will see in the next chapter many of those who emigrated across the world often found the working conditions on the ground considerably different to what had been described to them. For the New Caledonian Okinawans, many ran away from the grueling conditions of the mines and eventually marrying Kanak women.

---

150 *Kūhaku No Iminshi: Nyūkaredonia to Okinawa*, 120-121

20

LABOR OVERSEAS

Hawaiian Sugar and Manlian Hemp
The first Okinawan immigrants to Hawaii began their new life working on the sugar plantations where they would spend the day toiling in the fields under the watch of the plantation's overseer, always at his mercy if he should see fit to break out his whip. The whistle would sound in the early hours of dawn, and the immigrants were expected to begin work at six and worked for up to ten hours in the Hawaiian sun.

Many of the Japanese working on the plantations had multiple children, sometimes as many as seven to ten, and the sugar plantation work alone was not always enough to support their families, and women often took on side jobs. This included raising chicken or pigs, making tofu or washing the clothes of the many single men who worked on the plantations. These were all difficult tasks on top of the already strenuous work in the fields, particularly since there was no gas or lighting on hand. The single men usually sent money back to their families in Okinawa, although only about ten dollars could be saved a month.

From October each year, the labor would shift to the processing of the sugar. As on the plantations, an overseer would often shout at them in Portuguese to keep up the pace of work. Discrimination was the norm and immigrants would get paid a different salary depending on where they were from, and the

LABOR OVERSEAS

Okinawan immigrants women were paid a fraction of men's wages despite doing the same work.

Eventually the Okinawans working in Hawaii's plantations successfully saved up enough money to move into jobs where they would have more autonomy and better pay. A few examples are pig farming, opening a restaurant or starting a taxi business.

When Okinawan immigrants first arrived in Davao in the southern Philippines, it was largely undeveloped. The US administration of the islands sought to bring 'skilled agriculturalists' over to develop profitable hemp plantations. Compared to Hawaii, this put Japanese immigrants in a strong position, as they had the ability to buy or at least borrow land, paving the way for a more direct route to wealth, rather than laboring for someone else as was the standard in Hawaii.

Due to these circumstances, Okinawan women in the Philippines did not necessarily have to work on the plantations as they could instead marry into the ownership. The type of hemp that was grown on these plantations was Abacá, a species of banana prized for its fiber. These vast hemp plantations often meant that Okinawans living there could be an hour or more away from Davao itself, but with the fertile soil it was possible to grow and eat the food on one's own land — and it was often the women who raised such crops, including exotic fruits native to Southeast Asia such as the durian.

Those in the hemp plantations benefitted from the modern conveniences of the nearby city. One could drive or use taxis to get to nearby towns where rice, oil and canned goods could be purchased. Generally, the immigrants to the Philippines had a higher quality of life than their compatriots toiling in Hawaii's sugar plantations. Ginoza Masa, who went to the Philippines in 1929 reflected that "I thought to myself, is there really such a life [as good as this] on earth?"[151]

Maids in Taiwan and Spinning Mills in Japan

Most of the first contract migrants were overwhelmingly male, but neighboring Taiwan offered the chance for single women to work overseas, normally as maids in Japanese households there. Yaeyama was geographically closer to Taiwan than Okinawa, and now with both territories under a single Japanese Empire it made sense to many women to leave their rural island homes for the neighboring metropolis with its better job prospects. These workers generally moved to Taihoku (Taipei, as it was known during the Japanese era) or Keelung on the island's north coast. Yaeyaman girls going to Taiwan to work as maids became so prominent that an October 22, 1924 edition of the Yaeyama Shimpō commented that "Yaeyama has now become known as an area in which maids are made."[152]

In addition to a higher salary and more cosmopolitan living conditions, a maid in Taiwan would have her rent and food expenses covered, and as the scholar Matsuda Hirko, who has conducted extensive research into Okinawan immigration to Taiwan, has pointed out these women also benefited from working in a Japanese environment unlike their male peers. Okinawan men working as fishermen in Taiwan continued to hold onto Okinawan customs and traditions, but the women developed a stronger level of standard Japanese and a deeper understanding of Japanese customs.

From the 1920s, an increasing number of 'modern' jobs opened up to women from Okinawa, from switchboard operators, to office works and even teachers. Nevertheless, since few Okinawan girls had the education qualifications necessary

---

151 *Okinawa Ken Shi Kakuhen Ron 8 Joseishi*, 217
152 *Okinawa Ken Shi Kakuhen Ron 8 Joseishi*, 244

to become teachers in state schools in Taiwan.

Overall, Taiwan offered many women in Okinawa, and in Yaeyama in particular, a chance to leave behind what many at the time considered to be a rural backwater far from the capital of Tokyo. With Taiwan now part of Japan, Yaeyamans in particular began to reassess their place within the Ryukyu Archipelago and became proud to be so near such a metropolis as Taipei.

The cities of Japan were also a target of Okinawan immigration during this era. In particular this involved moving from Okinawa to the Kansai region which includes the cities of Kobe, Osaka and Kyoto. Until the 1920s, the population of cities in Kansai stayed relatively stable, but with increasing industrialization more workers were needed for factories. A 1935 survey by Okinawa Prefecture found 3,305 Okinawans living in Osaka at the time, up from only 91 in 1919.[153] Men who moved to Osaka could either find work in the factories, answering one of the many newspaper adverts looking for recruits, or rely on family members to introduce them.

For women, however, the means of finding work in Japan was quite different and focused on one industry in particular, spinning mills. The girls who labored in these spinning mills across Kansai were recruited in Okinawa, with most of them only in their teens. With the prospect of higher wages, these girls would move far away from their families and hometowns and move into dormitories owned by the mills in Kansai.

Discrimination was rampant during this era, many mills were divided into rooms of workers based on their ethnicity, such as having an 'Okinawan Room' and a 'Chosen (Korean) Room'. These young Okinawan girls also had the chance to become what the mill owners deemed 'model employees' but this involved

---

153 Tomiyama, Ichiro. *Kindai Nihon Shakai to Okinawajin: Nihonjin Ni Naru Toiu Koto*. Nihon Keizai Hyoronsha, 2015, 134

THE RYUKYUS

them not talking in Okinawan and abandon as many customs from Okinawa as possible.

In the mills, women freedom was heavily curtailed, and far from their families and the land they knew, they only had their fellow girls from Okinawa to rely on for support. By the 1920s, women working in the spinning mills had began to campaign for better labor conditions, demanding things such as the freedom to leave the premises and an end to discrimination.

By the 1930s, many of the girls who had worked in the Kansai spinning mills had gotten married and had children, mostly with Okinawan men in the region. The highest concentration of Okinawans in Osaka according to a 1935 survey was Taishō Ward with over 6,500 and there were between 26,700 and 26,800 Okinawans in Osaka as a whole. This 1935 survey also lists the professions of the women, with many moving on from the spinning mills to work as midwifes, elementary school teachers, hairdressers and waitresses. But even during this time, the majority of Okinawan women were employed at the spinning mills.[154]

Difficulties in South America's Plantation's and New Caledonia's Mines

Migration to South America resulted from a strong economic pull. In both Peru and Brazil, an Okinawan could make one yen a day (sometimes more), five times as much as the average Okinawan wage of 20 sen in 1907.[155]

As in Hawaii, labor on the plantations was the entry point to a better life, but this was not without its hardships. In Peru, malaria was a persistent problem, and the real sign of success was when one could move on from the initial plantation contract and find better work in the cities. Yafuso Uto was one such

---

154 *Okinawa Ken Shi Kakuhen Ron 8 Joseishi*, 265-66
155 *Okinawa Ken Shi Kakuhen Ron 8 Joseishi*, 228

worker who came to Peru in 1914. It was only three months after arriving that she contracted malaria. Since Yafuso had a child, she would do what all the women on the plantation did, carry her baby on her back as she continued to toil in the fields. When children were too big to be carried on their mother's backs they would instead be fastened to posts in the ridges of the fields. Yafuso eventually ended her contract and moved to Lima where she became a small-scale trader.

A 1930 survey of Japanese commerce in Peru showed that Japanese immigrants to the country were operating 28 general stores, 26 coffee sellers, 191 hairdressers, and 122 restaurants — with over half of these institutions being run by Okinawans.[156]

While Okinawans looking to immigrate to Brazil were promised one yen a day, the arrivals often found they had been deceived. Brazil had been described as a paradise by the salesmen of the immigration companies' back home, but the immigration companies cared little for the immigrants and often cheated them.

In Brazil's coffee fields, each worker was given a bag with a number on it and a ladder. They would enter the fields at eight in the morning, spread a cloth under a coffee tree and use the ladder to climb up and thresh the trees. Once the beans had fallen they would be sieved and packed into bags and the workers would move on to the next tree.

In this process, an adult man could on average fill about one 50-liter bag in a ten-hour shift, but to make the promised one yen, one would have to fill three or four such bags.

Japan Overseas – The South Seas Mandate
Since the South Seas Mandate was a Japanese colony, those who

---

156 *Okinawa Ken Shi Kakuhen Ron 8 Joseishi*, 237

moved here could expect a lifestyle similar to back in Japan. When in 1921 the South Seas Development Company was established by the Japanese government, Okinawans began to be recruited to fill this labor force.[cclxi] This led to a rapid rise in Okinawans migrating to these Japanese territories in the southern hemisphere, in 1922 there were only 702 Okinawans who left, but by 1923 this number had shot up to 2,391 and continued to increase in the years after.[157]

Much of the work Okinawans took up under the South Seas Development Company involved working in the sugar plantations or *Katsubosuhi* factories, skills that were familiar to these immigrants back in Okinawa. In contrast to the sugar plantations of Hawaii and South America, these Okinawans would become tenant farmers borrowing land from the company from which they would have to raise a crop on.

The company has a designated list of stipulations for anyone wishing to become a tenant farmer which included being married. As a result, many women came to the islands together with their husbands or were called over later.

While many women did work in agricultural roles as in South America, there were also opportunities to enter into hospitality roles due to the islands being part of the Japanese Empire. Women could take up work at Ryokan, guest houses, restaurants and some worked as Geisha's or prostitutes. Okinawans who were successful even ended up running such establishments.

Uezu Matsuko (born 1927) reflections on how one could live a life of prosperity overseas compared to back home encapsulates not only why Okinawans immigrated to the South Seas Mandate, but all across the world:

"We lived on Tinian, when I was five (our family) began

---

[157] *Okinawa Ken Shi Kakuhen Ron 8 Joseishi*, 249

operating a Ryotei. There was a street with Ryotei all long it, and cafe's had cafe street, everyone's place was decided... Each Ryotei had about two or three women working there, they were not particularly big establishments, the women had been bought along from Okinawa. Since life in Okinawa was poor, they wanted to come. The customers of the Ryotei were Okinawan farmers, people making sugarcane."[158]

Ryukyu in the Modern World

By the 1940s the centuries-long Ryukyu Kingdom had passed into history and Okinawa Prefecture had been part of Japan for six decades. It was during the war years as Japan headed into the Pacific War that the culture the people had inherited from the Ryukyu Kingdom came under further scrutiny by the Japanese state. The Okinawan language became increasingly frowned upon, Okinawan names and the custom of visiting a Yuta was discouraged in favor of an imperial policy that held the emperor of Japan at its zenith, this now went even further than the pre-war imperialization policy putting more value in self-sacrifice for the good of the nation.

This built on trends all ready underway, such as the militarization of education, and by the 1930s teachers at Okinawan schools were being ordered to go to Kagoshima for such training and both teachers and pupils would become the subject of the state's gaze. Sakiyama Hidesato was one such teacher who had to feign such allegiance. In a Yaeyama school, there was a small building erected to house a portrait of the emperor and the Imperial Rescript on Education. Both teachers and pupils were expected to bow top them when they walked past on their way into school. However Sakiyama would deliberately took a

---

[158] *Okinawa Ken Shi Kakuhen Ron 8 Joseishi*, 251

long route to avoid going directly past it. Another teacher with the same inclinations jokingly said to Sakiyama, "You are also avoiding it... a lot of students do the same."[159]

Despite this back and forth, we know that Ryukyu did not become a homogenised part of Japan, sharing for the most part, the same culture as the mainland as happened in Hokkaido, instead the culture of the Ryukyu Islands that we described in the introduction of this book remains vibrant today, and anyone who visits the Ryukyu Archipelago today are sure to experience this. After Okinawa's return to Japan, there was a boom celebrating Okinawan culture, from TV shows to food, and the unique differences that make these islands special became something to celebrate, a trend that is still going strong today. The prefecture continues to have the oldest population out of all prefectures in Japan often attributed to the Okinawan diet, more relaxed way of life, one more in tune with nature, in stark contrast to the bustling and crowded cities of the Japanese mainland.

There is also a trend to revive parts of Okinawan culture that have been targeted in the past, within the prefecture there has been an increasing interest in the local language, and in 2006, the 18th day of September of every year was declared to be the 'Shimakutuba Day' (literally 'words of the islands') and a 'Dialect Badge' with the Ryukyu royal family's crest became a symbol during the first of these celebrations, a reverse 'Dialect Tag' that had been used in schools in the past as a way of looking down on the local way of speaking.

Okinawa also has large international pull thanks to its expat community, and on average once every five years the World Uchinanchu Festival takes place from which those of Okinawan descent from all over the world attend. This involves a parade

---

[159] "証言集:沖縄戦関係資料閲覧室—内閣府—沖縄県史第9巻（1971年琉球政府編）及び同第10巻（1974年沖縄県教育委員会編."145

LABOR OVERSEAS

down the central street of Kokusai-dori.

The geopolitical legacy of the Ryukyu Kingdom remains just as prevalent today as ever, the Ryukyu Kingdom prospered precisely because of its location at the heart of Asia, allowing it to trade between major centres without being invaded by larger neighbours, that was until the samurai coveted the islands for this strategic region, still the Ryukyu Kingdom was able to remain in together in some shape for more than four hundred years. The islands today remain a central cornerstone in both Japan and America, the US could not have easily sent troops to Vietnam and Korea had there not been bases on Okinawa, and the waters around the Ryukyu Archipelago, which include the contested Senkaku Islands between Japan and China.

There is no Ryukyu Kingdom today, but the spirit, culture and history of this maritime cornerstone at the center of East Asia lives on in both the land and people of these islands and there seems little doubt that they will continue to hold a strategic position in international affairs.

Timeline

Around 14000 BCE: beginning of the Stone Age throughout the Japanese Archipelago (including Ryukyu)

Around 14000 BCE – 1000 BCE – Jōmon period throughout the Japanese Archipelago (including Ryukyu)

Around 5450-4350 BCE Akahoya eruption of the Kikai volcano

Around 5000 BCE – 1100 CE Shell Mound Period (Ryukyu)

Around 1000 BCE – 300 CE- Yayoi period in Japan

300-600: Kofun period (Japan)

538-645: Asuka Period (Japan) – the introduction of Buddhism

581-618: Sui Dynasty (China) – first Chinese records of 'Ryukyu'

618 – 907: Tang Dynasty (China) – golden age of Chinese cosmopolitanism

710-794: Nara Period (Japan) – Flourishing of Nara

794-1185: Heian Period (Japan) – Court culture (Tale of Genji), Ritsuryō codes

918 – 1392: Goryeo Kingdom (Korea)

920 – 1279 Song Dynasty

1100 – 1200: Gusuku Period (Okinawa)

1156: Hōgen Disturbance (Imperial infighting between the Emperor Go-Shirakawa and retired emperor Sutoku breaks out, the warriors who fight on each side became the foundation for the samurai class)

1185-1333: Kamakura Period (Japan) First era of the Samurai as de facto power moves from the Emperor to this warrior class. From now until the late 19th Century Shoguns not the Emperor will hold real power in Japan

1271-1368: Yuan Dynasty (China) – Mongol Dynasty of China

established by Kublai Khan
1293: Formation of the Majapahit Empire (Sumatra and Java)
1293: Beginning of the Majapahit Empire as Raden Wijaya defends against a Mongol invasion
1317: Miyako islanders going to what is today Singapore (theory)
1322-1429: Three Kingdoms Period (Sanzan Period) (Okinawa)
1333: Ashikaga Takauji captures the royal capital of Kyoto from the Kamakura Shogunate
1333: Kenmu restoration begins and last until 1336 — Emperor Go-Daigo attempts to restore the power of the imperial family and diminish that of the samurai
1336-1573: Muromachi Period (Japan)
1350: Reign of the Ayutthaya Kingdom begins in what is present day Thailand
1350: Birth of the Ayutthaya Kingdom (Thailand)
1368: Ming Dynasty (China)
1369: Ming China sends first envoy to Japan
1371: Ming maritime ban
1372: Ming China sends first envoy to Ryukyu (Kingdom of Chūzan) and Chūzan sends envoy to China in return
1372: Shō Hashi founder of the Ryukyu Kingdom is born
1380: King Shō-Satto of Nanzan pays tribute to the Ming
1383: King Haniji of Hokuzan pays tribute to the Ming
1383: Hongwu Emperor urges the kingdoms of Chūzan and Nanzan to end their conflict
1389: King Satto of Chūzan sends shipwrecked Koreans back to Goryeo
1390: Miyako chief Yonahasedo (Yonahashiido) Tuyumya comes to Chūzan learns the Okinawan language and pays respect to the king
1390: Miyako and Yaeyama pay tribute to the Ryukyu court
1392: Beginning of Joseon Kingdom (Korea)

TIMELINE

1392: Official Chinese settlement established in Kuninda with the arrival of '36' Fujian people—may predate this

1392: First Ryukyu students sent to China to study

1392: Goryeo sends a delegation of thanks to Ryukyu for returning shipwrecked Koreans

1394: The Kingdom of Chūzan asks Korea to send back the former king Shō-Satto of Nanzan

1396: King Satto of Chūzan passes away at age 75 and his son Bunei ascends the throne

1400: Formation of the Sultanate of Malacca (Malaysia)

1401: Shogun Ashikaga Yoshimitsu sends an envoy to Ming China

1402: Shō Hashi inherits the title of Sashiki Aji

1404: Siamese boat on way to Ryukyu runs adrift at Fuzhou

1405-1433: Admiral Zheng He makes several voyages around the world as far as the African continent

1405: Sultanate of Malacca makes first tribute to Ming China

1406: Shō Hashi overthrows King Bunei of Chūzan and installs his father on the throne

1407: Shō Shishō sends a delegation to China informing the Ming that he is the new king of Chūzan

1411: A Jiangxi retainer of King Satto of Chūzan requests permission to return to China in his old age

1411: The Sultan of Malacca journeys to China to pay respects to the Ming Emperor

1416: Shō Hashi captures the Kingdom of Hokuzan

1421: King Shō Shishō of Chūzan passes away and Shō Hashi becomes king of central and northern Okinawa

1422: Prince Shō Chū appointed custodian of Hokuzan

1428: First record of Ryukyu ships arriving in Palembang

1429: Shō Hashi leads an army against King Taromai of Nanzan

1430: Shō Hashi sends a delegation to the Ming declaring the

THE RYUKYUS

unification of Okinawa under the a single kingdom
1430: First record of Ryukyu ships arriving in Java
1433: The Ryukyu shipbuilders Ufuyaku and Saburō are sent to Korea to build a model ship
1441: Amami Ōshima becomes part of the Ryukyu Kingdom
1449: Mongol Esen Taishi captures Emperor Yingzong (China)
1453: Shiro-Furi Revolt—succession crisis within the first Ryukyu dynasty after the death of King Shō Kinpuku
1458: Gosamaru-Amawari revolt—Gosamaru or Amawari attempt to overthrow the first Ryukyu dynasty
1458: Bridge of Nations bell forged
1463: First record of Ryukyu ships visiting the Sultanate of Malacca
1467: Ōnin War breaks out and Japan descends into Warring States Period as the samurai fight amongst each other for power
1469: Kanamaru ascends the throne as King Shō En and the Second Shō Dynasty begins
1470: China limits tribute from Ryukyu to once every two years
1471: Kanamaru sends a delegation to China declaring himself the new king of Ryukyu
1472: Ryukyu Hall moved from Quanzhou to Fuzhou
1477: Shō Shin ascends the throne
1477: Korean sailors leave written record of Yaeyama in *Veritable Records of the Joseon Dynasty*
1478: Chinese delegation comes to Ryukyu for the enthronement ceremony of Shō Shin
1480: Ayutthaya returns Ryukyu sailors after their junks went alight in 1479 in Siam
1494: The Buddhist temple Enkaku-Ji is built
1500: Akahachi allegedly plans to stage a coup against the Ryukyu Kingdom

TIMELINE

1501: Construction of the royal mausoleum, Tamaudun is complete
1502: The Enkanchi Pond is created in the grounds of Shuri Castle
1507: King Shō Shin convinces China to increase Ryukyu's tributary allowance from once every two years to once a year
1511: Sultanate of Malacca falls to the Portuguese (Malaysia)
1511: Portuguese conquest of the Sultanate of Malacca
1516: Satsuma samurai kill Miyake Kunihide under the pretext that he was sailing south to overthrow the King of Ryukyu
1519: Stone gate erected at Bengadake-Utaki
1524: First Kuramoto in Yaeyama established on Taketomi Island
1527: Collapse of the Majapahit Empire (Sumatra and Java)
1536: The Satsuma send a letter to the Ryukyu Court stating that since they saved the kingdom from Miyake Kunihide they should send Japanese merchants from Naha if they did not carry the Shimazu seal
1543: Path from Shuri Castle to Bengadake-Utaki constructed
1569: Burmese attach the Kingdom of Ayutthaya and occupy the capital for the next 15 years
1570: Ryukyu sends its last tributary ship to Ayutthaya
1572: Satsuma send another letter to the King of Ryukyu ordering the kingdom to seize any Japanese ships without their seal
1587: Shogun Toyotomi Hideyoshi puts an end to Satsuma expansion in Kyushu
1591: Toyotomi Hideyoshi orders Ryukyu to send supplies for his invasion of Korea
1598: Death of Toyotomi Hideyoshi
1600: Battle of Sekigahara—Tokugawa forces triumph over Hideyoshi loyalists laying the foundations for Japan's final and longest lasting Shogunate
1602: Ryukyu ship washes ashore Sendai, Tokugawa Shogunate uses this as a pretext to connect with Ryukyu

THE RYUKYUS

1603: Beginning of the Edo period in Japan under the Tokugawa Shogunate, an era of 'no more wars' after the tumultuous Warring States Period

1604: Another Ryukyu ship washes up at Hirado but the sailors make their own way home before the Tokugawa Shogunate can capitalize on this

1605: Noguni Sokan introduces the sweet potato to Ryukyu

1605: Sunao Kawachi washes up in Fujian brings sugarcane o Amami

1609: Satsuma samurai invade the Ryukyu Kingdom

1609, March 4th: Satsuma army arrived at the island of Kuchinoerabu in Northern Ryukyu

1609, March 6th: Satsuma army arrive in Amami-Ōshima, Ryukyu officials surrender

1609, March 16th-22nd March: first ships of the Satsuma army arrives on Tokunoshima and begins first battle with Ryukyu soldiers

1609, March 24th: Divisions of the Satsuma army rendezvous at Okinoerabu to prepare for an invasion of Okinawa

1609, March 27th: Satsuma attack Nakijin Gusuku in northern Okinawa

1609, March 29th: Part of the Satsuma army set off from Unten in northern Okinawa and move off the coast of Yomitan

1609, April 1st: Ryukyu stations soldiers to protect Shuri and Naha who clash with Satsuma samurai at Naha

1609, April 4th: King Shō Nei surrenders to the Satsuma

1609, April 16th: King Shō Nei is taken to Naha where he meets the Satsuma generals

1609, May 15th-May 24th: King Shō Nei and his entourage are boarded onto ships and set sail for Japan at the port of Yamagawa

1609, June 23rd: King Shō Nei arrives in Kagoshima

TIMELINE

1610, August: King Shō Nei meets with Tokugawa Ieyasu and is forced to sign a vow expressing the Ryukyu Kingdoms fealty to the Satsuma

1610: Satsuma government established in Amami

1611: King Shō Nei is allowed to return to Ryukyu

1611: Satsuma finish a survey of the Ryukyu Archipelago

1612 & 1613: King Shō Nei sends tribute to China after the Satsuma invasion, China wary after Satsuma invasion and subsequently restricts the frequency of tribute from Ryukyu

1613: Creation of the Ōshima Magistrate in Amami

1614-1615: Tokugawa Ieyasu launches the siege of Osaka and disposes Toyotomi Hideyoshi's heir

1614: Tōrin-Ji Temple and Gongendō Shrine built in Ishigaki

1614: Sashiki Prince (later King Shō Hō) is sent to Kagoshima for ten years under the beginning of a hostage system, by 1626 this had been decreased to three years

1616: Creation of the Tokunoshima Magistrate in Amami

1622: China allows Ryukyu to increase tribute to once every five years once again

1623: Zama Shinjō introduces sugar wringers to Amami

1623: Satsuma order for the Yanchu system to be partially ended, although nothing comes of it

1624: Satsuma take direct control of Amami

1624: Spanish missionary Juan de los Angeles Rueda arrives in Ishigaki

1630: Hostage system reformed to allow member of the Council of three instead of prince

1633: Sakoku policy begins, Japan becomes semi-closed off from outside world

1633: King Shō Ho succeeds in convincing China to allow for Ryukyu tribute once every two years again

1634: Ryukyu official Ishigaki Eishō executed for converting to

THE RYUKYUS

Christianity
1636: Qing Dynasty (China) — China's last imperial dynasty established by the Manchus and replaces the Ming in 1644
1636: Satsuma introduce intermediate checks on the people of Ryukyu to make sure they have not converted to Christianity
1637: Poll tax begins in Miyako and Yaeyama
1637-1638: Shimabara Rebellion
1640: Foreign ship of unknown nationality kidnaps a women from Ishigaki
1641: Satsuma samurai dispatched to Ishigaki over a growing concern of foreign activity until 1648. After this the Saskishima beacons are installed
1644: Manchu's capture Beijing
1654: Ryukyu Hall established near Kagoshima castle
1660: Fire at Shuri Castle leads to the destruction of the palace, the rebuilt version uses a grey tiled roof
1660: Heirs to the throne of Ryukyu are now required to visit Satsuma for coronation, replacing the old hostage system which ended in 1646
1671: The construction of Shisei-byō, a Confucian temple begins being completed in 1676
1682: Dragon tiles installed on the roof of Shuri Castle
1682: An official role is established to inspect cultivation levels across the kingdom
1695: The Satsuma send a surveyor to Amami to determine its potential as a sugar plantation economy
1713: 300 Hateruma islanders moved to Ishigaki to create the village of Shiraho
1715: Palace at Shuri Castle once again burns down, the rebuilt versions uses a red tiled roof
1725: Miyako islanders forcibly moved to Ōgamijima to create a new village to increase production

TIMELINE

1732: 400 Kuroshima islanders moved to Ishigaki to create the village of Nosko

1734: 400 Hateruma islanders moved to Iriomote to create the village of Haimi

1745: Satsuma pass a law that citizens of Amami much pay a sugar tax, taxes shift from rice production to sugar

1755: Further 288 Hateruma islanders moved to Iriomote to create the village of Sakiyama

1755: 3,000 Tokunoshima islanders die due to crop failure

1764: King Hsinbyushin invades Ayutthaya from Burma, the city is sacked and much of it is burnt to the ground (Thailand)

1767: Collapse of the Ayutthaya Kingdom after invasion from Burma (Thailand)

1771: Meiwa Tsunami kills over 9,000 in Yaeama

1777: Buying and selling of sugar throughout Amami made illegal

1778: Captain Cook and his crew first visit Hawaii

1795: Kamehameha unifies Hawaii

1818: Captain Basil Hall writes an account of his experiences in Okinawa becoming one of the first English language books on the islands

1824: A British whaling ship arrives in Northern Ryukyu and run into tension with the local people and Satsuma officials

1825: Shogunate gives order to open fire on all foreign vessels

1830: Amami islanders ordered to not use any of the sugar the produce

1843: *HMS Samarang* arrives in Ishigaki

1852: Robert Bowne Incident

1853: Perry arrives in Ryukyu

1853: Perry arrives in Naha for the first time

1853: Satsuma extend sugar purchasing restrictions to Okinoerabu, covering even more of Northern Ryukyu

1853: New Caledonia becomes a French colony

THE RYUKYUS

1854: Perry once again comes to Ryukyu and treaty is signed
1854: March: Treaty of Kanagawa
1854, July: Convention between the Ryukyu Islands and the United States of America
1855: Ryukyu treaty with France
1857: Sugarcane planted in Yoronto the most southern island of Northern Ryukyu
1859: Treaty between Ryukyu and Holland signed
1864: Intabu Crusade (Tokunoshima Islanders rise up against the Satsuma officials)
1866: Final Chinese delegation comes to Ryukyu
1866: Satsuma-Chōshū alliance formed to overthrow the Shogun
1868: Meiji Restoration — The Emperor is reinstated as the head of state under the guidance of the Meiji oligarchs
1868-1869: Boshin War
1868: Edo is renamed Tokyo
1868: Tokugawa Shogunate defeated at the Battle of Ueno and agrees to surrender power to the Satsuma-Choshū alliance
1869: Shogunate forces in Hakodate surrender
1871: Abolition of old feudal domains and establishment of the Japanese prefecture system
1871: Mudan Incident — Miyako Islanders run aground on Taiwan creating an international stand off between Japan and China
1871: Government orders the Yanchu system to end and in 1872 the buying and selling of people is made illegal, although the Yanchu system continues
1872: The Meiji government declares that the Ryukyu Kingdom is now a feudal domain of Japan
1872: The Ryukyu Kingdom is reclassified as a 'feudal domain' of Japan
1872: Control of Ryukyu moves from Kagoshima Prefecture to the Ministry of Foreign Affairs, the Ryukyu officials in

TIMELINE

Kagoshima's Ryukyu Hall are sent back to Ryukyu

1872: Surnames are given to all Japanese citizens regardless of class

1873: Creation of the Ōshima General Trade Company under Kagoshima Prefecture seeks to continue the former Satsuma domains monopoly on cane sugar

1874: Ryukyu sends its last tributary ship to China

1874: Ōkuma Shinobu (he himself is opposed as he did not view Ryuykuans as Japanese) submits an investigation about a Japanese takeover of Taiwan to the Diet

1874: In July Japanese soldiers are sent to Taiwan, the jurisdiction of Ryukyu domain moves from the Ministry of Foreign Affairs to the Ministry of Home Affairs, two months before in May Japan sends troops to Taiwan. The battle does not last more than a few months due to British arbitration

1875: Japan once again orders King Shō Tai to stop sending tributary delegations to China, Ryukyu sent another delegation in 1887

1875: Kawarada Moriharu dispatched to Ryukyu by the Ministry of Home Affairs to assess the modernization of Ryukyu Domain

1875: Ijichi Seizaemon, a samurai from Satsuma organizes Amami-Ōshima islanders to no pay the sugar tax

1875: The Kingdom of Hawaii secedes Pearl Harbor on Ohau in exchange for a relaxation of US sugar tariffs, Reciprocity Treaty of 1875

1877: Ryukyu sends 109 men and women from the Spanish Philippines back after their ship runs aground on Hateruma

1878: Qing seek the help of Ulysses S. Grant to broker a deal over who owns Ryukyu

1878: The Ōshima General Trade Company is broken up

1879: Okinawa becomes a Japanese Prefecture, King Shō Tai is

THE RYUKYUS

exiled to Tokyo
1879, March: The Disposition of Ryukyu, King Shō Tai is exiled to Tokyo
1879, April: Okinawa Prefecture is born
1879, May: First governor of Okinawa Prefecture arrives, Nabeshima
1879, July: Police stations established throughout Okinawa Prefecture
1879: Okinawa's first middle school opens
1880: training of Okinawan teacher's to speak 'standard Japanese' begins with the creation of Instructor Schools to train teachers
1881: Governor Nabeshima is recalled to Tokyo
1881: King Kalākaua of Hawaii meets with Emperor Meiji and agrees to open the kingdom up to Japanese immigration, and an agreement is made in 1885
1883: Osaka Bōseki spinning company is established with the first steam powered looms in Japan
1884-1885: Sino-French War (conflict between China and France over Vietnam)
1884: Kikoeōkimi, the chief priestess, is abolished
1886: Education for girls in Okinawa begins
1887: Satsuma Rebellion (Seinan War)
1887: Goshinei go up in the Instructor Schools throughout Okinawa, and then later all of Japan
1887: French annex Vietnam
1889: vote granted to some male tax payers in Japan (1.13% o the population), but not to the people of Okinawa or Hokkaido
1889: Hajichi tattoos outlawed in Okinawa
1889 December: Tōyama Kyūzo leads the first Okinawan immigrants to Hawaii
1892: First 600 contract workers from Japan arrive in New Caledonia

TIMELINE

1893: The *Ryukyu Shimpō* newspaper is founded in September
1894-1895: First Sino-Japanese War
1895: Taiwan becomes a Japanese colony
1895 Treaty of Shimonoseki
1897: End of the Joseon Kingdom and beginning of the short lived Korean Empire
1897: Okinawa Prefecture decides to sell government land to private buyers under Governor Narahara
1897: First 34 Japanese emigrate to Mexico, followed by a 1901 movement
1898: Spanish-American War
1899: Education for girls becomes more practical to follow the mantra of 'Good Wife and Wise Mother'
1899: Okinawan immigration to Hawaii begins
1900: First girl's vocational school opens in Shuri
1900 January: First 26 Okinawan immigrants arrive at Oahu
1903: Poll tax is abolished in Miyako and Yaeyama
1903: Meiji government ends the policy of 'Preserving the Old' in Okinawa
1903: Second wave of Okinawan immigrants (41) come to Hawaii
1904: As Immigration Supervisor to the Philippines, Ōshiro Kōzō leaves Kobe for Manila
1904: immigration to the Philippines begins
1904: First Okinawan immigrants leave for Mexico
1904: First Okinawans immigrant to the Philippines
1905: First Okinawan immigrants leave for New Caledonia
1906: Immigration to Peru begins
1908: Immigration to Brazil begins, although possibly earlier
1910: State payments to Noro come to an end
1912: The death of Emperor Meiji, his son ascends the throne and the Taishō Period begins
1912: Fall of the Qing Dynasty (China)

1912: Right to vote granted to some in Okinawa, but not Sakishima
1913: Immigration to Argentina begins
1914-1918: World War I, Japan join the Triple Entente and captures Germany's colonies in Micronesia
1916: Ōshiro Kōzō founds the Okinawa Davao Association, and then also founds the Davao Japanese Association in 1918
1918: Ōshiro Kōzō founds the Davao Japanese Association in the Philippines
1919: Japan acquires Germany pacific island territories and establishes the South Seas Mandate
1919: Treaty of Versailles, formal start of the Japanese South Sea Mandate
1920: Right to vote granted to some in in Sakishima (Miyako and Yaeyama)
1924: Immigration Act bans Japanese immigration to the US
1926: Passing of the Taishō emperor, his son and grandson of Emperor Meiji, Hirohito (The Shōwa emperor) ascends the throne
1940: Nanyō Shrine constructed at Koror on Palau
1945: Battle of Okinawa at least 200,000 Okinawans die
1945: American Period begins throughout the entirety of the Ryukyu Archipelago
1953: Amami rejoins late Shōwa Period Japan under Kagoshima Prefecture
1972: Okinawa rejoins late Shōwa Period Japan and once again becomes a Japanese prefecture

Bibliography

Books
- Akamine, Mamoru. *Ryūkyū ōkoku: Higashiajia No kōnāsutōn*. Kōdansha, 2004.
- Edward Belcher, 'Narrative of the voyage of H.M.S'. Samarang, 1848
- Eiji, Oguma. *"Nihonjin" No kyôkai Okinawa, Ainu, Taiwan, Chôsen: Shokuminchi Shihai Kara Fukki undô Made*. Shinyôsha, 1998.
- Francis L. Hawkes, 'Narrative of the Expedition of an American Squadron to the China Seas and Japan: performed in the years 1852, 1853, and 1854, under the command of Commodore M.C. Perry, United States Navy, by order of the Government of the United States'
- Furukawa, Chikashi, Shusetsu Rin, and Takayuki Kawaguchi. *Taiwan Kankoku Okinawa De Nihongo Wa Nani o Shitanoka: Gengo Shihai No Motarasu Mono*. Sangensha, 2007.
- Harada, Nobuo. *Ryūkyū To chūgoku: Wasurerareta sakuhōshi*. Yoshikawakōbunkan, 2003.
- Higa, Masao. *Okinawa Kara Ajia Ga Mieru*. Iwanami Shoten, 1999.
- Iha Fuyū. *Watashi No Kodomo Jibun* (伊波普猷全集 第十巻). Heibonsha, 1976.
- Kamiya, Hiroshi. *Amami Motto Shiritai: Gaidobukku Ga Kakanai Amami No Futokoro*. Nanpō Shinsha, 1999.
- Kuba, Mayumi. "首里城の赤瓦." 首里城公園. http://oki-park.jp/sp/shurijo/about/3798/3828.
- Machida, Munehiro, Kinjō Hiroyuki, and Hisamitsu Miyauchi.

- *Yakudō Suru Okinawakei Imin: Burajiru Hawai o Chūshin Ni.* Sairyūsha, 2013.
- Mainichi Shimbun. *Okinawa, Sensō Mararia Jiken: Minami No Shima No Kyōsei Sokai.* Tōhō Shuppan, 1994.
- Miki, Takeshi. *Kūhaku No Iminshi: Nyūkaredonia to Okinawa.* Shinema Okinawa, 2017.
- Shinoda, Kenichi. *Nihonjin Ni Natta Sosen Tachi: DNA Kara Kaimei Suru Sono Tagenteki Kōzō.* NHK Books, 2007.
- Nagoshi, Mamoru. *Amami No Saimu Dorei Yanchu.* Nanpō Shinsha, 2006.
- Nakata Ryūsuke. *Yaeyama Rekishi Dokuhon.* Nanzansha, 2004.
- Oguma, Makoto. *Kyokai o Koeru Okinawa: Hito Bunka Minzoku.* Shinwasha, 2016.
- Okinawa Ken Kyoikuchō Bunka Zaika Shiryō Henshūhan, ed. *Okinawa Ken Shi Kakuhen Ron 8 Joseishi.* Haebaru : Okinawa ken kyōiku iinkai, 2016.
- Ōhama Shinken. *Yaeyama No Mararia Bokumetsu: Zuihitsu Anohi Anokoro.* Ōhama Shinken, 1968.
- Ōhama Shinken. *Yaeyama No Nintōzei.* Sanichi Shobō, 1971.
- Ōta Masahide. *Minikui Nihonjin: Nihon No Okinawa Ishiki.* Saimaru shuppan, 1995.
- Takara, Kurayoshi, Kenichi Tanigawa, and Ringorō Ōyama. *Okinawa Amami to Yamato.* Doseisha, 1986.
- Takara, Kurayoshi. *Ajia No Naka No Ryūkyū okoku.* Yoshikawako bunkan, 1998.
- Takara, Kurayoshi. *Ryūkyū No Jidai: ōinaru rekishizō o Motomete.* Chikuma Shobō, 2012.
- Takara, Kurayoshi. *Ryūkyū Ōkoku.* Iwanami Shoten, 2005.
- Tomiyama, Ichiro. *Kindai Nihon Shakai to Okinawajin: Nihonjin Ni Naru Toiu Koto.* Nihon Keizai Hyoronsha, 2015.
- Tomiyama, Kazuyuki. *Ryūkyū, Okinawa Shi No Sekai.* Yoshikawa

BIBLIOGRAPHY

Kōbunkan, 2003.
- Torigoe, Hiroyuki. *Ryūkyūkoku No metsubō to Hawai Imin.* Yoshikawa Kōbunkan, 2013.
- Uehara, Kenzen. *Shimazu-Shi No Ryūkyū Shinryaku: mō Hitotsu No Keichō No Eki.* Yōju Shorin, 2009.
- Yamashita, Shigekazu. *Zoku Ryūkyū, Okinawa Shi Kenkyū Josetsu.* Ochanomizu Shobō, 2004.
- Yoneshiro, Megumu. *Yomigaeru Dunan: Shashin Ga Kataru Yonaguni No Rekishi.* Nanzansha, 2015
- Yoshinari, Naoki, and Hiromi Fuku. *Ryūkyū Ōkoku to Wakō Omoro No Kataru Rekishi.* Shinwasha, 2008.
- 『海のクロスロード 八重山』沖縄県立美術館 2010年
- 山畠 正男『琉球王国と蝦夷地（沖縄国大ブックレット沖縄国際大学公開講座（No 3）』1998年
- 八重山毎日新聞『「唐人墓」説明文は正しいか』3月5日2008年
- Homer, and Emily R. Wilson. *The Odyssey.* W.W. Norton & Company, Inc, 2018.
- Nakayama, Yoshiaki. *Nihon no Shiro .* Seitōsha, 2015.
- *Ryūkyū* Shinpō. Okinawa Konpakuto Jiten. *Ryūkyū* Shinpōsha, 2003.
- Ishikawa, Tomonori. *Nihon Imin No Chirigakuteki Kenkyū: Okinawa Hiroshima Yamaguchi.* Yōjushorin, 1997.
- 'Documents Concerning Psychological Warfare in the Battle of Okinawas' cited in 『沖縄県史 資料編2 THE OKINAWANS OF THE LOO CHOO ISLANDS, etc.』沖縄県立図書館史料編集室 1996, 91
- Ono, Mitsuaki. *Okinawa Toso No Jidai 1960/70: Bundan o Norikoeru Shiso to Jissen.* Jimbunshoin, 2014.
- Tsurumi Okinawan Association, ed. Yokohama, *Tsurumi Okinawa Kenjinkaishi: Tsurumi Okinawa Kenjin Hyakunen No Ayumi.* Yokohama Tsurumi Okinawa Kenjinkai, 2016.

- McKenna, Rebecca Tinio. American Imperial Pastoral: the Architecture of US Colonialism in the Philippines. The University of Chicago Press, 2017.
- Murata, Kazunosuke, and Shigeru Kinugasa. Sekai no Rekishi 4 Girishia. Kawadeshobōshinsha, 1989.
- Jared Diamond, *The Worst Mistake in the History of the Human Race*, Discovery Magazine, UCLA School of Medicine, 1987, 64-66.
- 那覇市. "玉陵." https://www.city.naha.okinawa.jp/kankou/bunkazai/tamaudun.html.
- Polo, Marco. The Travels of Marco Polo. Oliver & Boyd, 1845.
- Pires, Thome, and Francisco Rodrigues. The Suma Oriental of Tome Pires and the Book of Francisco Rodrigues. J. Jetley for Asian Educational Services, 1990.
- Umi No Curosurōdo Yaima. Okinawa Prefectural Museum & Art Museum, 2010.
- Meyer, Milton Walter. *Japan a Concise History*. Rowman & Littlefield, 1992.
- Okuno Shūji. Natsuko: Okinawa Mitsubōeki no Joō. Bungei Shunjū, 2007.
- Spickard, Paul R. Japanese Americans: the Formation and Transformations of an Ethnic Group. Rutgers University Press, 2009.
- Hokkoku, Ryōsei. Bakumatsu Ishin Ezochi Ibun: Gōshō, Mononofu, Ikokujintachi No Yūhi. Hokkaidō Shuppan Kikaku Sentā, 2014.
- Aldrich, Robert, and John Connell. *France's Overseas Frontier: Départements Et Territoires D'outre-Mer*. Cambridge University Press, 2006.
- Blakeslee, George H. "The Mandates of the Pacific." *Foreign Affairs* 1, no. 1 (September 15, 1922): 98–115.
- 大田昌秀、新川昭、稲嶺恵一、荒崎守輝『沖縄の自立と日

BIBLIOGRAPHY

本―「復帰」40年の問いかけ』岩波書店2003年
- 林博文『沖縄戦 強制された「集団自決』吉川弘文館2009年
- 大田昌秀『醜い日本人:日本の沖縄意識』サイマル出版、1995年
- 川平 成雄 『沖縄 空白の一年 1945-1946』吉川弘文館 2011年 Kabira, Nario. *Okinawa kuhaku No Ichinen: 1945-1946.* Yoshikawakobunkan, 2011.
- Ono, Mitsuaki. *Okinawa Toso No Jidai 1960/70: Bundan o Norikoeru Shiso to Jissen.* Jimbunshoin, 2014.
- 北村 毅 『死者たちの戦後誌 ‐ 沖縄戦跡をめぐる人々の記憶』御茶の水書房2009年 (Kitamura Tsuyoshi)
- Furukawa Chikashi, Lin Chu-Sheue, Kawaguchi Takayuki) Furukawa, Chikashi, Shusetsu Rin, and Takayuki Kawaguchi. *Taiwan Kankoku Okinawa De Nihongo Wa Nani o Shitanoka: Gengo Shihai No Motarasu Mono.* Sangensha, 2007.
- 前田 哲男 (編集), 我部 政明 (編集), 林 博史 (編集)『"沖縄"基地問題を知る事典』吉川弘文館 2013年

Websites

- 沖縄県. "沖縄と移民の歴史," https://www.pref.okinawa.jp/toukeika/so/topics/topics457.pdf.
- "Loochoo (Ryukyu) Commerce and Navigation," Library of Congress, 1854 https://www.loc.gov/law/help/us-treaties/bevans/b-loochoo-ust000009-0692.pdf.
- Blakemore, Erin. "ハワイ王国最後の「悲劇の女王」、リリウオカラニの物語." Translated by 和博 鈴木, June 6, 2021. https://natgeo.nikkeibp.co.jp/atcl/news/21/051700236/?n_cid=nbpnng_mled_html&xadid=10005.
- Ryukyu Cultural Archives"大城孝蔵." Ryukyu Cultural Archives. http://rca.open.ed.jp/city-2001/emigration/person/e_2h.html.

- "大阪にリトル沖縄、誕生の理由　住民4分の1が出身者." NIKKEI STYLE. August 17, 2011. https://style.nikkei.com/article/DGXZZO34037380X10C11A8000000.
- Iha, Fuyū. "私の子供時分" 青空文庫 Aozora Bunko. https://www.aozora.gr.jp/cards/000232/files/54136_53806.html.
- "沖縄の民権運動の父。謝花昇." 琉球文化アーカイブ. http://rca.open.ed.jp/city-2001/person/07jyahana/index.html.
- "謝花昇　近代日本人の肖像." 国立国会図書館 National Diet Library, Japan. https://www.ndl.go.jp/portrait/datas/512.html.
- 沖縄県立総合教育センター. "野底マーペー" 琉球文化アーカイブ. http://rca.open.ed.jp/city-2000/minwa/story1.html.
- Chang, Richard T. "General Grant's 1879 Visit to Japan." Monumenta Nipponica 24, no. 4 (1969). https://doi.org/10.2307/2383879.
- 浦添市教育委員会. "浦添市指定文化財　史跡　経塚の碑 - Monumento(モニュメント)." みんなでつくる案内板データベース, July 1, 2015. https://monumen.to/spots/4040.
- 補陀洛山寺. "熊野の神域・那智." https://www.nachikan.jp/kumano/fudarakausan-ji/.
- 友紀石川 "メキシコへの沖縄県出身移民の歴史と実態." CiNii Articles. https://ci.nii.ac.jp/naid/120006729891/ja/?range=0&sortorder=0&start=0&count=0.
- "奄美大島の基本データ." JAPAN WEB MAGAZINE, July 20, 2015.
- 日刊OkiMag. "日秀上人【金武町】." 沖縄人(OKINAWAN.JP). https://okinawan.jp/minwa/minwa009.htm.
- み熊野えっと "補陀落渡海." February 28, 2008. https://www.mikumano.net/keyword/fudaraku.html.
- "移民人物伝2." 琉球文化アーカイブ. http://rca.open.ed.jp/city-2001/emigration/person/e_2h.html.
- "八重山新時代～20世紀から21世紀へ～　-　やいま特集." や

BIBLIOGRAPHY

- いまタイム, June 21, 2017. https://yaimatime.com/yaima_special/27125/.
- 沖縄県公文書簡 "土地と移民." 沖縄県公文書館, October 25, 2016. https://www.archives.pref.okinawa.jp/event_information/past_exhibitions/6246.
- Kousyou. "「薩摩島津氏の琉球侵攻」(1609年) まとめ." 歴史の呼び声ー. 歴史の呼び声ー, May 18, 2018. https://call-of-history.com/archives/15591#toc2.
- "海外の沖縄県系人、約41万5千人　県が5年ぶり推計： 5年に一度の祭典「世界のウチナーンチュ大会」特集." 沖縄タイムス. Accessed June 28, 2021. https://www.okinawatimes.co.jp/articles/-/66205.
- "海外の沖縄県系人、約41万5千人　県が5年ぶり推計: 5年に一度の祭典「世界のウチナーンチュ大会」特集." 沖縄タイムス. https://www.okinawatimes.co.jp/articles/-/66205.
- "The New Caledonia Weekly, 22-29 August 2008," August 2008. http://www.newcaledonia.co.nz/wp-content/uploads/2019/04/newcal-weekly-08-08-22.pdf.
- https://ryukyushimpo.jp/news/prentry-184003.html
- "沖縄県人ブラジル・アルゼンチン移民100周年と世界に広がる沖縄ネットワーク." 全国知事会. December 2008. http://www.nga.gr.jp/pref_info/tembo/2008/12/post_183.html.
- "「沖縄の家」が落成　ニューカレドニア３００人が開所式." 琉球新報, November 13, 2011. https://ryukyushimpo.jp/news/prentry-184003.html.
- "Communautés - Une Mosaïque Pluriethnique." Institut de la statistique et des études économiques Nouvelle-Calédonie, 2020 https://www.isee.nc/population/recensement/communautes.
- https://www.pref.okinawa.jp/site/bunka-sports/bunka/r2simakutolubakenminisikityousa.html

Endnotes

i As of 2018 there are 113 uninhabited islands in Okinawa Prefecture and 47 inhabited islands. This number will increase if the islands of Southern Kagoshima Prefecture are also counted

ii If the Minatogawa man had entered Ryukyu from the south and his peoples continued to go north, he will also be a direct descendent of mainland Japanese as well.

iii 爪形土器

iv 轟式土器 & 曽畑式土器

v 市来式土器

vi 遮光器土偶

vii 中空土偶 & 縄文のビーナス

viii 蝶形骨製品

ix 下田原式土器

x The historian Akamine Mamoru has proposed that this early iron and Chinese porcelain could have entered Ryukyu from Kyushu, but also recognizes that Fujian was a major center of iron production in Asia

xi The two Utaki's located within Katsuren Gusuku are Nomiuchi Utaki and Kimutaka-no Utaki. At Kimutaka-no Utaki, annual events known as umachii were carried out by priestesses to offer prayers for harvests.

xii 須恵器 Sue Pottery was produced in parts of Japan and southern Korea beginning around the Kofun period (300-538).

xiii カムイヤキ kilns can also be found throughout Amami

xiv In Yaeyama, the Gusuku period is called the Suku Period (Suku is the Yaeyaman word for Gusuku) and lasted from the 12th to 16th Century.

xv Some believe the Furusutobaru Castle site to be the base of Yaeyama's last hegemon before it became integrated into the Ryukyu King, Akahachi. Although, there is no conclusive evidence regarding whether this is true or not

xvi Hokuzan is sometimes referred to as Sanhoku, and Nanzan as Sannan. The alternate names a result of later Ryukyu scholars modifying names first found in Chinese documents, 山北 'Sanhoku' was first written in Chinese documents, later being reversed to 北山 'Hokuzan'. The same is true for 山南 'Sannan' first written in Chinese, which was later reversed to 南山 by Ryukyu scholars

xvii Nakijin Gusuku was declared a World Heritage site in November 2000, alongside the remains of Shuri Castle

xviii Omoro means songs handed down in the Okinawan language

xix Shuri Castle, as the center of the Ryukyu Kingdom is the only castle in Okinawa to be called 'castle' in Japanese instead of Gusuku. Both words use the same Chinese character

xx 隋書

xxi 明実録

xxii For example, 新元史 writes Ryukyu as 琉求, while元史 writes it as 瑠求

xxiii 大琉球&小琉球

xxiv 明史

xxv 高麗史節要

xxvi 季朝実録

xxvii Unlike Ryukyu, Japan would not send tribute to China for long stretches of time

xxviii 中山世鑑 Chūzan Seikan (Mirror of Chūzan) was compiled by Haneji Chōshū in 1650 and it is the first official history of the Ryukyu Kingdom and is written largely in Japanese. Later official histories such as 中山世譜Chūzan

Seifu (Genealogy of Chūzan) 球陽Kyūyō and are written in Chinese. Haneji Chōshu is the individuals Japanese name, he would also use the Chinese name 向象賢(しょうじょうけん) with the 向 being a simplification of the 尚 character used by the kings of Ryukyu, to indicate his blood connections

xxix There are a few theories about why Shō-Satto of Nanzan has such a similar name to Satto of Chūzan. It is possible that Satto was not a name but a title for kings, other theories see the name of Ufusato as phonetic characters that match the area Shō-Satto would have reigned over

xxx 皮弁冠 also known as Tamanchaabui タマンチャーブイ in Okinawan

xxxi The bestowment of royal clothing and a crown was a Ming custom and the practice came to a halt with the Qing dynasty. However the Ryukyu Kingdom continued the custom locally, using textiles with the Qing's dragon symbol to fashion royal clothing

xxxii 国子監 Under the Ming dynasty the Imperial University was located in Nanjing, under the Qing it was moved to Beijing

xxxiii 玉之 Utsuchi is also sometimes written as 完玉之 Kangyokushi. I have chosen to use Utsuchi following Takara Kurayoshi's style in 『琉球の時代』

xxxiv While Shō Hashi is the founder of the first Ryukyu Dynasty, his father, Shō Shishō is technically the first king

xxxv Shuri Castle was built at the beginning of the 14th Century, it would burn down and be rebuilt multiple times, until it was abandoned during the disposition of Ryukyu in 1879. The 1945 Battle of Okinawa destroyed much of the historical castle. Under the American occupation of Okinawa, the University of Ryukyu was built on the site of the castle, it would later be relocated. In 1992 the castle was rebuilt at last, this version of Shuri ultimately met its end in November of 2019 when faulty electrics led to it going up in flame. After the 2019 fire, donations came from across Okinawa, Japan and around the world to reconstruct it

xxxvi 懐機

xxxvii 安国樹花木記

xxxviii 他魯毎 Taromai/Tarumii's tomb can be found in Itoman today

xxxix 日本書紀＆続日本紀

xl The Amami native and historian Ōyama Ringorō recalled how after spending 20 years in 'Yamato' he heard a wonderful folk song in his home town that was like nothing that could be heard on the mainland. Many people in Amami also support Okinawa during the Kōshien high school baseball tournaments despite being members of Kagoshima Prefecture

xli 志魯・布里の乱

xlii 護佐丸・安麻和利の乱

xliii 百度踏揚（ももとふみあがり）

xliv Other versions of this story have it so that it is actually Gosamaru who is planning the coup, or that Gosamaru hides a note in his mouth with the truth that is discovered when his head is bought back to the Ryukyu court, or that Gosamaru dies trying to stop Amawari. In some versions the daughter of Shō Taikyū runs from Katsuren to warn Shuri of the rebellion in order to save her family. There are other theories as well, it is possible that Shuri aimed to purge both Gosamaru and Amawari to remove potential usurpers in a period in which the legitimacy of any one family on the throne was still loose

xlv The official name of this position was 'Omono-gusukū-usasunusuba' 御物城御鎖側

ENDNOTES

xlvi 鮫川

xlvii 君手摩

xlviii 宇喜也嘉

xlix 冊封使

l 天使館 A sign marks the location of the Tenshikan today and is a short walk from Asahibashi Station on the municipal monorail. In 1896 the Tenshikan became the city hall for Naha, until a new building was built in 1917. The Tenshikan was destroyed during World War II during the October 10, 1944 bombing of Naha

li 守礼門 Shurei Gate was not build until the reign of Shō Sei (1497-1555), who is the fifth son of Shō Shin

lii 百浦添御殿（ももうらそえうどうん）

liii 浮き道 The Ukimichi (floating path) in Shuri castle today is only raised five centimeters above the ground as opposed to the fifteen centimeters in the days of the Ryukyu Kingdom

liv 首里森御嶽 It is likely that Shuri Castle was built around this particular Utaki

lv 張学礼

lvi 徐葆光

lvii 朝鮮王朝実録

lviii 仲宗根豊見親&遠弥計赤蜂 In Kyūyō Akahachi is described as one individual but in 八重山年来記 (Chronicles of Yaeyama) Oyake Akahachi is described as one individual with Hongawara as another. I have chosen to write about Akahachi as one individual as this is how he is remembered throughout Yaeyama today

lix There is also a theory that Akahachi came from as far as South-East Asia to Yaeyama, although no evidence to support this, much about Akahachi remains a mystery

lx The narrative surrounding Akahachi remained the one of the Ryukyu Court for most of Yaeyama's history, that of a usurper. However in the Meiji period scholars such as Iha Fūyū and

Yanagita Kunio's more modern reinterpretation of the sources painted a more complicated picture with Akahchi becoming a figure of resistance. In Yaeyama today he is portrayed as a hero

lxi 百浦添の欄干之銘 This is an inscription on the front parapet in the palace at Shuri that records the successes of Shō Shin, including his subjugation of Yaeyama, and the use of different colored Hachimachi and Kanzashi hairpins to denote rank

lxii It is Nishitō who is credited for building the stone gate at the world heritage 園比屋武御嶽Sonohyan-Utaki

lxiii 国仲御嶽

lxiv Textiles from Sakishima were designated as 大平布 by the Ryukyu Kingdom. 大平山 was the word used to refer to Sakishima. While the Ryukyu Kingdom's name for cloth produced in Sakishima was the same, there were differences between cloth produced in Yaeyama and Miyako. Yaeyama was notable for白細上布and 赤島上布, while Miyako was notable for 紺地細上布. Cloth from both Yaeyama and Miyako was rated as 'high-quality' by the Kingdom (上布)

lxv Those under the same Mōnchu would be enshrined in the same grave.

lxvi 親方（ウエーカタ）

lxvii 親雲上(ぺーちん) Pēchin was a rank below Uēkata but higher than that of Satonushi

lxviii 里之子(さとぬし)& 筑登之親雲上 (ちくどぅん)Satonushi and Chikudun ranks

lxix 間切 In the Okinawan language Magiri are known as Majiri

lxx 大屋子&与人

lxxi 辞令書

lxxii 毛遊び

lxxiii 馬手間

lxxiv 聞得大君 also called チフィジン Chifijin in Okinawan

ENDNOTES

lxxv 音智殿茂金

lxxvi 三十三君

lxxvii 佐司笠

lxxviii ノロ&阿母

lxxix If the Noro resigned from this role, the land would go to her successor

lxxx The names for the Ōamo position have a great deal of variation, for example at the island of Kumebe the title is called 君南風（きみはえ）Kimihae

lxxxi Mihira-no-Ōamoshirare oversaw Kamichu in Naha, Haebaru Isena, etc, the Makabe-no-Ōamoshirare oversaw Kaminchu at Urasoe, Ginowan, Kerama and Katsuren etc. and the Gibo-no-Ōamoshirare oversaw Kaminchu at Kumejima, Yomitan, Miyako and Yaeyama

lxxxii 玉御殿

lxxxiii Tamaudun was damaged by the Battle of Okinawa, but was restored after three years of work in 1974. In 2018 it was registered as a National Treasure, the first such building in Okinawa Prefecture

lxxxiv Kuba, Mayumi. "首里城の赤瓦." 首里城公園

lxxxv When the Shuri Castle burnt down in 2019, these stone dragons were one of the only things still standing around the palace

lxxxvi 円鑑池

lxxxvii Benzaiten is derived from the Hindu goddess Saraswati

lxxxviii 真珠 'Madama' is the Okinawan word for pearl

lxxxix A recreation of this serpentine platform of Mii Gusuku can be visited at Yomitan today, where it was created for the period drama 'Ryukyu No Kaze' in 1993

xc 長虹堤

xci Penglai or Hōrai in Japanese, is an immortal island that appears in Chinese mythology. On Hōrai there is no agony nor winter, rice bowls and wine glasses that never become empty no matter how much people eat or drink from them; and the enchanted fruits growing there can heal any ailment. Those on Penglai are granted eternal youth, and even the dead can be bought back to life.

xcii 万国津梁の鐘 — The Bridge of Nations Bell is located in the Okinawa Prefectural Museum today miraculously surviving the Battle of Okinawa while the rest of Shuri Castle went up in flames around it. Today a replica of the bell is housed at Shuri Castle, housed in a special building called the Tomoya 供屋 in front of Kōfukumon gate, instead of hanging from the palace itself as it did in when it was first forged. The bell once again took on significance as an international symbol during the 2000 G8 Okinawa Summit in which the meeting room was named after the bell (Bankoku Shinryokan)

xciii 京の内 The Kyō-no-Uchi was one of the most sacred locations within Shuri Castle, where the Kikoeōkimi and Ōamoshirare would prey to the gods for the prosperity of the royal family, save naval passage, and bountiful harvests. The Kyō-no-Nai can be found south of Hōshinmon

xciv The Muromachi Period takes its name from the district of Kyoto in which the shogunate made its base, this is similar to the later Edo Period under the Tokugawa Shogunate, with Edo the base of Japan's longest shogunate

xcv 大明会典

xcvi Horses appear to be present throughout the Ryukyu Archipelago since at least the Shell Mound period, were horse teeth have been excavated. The horses of Okinawa are stout, in Yonaguni, this island's particular type of horse has become a tourist attraction. The males have an average height of one-hundred-and-twenty centimeters, the females, one-hundred-and-sixteen centimeters.

ENDNOTES

xcvii Off the coast of Iōtorishima, and not present in Ryukyu times is the even tinier island of Shōwa-Iōtorishima — Shōwa-Iōtorishima came into existence during an eruption in 1934

xcviii 歴代宝案 The documents in the Rekidaihōan span a period of four-hundred-and-forty-three years

xcix Okinawa Prefecture and Fujian Province have a relationship of over four-hundred-years, and this can still be seen today. Naha and Fuzhou are sister cities, while Urasoe and Quanzhou are friendship cities. In 2001, the then governor of Fujian, Xi Jingping (presently head of the Chinese Communist Party) visited Okinawa Prefecture, with the governor of Okinawa Prefecture, Inamine Keiichi visiting Fujian in 2002

c 来遠駅

ci 土通事

cii This is also the reason many scholars in the 19th Century mistakenly thought Marco Polo's description of 'Zai-tun' was about Xiamen (Amoy)

ciii 柔遠駅 The Fuzhou Ryukyu Hall, while no longer standing, can be visited in a smaller reconstructed museum in its place today in the Taijang district of Fuzhou today, it is about a twenty minute walk east of the Fuzhou Chating Park

civ 五虎門

cv These characters can be seen on the museum that is constructed in the Fuzhou Ryukyu Hall place

cvi Most of the site where the Fuzhou Ryukyu Hall stood was a factory during the Second World War. Alongside the museum, there is also a monument which charts the relationship of Ryukyu and Fujian

cvii 崇報祠

cviii 会同館

cix Under the Qing the practice of sending Hibenfuku (royal clothing) for the king stopped. Instead the Ryukyu Kingdom received fine cloth form which the Ryukyu Kingdom continued the tradition by making it within the kingdom

cx Chinese records also refer to the Ryukyu Archipelago as having 'thirty-six' islands, despite there being more than fifty throughout the archipelago

cxi The Rekidaihōan was compiled by individuals from Kuninda

cxii 唐栄

cxiii Sai On (Bunjaku Gushichan), who was descended from Chinese who had first come to Ryukyu in 1392, first went to China as an interpreter in 1708, where he studied Confucianism and among other things forestry and agriculture. In 1713 he returned to Ryukyu and became the teacher to the 13-year-old Shō Kei, and was granted a residency in Shuri in the area around what is now Gibo station in Naha. In 1728 he ascended to the role of Council of Three, and would continue working in the capacity for 25 years until 1753. Sai On led forestry and agricultural reforms such as 『杣山法式帳』『農務帳』 which sort to increase the standard of living in Okinawa through reforms such as windbreaker trees and tidal forests (mangroves). Other land reforms included the reclamation of land for agriculture, the relocation and establishment of settlements, the creation of forestry on islands lacking trees by bringing them from central and northern Okinawa, lining the coast with Fukugi tree and pines. Even today the around Hedo-Misaki (the most northern part of Okinawa) the pine trees are called Sai-On-Matsu (Sai-On Pine Trees). Within Sai On's reforms the kingdom was able to produce more than ever before

cxiv Gishitetsu (Tokumei Takamine) went to China in 1688, where he worked as an interpreter and studied medicine.

ENDNOTES

In 1689, he returned to Ryukyu where he treated the crown prince Shō Eki (1678-1712) of clef lip successfully, and was promoted to the highest position in Kuninda because of

cxv this Ishigandō are known as Shigandang in Chinese

cxvi 奏山石石敢當

cxvii One example is of a large Ishigandō outside Kawasaki JR Station. This was built after multiple typhoons struck Okinawa in 1966, the Kawasaki City Assembly passed a unanimous resolution to send to badly hit Miyako. In their thanks, the people of Miyako sent this Ishigandō made of travertine a rock characteristic of Miyako

cxviii 晴明の節 (シーミー)

cxix 勢治荒富 (せじあらとみ) 世高富(せだかとみ) 浮豊見 (うきみとみ)

cxx Yoshinari Naoki has proposed that the name of the Hokuzan king, Hanaji comes from Hachiman Aji

cxxi The Tripiṭaka Koreana was printed on over 80,000 wooden printed blocks. The text was inscribed in the UNESCO Memory of the World Register in 2007

cxxii The Benzaiten-Dō is the only building in Okinawa that can be seen today that directly relates to the Korean Peninsula

cxxiii 波上宮Nami-no-Ue shrine is one of the most important religious sites in Okinawa. It was prayed to when leaving Naha port for a safe journey, and during the New Year Celebrations the king would visit the shrine himself. Nami-no-ue was also the head of the 8 shrines of Ryukyu. Even before the site became a shrine it was sacred for its connection to Nirai Kanai, which is a paradise under the sea and one of the realms from which the gods came. There are myths about Nirai Kanai being the origins of fire and rice, since the Gods would come from Nirai Kanai to bring bountiful harvests. Numerous Ryukyu religious events and ceremonies took place on beaches, such as Yaeyama, and also Nami-no-ue, and this is because of the ocean's connection with Nirai Kanai

cxxiv 金武観音 There is a legend that a gigantic snake was living in a cave and drinking the spring water. At times it would slither out of the cave and devour the people's livestock. It is here that the Shingon Priest Nishū Shōnin makes an appearance, and by chanting Buddhist sutra he is able to seal the snake inside the cave (which is now called Nishū Cave). In honor of these events the Kinkannon-Ji temple is constructed on the site

cxxv 補陀洛山寺 Fudarakusan-Ji in Wakayama Prefecture

cxxvi 補陀洛 Fudaraku or Potalaka in the original Sanskrit

cxxvii If one visits Fudarakusan-Ji today you can find graves for some of the monks who were cast adrift on the Fudaraku boats, and also one of the boats within the temple grounds

cxxviii These gates are 'The Gate of Religious Awakening' 「発心門」 'The Gate of Aestheticism' 「修行門」 'The Bodhisattva Gate' 「菩薩門」 and 'The Gate of Nirvana' 「涅槃門」

cxxix 金剛経

cxxx 南蛮 The same word as 'Nanban' (southern barbarian) in Japanese. This term would later be applied to the Portuguese and Spanish and then all Europeans as they appeared in both Ryukyu and Japan from the south

cxxxi The Majahapit Empire was the first regime to bring the Indonesian archipelago under one rule, and is considered by many Indonesians today to be the foundations for their modern nation state

cxxxii As with Awamori, the snakes throughout the Ryukyu Archipelago are small, and the snake skin for the Sanshin seems to have been bought back from Southeast Asia

ENDNOTES

cxxxiii There are different accounts the origins of the Sultanate of Malacca's founder. In the Malay Annals (circa 15th to 16th century) a genealogy of the Sultanate of Malacca, Iskandar Shah is described as a descendant of the founder of Singapura, however there are also accounts of a prince arriving in Singapura from Sumatra and it is not clear whether this is referring to the founder of the Sultanate of Malacca

cxxxiv Iskandar is the Persian word for 'Alexander' and Shah 'King'. This Iskandar would be Alexander the Great showing how South East Asia was connected to a wider near eastern and European world and how Ryukyu was indirectly connected to this

cxxxv 呉実堅

cxxxvi A reconstructed Malacca Palace which is also a museum can be visited in Malaysia today

cxxxvii It is possible that Pires may have never met Ryukyuans in Malacca and was basing his accounts off what others said about the Ryukyuans

cxxxviii Malacca would finally lose its capital city status when the British moved their straits colony to Singapore.

cxxxix The Mamluk Sultanate was the main middleman between spice producing India and Venetian buyers in the Mediterranean

cxl Both Hokkaido and what is now Okinawa Prefecture would not come under the direct rule of the Japanese government until the Meiji Period (1868-1912)

cxli Hyūga, Ōsumi and Satsuma make up much of present-day Kagoshima Prefecture, the other parts of Kagoshima Prefecture are of course the Amami Islands (Northern Ryukyu)

cxlii The historian Uehara Kenzen has used the Satsuma records to provide exact dates down to the day for the progression of the Satsuma invasion of Ryukyu, and I have used mainly his used his dates in this section

cxliii There is a story about resistance in Amami, although this may have been created after the invasion itself. It is said that the village of Yakiuchi (present day Uken), whose first character 焼 'burn', got its name because the village was burned down by the Satsuma

cxliv 南聘紀考 The *Nanpeikyō* was written by the Satsuma historian Ijichi Kian, the book consists of three sections that covers events from the period 607 to 1832. It is thought that it was written to make clear the historical events that happened whilst the Ryukyu Kingdom was under Satsuma rule.

cxlv 琉球渡海日々 *Ryukyu Tokai Hibi*

cxlvi Shō Nei was interned at a royal residency in Urasoe 浦添美御殿

cxlvii Uehara Kenzen has proposed that while Shō Nei and his entourage were at Yamagawa a mansion for the king was being constructed in Kagoshima

cxlviii Sakurajima's highest point is 1,117 meters compared to Iōtorishima 212 meters. Sakurajima remained an island until lava flows during the 1914 eruption caused it to join to the mainland

cxlix 謝名利山

cl 大島奉行所 The remains of the Ōshima Magistrate can still be seen in the Kasari district of Amami City, this is also probably why the biggest city in Amami (Amami City) is located in the central and north of the island, facing Kagoshima Prefecture rather than Okinawa Prefecture

cli 琉球檢地

clii 桃林寺&権現堂 In the Gongendō Shrine there is a bronze mirror cast in 1772 which is the oldest within Okinawa Prefecture. Both The Gogendō shrine and Torin-Ji were washed away by the Meiwa Tsunami in 1771, but were reconstructed in 1786, and many more times since

cliii In a similar manner, three temples were built in Hokkaido which had the aims of converting the Ainu to the Buddhist faith, these 'Three Ezo Temples' could also be used when the Shogunate was debating that Hokkaido was a Japanese territory

cliv In 1604 the Tokugawa Shogunate bestowed the Matsumae samurai with the Black Seal, a document that gave them exclusive rights to trade with the Ainu. The Matsumae samurai then monopolized this trade, just as the Satsuma did to Ryukyu

clv 仕上世 (しのぼせ)

clvi 道之島

clvii 中城王子の上国

clviii 羽地朝秀

clix 耕作主取

clx 野国総管 Noguni Sōkan is the name of an official position, with the title of Sōkan related to tributary ships. The individuals name may have been Yohana Machū (与那覇 松) although Noguni Sōkan has become the general name under which the individual is celebrated in Okinawa today. In Kadena there is a shrine dedicated to him with stone lions from Fujian

clxi 義間真常 Zama Shinjō is enshrined at the Yomochi Shrine in Naha, along with Sai On and Noguni Sōkan, who are subsequently three of the five 'Great Men of Ryukyu' as decided by Iha Fuyū in 1916. The other two great men of Ryukyu are Haneji Chōshū and Giwan Chōho (1862-1875) a member of the Council of Three during the kingdom's final days before its annexation by Japan

THE RYUKYUS

clxii 琉球館 A stone monument marking the former Ryukyu Hall can be found a short walk from Kagoshima Station today. The Ryukyu Hall in Kagoshima was also called 御仮屋

clxiii Rekidaihōan was compiled using diplomatic documents from China and other countries in 1678 and Ryukyukoku Yūraiki (The origins of the Ryukyu Kingdom 琉球国由来記) in 1713、Kyūyō from 1743 to 1745. The Niyokanosōshi between 1706-1713 (女官御双紙) which describes the priestess system of Ryukyu

clxiv 日流同祖論

clxv It is also possible that Haneji felt compelled to write positively about Japan since it the Satsuma who were ultimately in control of the Ryukyu Kingdom

clxvi 鎮西八郎

clxvii Chūzan Seikan would later be an important document used by the Japanese sides in negotiations with Qing China about who the Ryukyu Archipelago belonged to in the late 19th Century

clxviii 御教条 The Articles of Instruction or Gokyōjō was written in 1732, with all members of the Council of Three as co-signers

clxix 至聖廟

clxx This name is sometimes written as Kantsume, or Kantiimi/Kantimi

clxxi かんつめ節の碑

clxxii カンティミ節

clxxiii While Sunao Kawachi is the first person officially credited with bringing sugar to the Ryukyu Archipelago, Takara Kurayoshi argues that sugar, while not on a mass-produced scale, was already happening throughout the archipelago long before this. Takara's evidence is that a 1470 Ryukyu envoy to Korea gave an alcohol called 'Tenjikushu' (天竺

ENDNOTES

酒) which likely had sugar as an ingredient

clxxiv 家人 are the characters for 'Yanchu'. The name for Yanchu varied throughout Amami, in Tokunoshima Yanchu were called 'Chikeben' and in Okinoerabu they were called 'Niza'

clxxv 大島置目条々 under this the Yanchu system was to be abolished in part preventing Noro from owning Yanchu, but not powerful clan within Amami

clxxvi 換糖上納制

clxxvii 高割り

clxxviii 第一次砂糖総買い入れ制 1777

clxxix 第二次砂糖総買い入れ制 1830

clxxx ヤンチュ札

clxxxi 福重

clxxxii 新山為盛

clxxxiii The general term for the incident is 犬田布騒動, the word '騒動' (sōdō) indicates an uprising or rebellion

clxxxiv 犬田布義戦, 義戦 (gisen) holy or righteous war

clxxxv のそこマーペー/ヌスクマーペー

clxxxvi Unfortunately there is no English text on this sign

clxxxvii The tragedy of forced movement to malarial zones in Yaeyama would repeat itself during the Second World War in Yaeyama, something outside the scope of this book

clxxxviii The Meiwa Tsunami was roughly eight meters tall, and had a magnitude of 7.4. The Tsunami was so intense that it carried boulders across Yaeyama and Miyako, such as the seven-hundred-ton boulder that can now be found in Sakihara Park in Ishigaki City

clxxxix In Miyako this role was a male village official instead

cxc 白保村、野底村、南風見村＆崎山村

cxci 崎山節 This song can often be found if one goes to the CD

section of an Okinawan Convenience store, and even from many international streaming services

cxcii The Pai-Patirōma legend is well known throughout Yaeyama. There is a restaurant in Ishigaki city called Pai-Patirōma which serves specialties from Hateruma island. Likewise, there is a ferry which runs between Ishigaki and Hateruma called the 'Pai-Patirōma'

cxciii 切支丹門手札改

cxciv 八重山島年来記

cxcv 節祭

cxcvi The local people called this the battle of 'British Hill' and there is a monument on its site in Takarajima today

cxcvii 異国船打払令

cxcviii The captain of the Blossom was Captain F.W. Beechey who wrote *Narrative of a voyage to the Pacific and Bering's strait* (1831)

cxcix For example, Belcher refers to Iriomote as Kokiensan, Ishigaki as Patchungsan and Miyako as Typinsan which are miss pronunciations of Chinese names for the islands. Throughout this work I have added the correct names where contemporaries miswrote them

cc 唐人墓 Tōjinbaka 'the grave of the Chinese'

cci *Narrative of the Expedition of an American Squadron to the China Seas and Japan* was coauthored with the priest Francis L. Hawkes, who compiled the work together with Perry as well as accounts from his crew

ccii The people of Ryukyu were wary of Bettelheim and his family. When he went to the market people would leave their good as they were and flee, Bettelheim would place what he deemed to be appropriate payment and take what he needed during these occasions

cciii It is unknown whether this exile was enforced after Perry

ENDNOTES

left the Ryukyu Kingdom

cciv 尊王攘夷

ccv In reality the Meiji Emperor would largely be controlled by the former samurai from Satsuma and Chōshū who led the Meiji Restoration

ccvi 廃藩置県

ccvii The Meiji Emperor relocated from Kyoto to Tokyo in 1869

ccviii Many of Okinawan surnames were transposed from the Ryukyu Languages into standard Japanese, although this was a gradual and not sudden process. For example, the Okinawan name 'Fija' became 'Higa' with the surname containing 'Gushuku' becoming 'Gusuku'. Other examples of making the surname more 'Japanese' involved changing the reading of a character to make it more in line with Japanese reading 城 going from 'Gusuku' to 'Shiro'. Dozens of surnames from Okinawa today continue to be tied to a particular region, Just two examples are 喜屋武 (Kyan) from Itoman and 饒平名 (Yohena) from Yagajishima, although there are many more. This is also a time in which place names became more in line with standard Japanese readings, with Naha replacing Nāfa

ccix 春立船

ccx 台湾蕃地処分要略

ccxi 大日本琉球藩民五十四名墓 This monument still stands in Taiwan today, having been renovated numerous times

ccxii The names Minamoto (or Genji) along with Taira were given to the children and grandchildren of emperors who were not eligible for the throne during the Heian period during the reign of Emperor Kanmu (reign 781-806). This was as the imperial court was to limit the court growing larger with the descendants of a previous emperor no longer being princess, and this gave birth the samurai clans of the Minamoto and Taira

ccxiii This legend was also recorded in *Dai Nihonshi* (大日本史 Great History of Japan) written during the Edo period. A similar myth was also applied to justify the Japanese takeover of Korea. The argument was that the King of Chosen descended from Susanao, the younger brother of the son goddess Amaterasu who the emperor traced his lineage to

ccxiv A similar argument about the Ryukyu Languages being a dialect of Japan was made in Korea also. Today the majority of people in the Ryukyu Archipelago refer to their languages as 'dialects', although others still insist that they are languages. UNESCO has recognized all the languages of the Ryukyu Archipelago as endangered. I should also add that the languages/dialects of the Ryukyu Archipelago are mutually unintelligible with standard Japanese. As in other countries in the world, what to classify as a dialect or language is often a political and historical decision

ccxv The Chamber of the Left (左院) was replaced by the Chamber of Elders (元老院) which in turn was replaced by the Imperial Diet in 1890

ccxvi It was after the royal family vacated Shuri Castle that precious manuscripts within were carried off to Tokyo. This included the Rekidaihōan, which was stored at the Ministry of Home Affairs, and was little interest to researchers at the time. With the 1923 Great Kanto Earthquake this building, and all inside, went up in flames. Fortunately, a copy in Kuninda was also held that was kept hidden by those in Kuninda from the government under fears it would be confiscated. The Kuninda existence of the Kuninda version of Rekidaihōan only became public knowledge once it was given to the Okinawan Prefectural Museum in 1933, however during the Battle of Okinawa this also went up in flames. It was a researcher at the Imperial University in Taiwan who had made copies of most of the manuscript that made it possible to reassemble the text. In 1989, Okinawa Prefecture formed a committee to reassemble the text, and throughout the 1990s Rekidaihōan was reintroduced using copies from Taiwan, China and Japan, with all thirteen volumes being published by 2003

ccxvii Okinawa is classified as 'ken' 県 prefecture (沖縄県) but there is no corresponding character for Hokkaido which is classified by the last character In the word 'Dō' 道 (北海道). Hokkaido is the only region in Japan with this classification, although in English it is sometimes refered to as 'Hokkaido Prefecture'

ccxviii The last Kikoeōkimi was Nozu Keiko (1947-2019) who was the great-great granddaughter of Shō Tai. Of course, the Kikoeōkimi had lost its official status in 1884

ccxix In Miyako there are 'Kankakariya' and in Yaeyama 'Nigaibī' both are similar to the Yuta in Okinawa. Both the Kankakariya and Nigaibī were persecuted under the Ryukyu Kingdom, and numerous royal decrees in the 17th an 18th century banned the practice

ccxx 開墾結社

ccxxi What was more of a success in Yaeyama during this era was the fisherman and itinerant merchants from Okinawa

ccxxii ヤンチュ解放令&人身売買禁止令

ccxxiii 伊地知清左衛門

ccxxiv 勝手世運動

ccxxv Meirin-dō was the first public school in Ryukyu where students of Kuninda learnt Mandarin, Confucinaism and how to write diplomatic documents

ccxxvi Even the regional accents in Japan can have quite a degree of difference, the most well known example is between Tokyo and Osaka, with the negative on the end of verbs in standard Japanese being 'nai' in Kansai this is 'hen'. Japan continues to be a country of strong regional accents today

ccxxvii 会話伝習所
ccxxviii 沖縄師範学校
ccxxix 御真影
ccxxx 良妻賢母
ccxxxi 実業補習学校規定
ccxxxii 高等女学校令
ccxxxiii 首里女子実業補習学校
ccxxxiv Mōashibi is the gathering of young people in the evening along the seaside and planes to sing and dance. The practice was a means for young people who were not of noble rank to chose their partners. This was in contrast to the nobles of the Kingdom who had their future spouses chosen by their parents
ccxxxv 高等女学校令
ccxxxvi The Kumamoto Garrison Outpost had dispatched an army to this site in May of 1875 under the pretext of protecting Ryukyu. Here there were hospitals, barracks and drill grounds. The site fell out of use after July 1896. The center for the army was later transferred to Shuri Castle after the Disposition of Ryukyu which became the main garrison in Okinawa, and because of this the castle was the target of US bombardment during the Battle of Okinawa
ccxxxvii 海軍条例
ccxxxviii 蛍の光
ccxxxix 沖縄県私立教育界
ccxl 琉球教育
ccxli 方言札

ENDNOTES

ccxlii The use of the Okinawan language continued well after the Meiji era. In 1970 Higa Masao was working as a teacher at a high school and was attending a national Red Cross event in Gunma Prefecture with some students. While they were staying at a hotel near Ueno station, the kids were speaking in the Okinawan language, the owner of the lodging who was guiding them to their room asked, "did you come from Korea?" This is because Korean often ends with the ン sound and so does the Okinawan the children were speaking: (to be) Okinawan: An, Japanese Aru, (To be different) Okinawan Aran, Japanese Chigau, (To walk) Okinawan: Acchun, Japanese: Aruku (アン ある / アラン 違う / アッチュン歩く / チュラサン 美しい)

ccxliii Traditional Okinawan clothing is known as Uchinā Sugai(ウチナースガイ)

ccxliv Reversing the trend of the pre-Pacific war era there was a boom in the post-war era in Okinawan fashion that continues to this day. Today in Okinawa, the colorful Bingata kimono's can be seen throughout the prefecture, and Bingata shirts full of colorful floral designs are common in offices.

ccxlv Under the Ryukyu Kingdom and even sometimes in Okinawa today, the top knot hair style is called Kanpū

ccxlvi As of 2011, there were 922 Mexicans of Okinawan descent

ccxlvii By 1935 the number of Okinawans in Taiwan was just under 10,000, in contrast to New Caledonia which was mainly men, most of these immigrants were women

ccxlviii The Soma-Yama were a policy of Sai On, member of the Council of Three

ccxlix 沖縄倶楽部

ccl 熊本移民会社

ccli 謝花昇先生之像

THE RYUKYUS

cclii 大阪紡績会社
ccliii 関西沖縄文庫
ccliv In Yokohama's Tsurumi Ward today there remains an Okinawa town today. A detailed guide to this history can be found in the book 横浜・鶴見沖縄県人会史 by the Tsurumi Okinawan Association (鶴見沖縄県人会)
cclv 太田興業株式会社
cclvi ダバオ日本人会
cclvii 皇国殖民合資会社
cclviii 大城カメ
cclix 日本吉佐移民会社
cclx The Plateau of the Thio Mine is one of the largest nickle deposits in the world, and a museum is on site now
cclxi 南洋興発

About The Author

Ibrahim Jalal completed his postgraduate studies at Waseda University's Graduate School of Asia and Pacific Studies. He has lived throughout Japan, in Kurashiki, Yokohama and Tokyo, and currently resides in Cambridge in the United Kingdom. He is also the author of *Hokkaido – A History of Japan's Northern Isle and its People*.

www.ingramcontent.com/pod-product-compliance
Lightning Source LLC
LaVergne TN
LVHW030317070526
838199LV00069B/6486